HEALING
THE
BLUE PLANET
AN INFORMED CONSENT

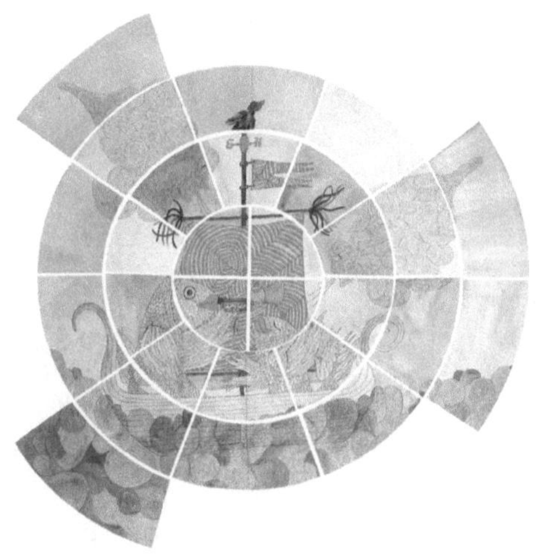

BANE SINGH

Wordizen Books

ISBN 978-9381836-74-3
© Text: Bane Singh, 2012
© Cover Art: Ritika Merchant, *Fish Out Of Water*, 2012

Cover Art   Ritika Merchant
Cover Design   Fravashi Aga
Layouts   Ajay Shah
Printing   Repro India Pvt Ltd

Published in India, 2012
WORDIZEN BOOKS
An imprint of
LEADSTART PUBLISHING PVT LTD
Trade Centre, Level 1
Bandra Kurla Complex, Bandra (E), Mumbai 400 051, INDIA
T + 91 22 40700804   F +91 22 40700800
E info@leadstartcorp.com W www.leadstartcorp.com

US Office
Axis Corp, 7845 E Oakbrook Circle, Madison, WI 53717, USA

Disclaimer The views expressed in this book are those of the Author alone and do not purport to be those held by the Publishers.

This work is an offering to Mother Earth, who has, ever so wholeheartedly and generously, lavished on me her bountiful biotic and abiotic resources through this beautiful journey called Life! This is a gesture, however feeble, to acknowledge that great maternal debt in my own little way.

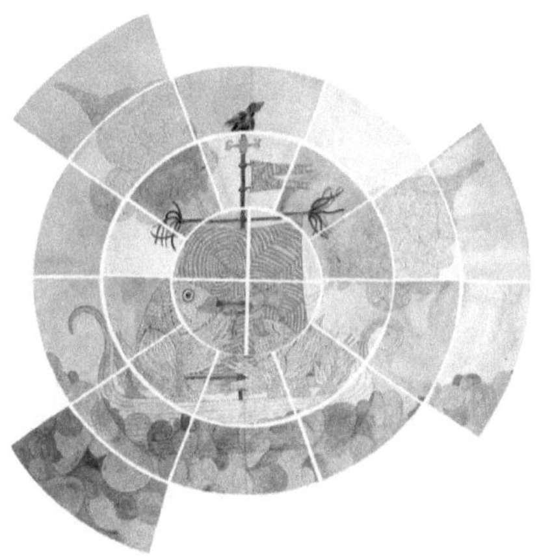

The book is also dedicated to all those conscientious people who have strived unflinchingly to heal this planet and in doing so, have sacrificed something today for the lasting benefit of future generations, which posterity might someday, choose to record with approbation and some degree of gratitude. A few words of thanks to them.

About the Author

BANE SINGH is a Civil Engineer and Ecologist by professional training and an environmentalist by leaning. A scholar and thinker, he began his career with the Water Resources Department(WRD). Thereafter he developed an abiding passion for the environment and since 1992, has significantly consolidated his knowledge of the subject. He has been associated with numerous environmental /technical reports/volumes during his professional career, holding multi-chromatic assignments.

Bane's innovative yet viable ideas on 'environmental enhancement' have won him widespread acclaim as have his articles in the *Time of India*, written to galvanize environmental rethinking. He has travelled globally to research numerous environmental parameters and gained an incisive understanding of national and international environmental/ ecological issues. He frequently lectures on Environmental Awareness, Water Conservation and Sustainable Development. His green ideas, thoughts and messages can be found on 24 different green pages which he contributes to, in addition to his own page that also offers an interactive platform for the environmental aficionados across the globe.
http://www.facebook.com/ENVIRONMENTALIST.BANE.SINGH
Bane Singh can also be contacted at: bsdauphin@gmail.com.

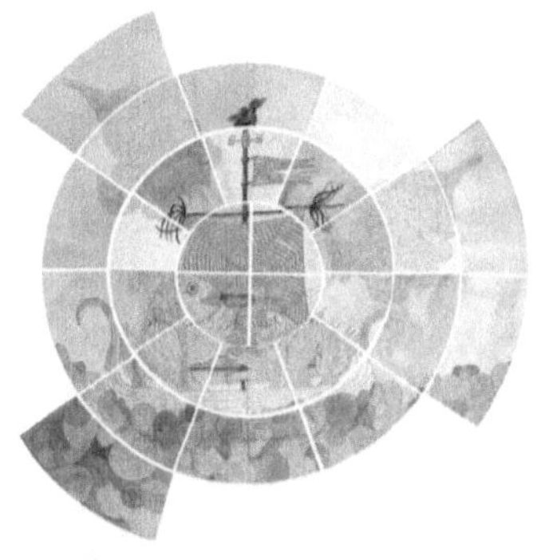

CONTENTS

Ecocide is rampant across the globe and now perceived as a grave threat. The Planet has been rapidly changing and the complex eco-web and life-supporting resources are increasingly at peril. This is a detailed and incisive insight into each burning issue: Global Warming, Climate Change, Depletion of Biodiversity, Retreating Glaciers, Threatened Wetlands, Urbanization, and the less- known problem of Ocean Acidification. A holistic treatment of global trends with specific reference to India, has been used with condign prescriptions intertwined.

The very basis of life is water. This 'Blue Gold' now needs to be managed with scientific innovations, rigorous regulations and modern management techniques. There is a critical need to complement technology with a consciousness, responsibility and genuine humility towards water usage. The future of water is precarious. Over 3 dozen innovative, viable and practicable multidisciplinary solutions have been presented here.

Ozone has been a mystery. The majority of people do not know whether it is friend or foe. Its behaviuor is quite anomalous in different atmospheric layers. Why do Ozone holes occur only over Antarctica? What is an Ozone Hole? Do we have a role in Ozone layer protection? How is Ozone depleted? The answers to these and many other questions are presented in this in-depth chapter.

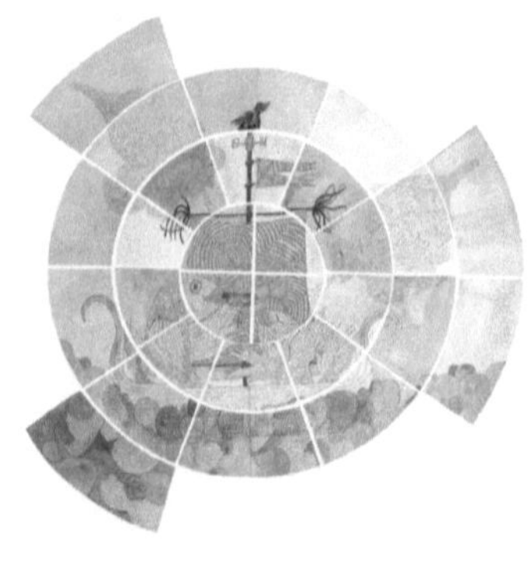

PREFACE

The saga of the evolution of life from Cambrian arthropods through Jurassic dinosaurs and so on, to modern homo-sapiens, has been a phenomenally exciting one. Given the astounding pace of current progress, the sky indeed seems to be the limit, quite literally, because human genius and endeavour may conceivably catapult terrestrial life to far-flung colonies in outer space. But before all that, the looming dangers inherent in the ongoing environmental upheaval and immense degradation in ecology wrought by man's actions, need to be clearly understood and adequate measures taken urgently to arrest the same. In the success of such a global mission lies the only hope for the survival and continuity of the human race.

This planet of ours has been devastated five times in the past. The first four (in the Ordovician, Devonian, Permian, and Triassic Periods), were brought about by various phenomena of climate change; the fifth (in the Cretaceous period), was by common consensus, caused by a gigantic meteoric crash. The sixth extinction, which portends our collective and sinister doom, would in all probability be caused solely by human-induced climate change. Around 74 species are becoming extinct every day! Unless thoughtful conservation measures are undertaken expeditiously, we may soon witness a phase wherein some 50 to 150 species would be disappearing each day! Two thousand species of animals and 60,000 species of plants are already tottering on the verge of extinction. All these are precursors of an ominously bleak future. The very existence of human civilization is now at stake.

The global temperature has recorded a rise of 0.74^0C over the past century. A significant rise of 1.8 to 4 degree Celsius is expected by the turn of this century. The increased temperature coupled with other parameters has apparently resulted in a rise in the incidence of storms, hurricanes and floods that is typically exemplified by an ascendant pattern in hurricanes of category '4' and '5'.

The years 1998, 2005 and 2010 have been the hottest in the last 200 years, and for that matter, 11 out of the preceding 14 years, have shown temperature anomalies greater than 0.5 degrees. Consequently, glaciers have retreated by 50 percent since 1950.

The Sea Surface Temperature (SST) has registered an increase of 0.2 degree to 0.3 degree Celsius over the last 45 years. It is projected to rise further by 2.0 to 3.5 degree Celsius by the next 90 years. The sea levels too have recorded a phenomenal rise of 18 cm between 1900 and 2000. It is estimated that sea level would rise up by 5 mm/year in the coming decades, resulting conceivably in a whopping 450 mm rise in sea levels by the turn of this century.

Due to highly erratic rainfalls, lesser run-off would be generated in majority of rivers, thereby reducing availability of surface water. This is substantiated by one recent research conducted at the National Centre for Atmospheric Research, Colorado USA, which carried out studies on water flow of 900 rivers over 50 years up to 2004. The study revealed signs of reduced flow in major rivers like the Ganga, the Niger, and the Yellow river (China).

According to one estimate, the amount of water being used in India is approximately 45% more than what nature's system or artificial recharge can replenish. Hence, the ground water table is depleting rapidly. At some places it has fallen below 100 feet. Some parts of NCR-Delhi are witnessing an abnormal drop of more than 6 ft. per year. In Punjab, Rajasthan and Haryana, it has been depleting by 1 ft. per year. Such huge extractions are not sustainable and presage a serious threat to the habitat. Ground water is increasingly being contaminated, as is starkly brought out by many reports and available data. Ground water would be depleted even further and rendered grossly polluted due to over-exploitation or contamination or both.

Total rainfall has been increasing and decreasing in different pockets. The future would be marred by recurrent droughts in some areas and flooding in others– a bleak scenario indeed.

Greenhouse gas emissions (GHGe) continue to rise year after year with no signs of abatement, no respite being seen in near term as well. The carbon di-oxide concentration, which stood at 284 parts per million in 1832, has crossed 390 ppm, surpassing the critical limit of 350ppm. It is anticipated that the value may further increase to a staggering 585 ppm by 2085.

Newer pests would be encountered. Climate change would continue to alter the 'periodicity' as also the 'intensity' of rainfall in coming years. Rapid increases in night temperature and higher levels of warming have been observed in the northern parts. Dew precipitation is gradually diminishing in northern rain-fed regions. Both 'evaporation' and 'evapo-transpiration' are likely to soar. All this would result in decreased agriculture production which is likely to go down by 18-20 % in coming decades. Rice production would decrease by 0.6 tones/ha for every 1 degree rise in temperature.

Storage capacity of dams would diminish year after year due to erosion (land degradation) and consequent greater silt deposition. *Eutrophication* would increase. Oceans would tend to be more acidic. Moreover, *Poikilothermic* aquatic animals have been experiencing *Phenological* changes such as spawning. Lakes would gradually be rendered highly polluted and in extreme cases disappear. Aquatic life would be in danger and some might face extinction.

Coral reefs and *wetlands* are threatened everywhere. Rain forests, the so-called *lungs of the Earth* and the *world's largest pharmacy*, have been largely decimated. They constituted 14% of the world's land surface 50 years ago, but are now reduced to merely 6%. It is argued that one-fifth of the world's tropical forest was destroyed between 1960 and 1990. Originally 6 million square miles of tropical rain forest existed worldwide, now only 2.6 million square miles remain.

The possible slowing down of the ocean current system – the Great Ocean Conveyor , would alter the *season pattern*, thereby affecting agriculture, living organisms, and industries in varying proportions. The list is never ending. Against the backdrop of such a long list of afflictions, this treatise seeks to address the cardinal issues. It is hoped that this book, in its entirety, will offer an engaging and wholesome repast to proactively thinking minds. Readers will hopefully acquire, after their cerebral journey through its pages, extra awareness and subsequently feel inspired and motivated to do something meaningful towards the greater cause of the environment. That in itself would be vindication of the author's efforts.

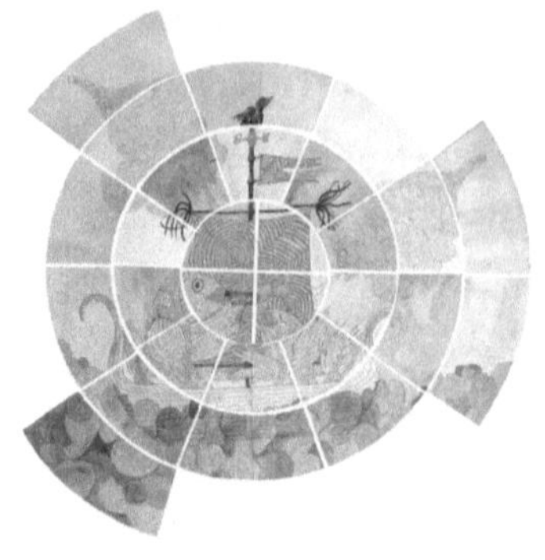

I
AN OVERVIEW OF GLOBAL ENVIRONMENTAL ISSUES

Rapid environmental change is all around us. The most obvious example is climate change. But that is not the only threat. Many other clouds are on the horizon. This assault on the global environment risks undermining the many advances human society has made in recent decades – it could even come to jeopardize international peace and security. ~ Ban Ki-Moon, Secretary General, United Nations

The world has for some time now, been facing an environmental crisis that threatens the very survival of the human race and civilization on this lovely, blue planet. What is even more worrisome, the clock of environmental degradation is now ticking at a pace faster than ever before.

The height of panic and the depth of despair, wide ranging research and intellectual polemics, concerning the impending collapse of civilization owing to inexorable environmental degradation, attributed to multifarious factors, have created a baffling conundrum about the course of action humanity should take to overcome the challenges to its very existence. The myriad responses that have been elicited range from technological fantasies to pessimistic resignation about the inevitable destruction of humanity. The remedies often cited include colonizing and inhabiting new planets, as well as constructing polar townships to sustain life on earth. Most of the conceptual models relate to a doomsday projection, involving the end of civilization and cessation of human existence. The battle is increasingly turning out to be a fight against time!

Despite a plethora of thought-provoking discussions about the influence of global warming and climate change on human existence and the possible solutions to tackle the same, we have been hurtling on a downhill slope towards major disaster and the options for solutions are narrowing with alarming rapidity. The increasing natural calamities, the concern about ever increasing carbon emission and its adverse effects on the habitability on earth have all caused immense environmental worries.

A recent report by the National Center for Atmospheric Research (NCAR) mentions that 'the rate of climate warming over northern Alaska, Canada and Russia could more than triple during the periods of rapid sea ice loss'. This has raised concerns about the thawing of permafrost resulting in potential consequences for sensitive ecosystems, human infrastructure and additional release of greenhouse gases. As the IPCC Chairman says: 'If there is no action before 2012, that's too late. What we do in the next two or three years will determine our future'.

Moreover, to aggravate an already precarious situation, fresh economic crisis in Europe and the US, triggered by the American mortgage crises, the worldwide fall in share markets, the plunging value of currencies and the rising prices of fossil fuels, have all created great uncertainty and concern about bankruptcy and serious economic consequences on society. At the same time widening income disparities have caused a serious rift between the social classes, as witnessed of late in Britain where the so called have-nots resorted to widespread looting, arson and torching of shops and properties.

Depletion in precious natural resources, including water and agricultural yield that are essential to sustain life, have resulted in rising food prices, poverty, inflation, refugee crises and food riots in many countries. To make matters worse, knee-jerk reaction to counter climate change that has resulted in many countries investing large portions of land for bio-fuel cultivation has also influenced the global food crises and price rise. The reducing carrying-capacity of earth due to rising population and over exploitation of natural resources due to capitalist model of economic development and consumer culture have also added to the crises. The unrestricted profit-driven lust of multinational companies and corporations, notwithstanding the pollution and damage caused to air, water and land by their activities has only added fuel to the fire.

What with the complications presented by all these factors, coupled with the ever growing deterioration in the habitability of earth due to environmental decadence and its multidimensional ramifications on the existence of humankind, concrete and carefully planned actions to counter the crises are the need of the day. But such actions have not really taken off owing to a strangle-hold of concepts and attitudes afflicting modern society, such as abdicating socio-economic responsibilities to unbridled market forces; perennially chasing the fetish of higher GDP; giving in to the lure and comfort of soft options where hard remedies are called for, including the need to contain the antipathies that bedevil the relationship between individuals, societies and nations.

The cardinal question is, if all these developments are symptomatic of a gathering storm that threatens to cause the collapse of civilization and perhaps the end of human existence on this planet, what are the obstacles that are hindering effective actions to confront the crisis?

Global Environmental Problems & Issues

An in-depth analysis of the present predicament would make us realize that the various environmental problems are basically interrelated. Let's cast a glance over the major climatic concerns that confront today's world:

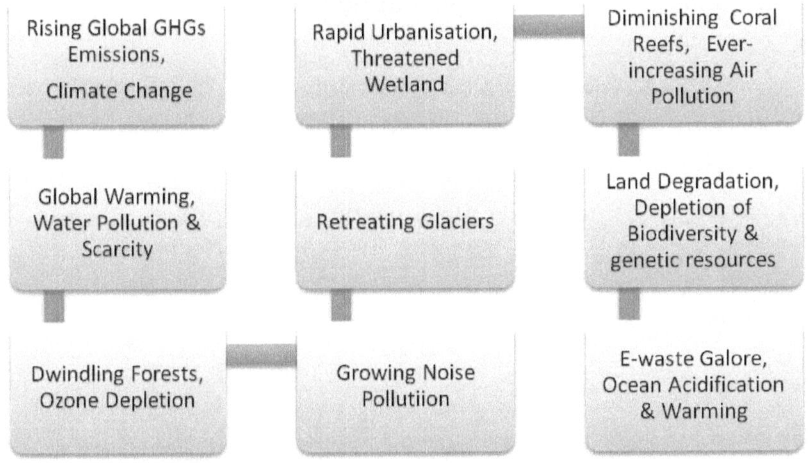

Raging Global Environmental Problems and Issues

An attempt has been made to depict in the above diagram the principal environmental issues the present world has been facing. In this chapter, we shall now examine each of these main issues in its minutiae. The inter-se order of listing does not signify much and has nothing to do with the severity or graveness of an issue, because every problem is unique and has its own importance and consequences. It needs to be emphasized, however, that collectively these inter-related (or cognate) problems put an immense burden upon our planet. Here is our running list of environmental woes:

1.01   RISING GLOBAL GREENHOUSE GASES (GHC) EMISSIONS

DEVELOPING FIRST, DEVELOPED NEXT
RICH FIRST, POOR NEXT!
WE CAN ARGUE, DITHER, AND PLAY BILLIARD
WE DON'T HAVE TIME TO CHANGE THIS PERIOD!

The mood of the majority of the nations of the world, is pretty well summed up in the above verse. Rising emissions is turning out to be the most dreadful and complex issue before today's environmentalists. Available data released by IEA (International Energy Agency) and CDIAC (Carbon dioxide Information Analysis Center) of US amply attest to that.

Emissions have a lot to do with energy use and the same has been increasing with economic development, greater prosperity and higher quality of life. Since 1751, around 337 billion tons of carbon has been injected into the atmosphere from the consumption of fossil fuels and cement production. Half of these emissions have occurred since the mid-1970s. The 2007 global fossil-fuel carbon emission estimate was 8365 million metric tons of carbon, representing an all-time high and a 1.7% increase from 2006.

Globally, liquid and solid fuels accounted for 76.3% of the total emissions from fossil-fuel burning and cement production in 2007. Combustion of gas fuels (e.g., natural gas) accounted for 18.5% (1551 million metric ton of carbon) of the total emissions from fossil fuels in 2007 and reflects a gradually increasing global utilization of natural gas. Emissions from cement production (377 million metric ton of carbon in 2007) have more than doubled since the mid-1970s and now represent 4.5% of global CO_2 releases from fossil-fuel burning and cement production. Gas flaring, which accounted for roughly 2% of global emissions during the 1970s, now accounts for less than 1% of global fossil-fuel releases. As per latest officially released figures of 2009, total CO_2 production now stands at a whopping 29.4 Gt (Gigatonne).Within the fuel sector, emission is largely contributed by three large sub-sectors which are:

- Combustion of Coal 43%
- Combustion of Oil 37%
- Combustion of Gas 20%

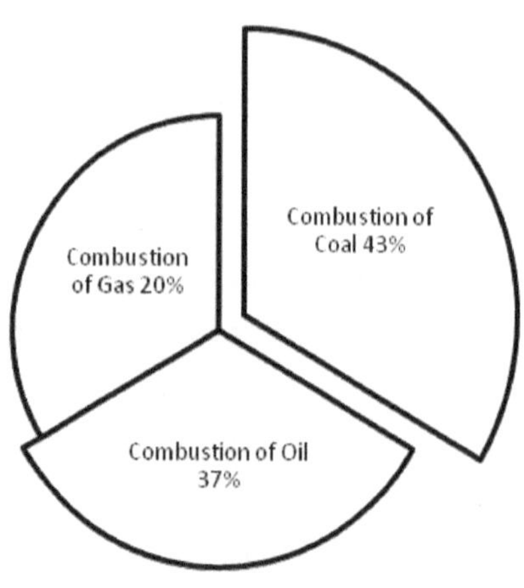

Contributing sectors and their percentage in global CO_2 emissions

As per CDIAC (Carbon dioxide Information Analysis Center), Top 10 emitting countries by total fossil fuel Carbon dioxide emissions in the year 2008 are : 1. China 2. USA 3. India 4. Russian Federation 5. Japan 6. Germany 7. Canada 8. Iran 9. United Kingdom 10. South Korea. The top 10 emitting countries account for about two-thirds of the world carbon dioxide emissions. It is amply evident from the released data that China and the US surpass all other countries. These two countries together produce 12.1 Gt (gigatonne) of carbon dioxide, constituting a staggering 41% of total carbon dioxide emissions.

Coming to the figures of per capita emission, they vary, ranging from 1 ton for India, 5 ton for china to as much as 18 ton for the US. A small but prosperous country like Qatar, has 53 ton per capita emission, which is indicative of the disproportionate impact on global ecology caused by prosperity of few. Not only that. Emission, as has been already mentioned, is the currency of today's model of economic development as well. It is noteworthy that in the past two decades, per capita emission has nearly doubled for large developing countries like India and China. The top 10 countries according to per capita emissions are ranked in the next table.

New statistics paint a very dismal picture of escalating carbon emissions. Estimates from the International Energy Agency (IEA) show greenhouse gas emissions grew by a record amount last year (2010), to the highest level in recorded history: 30.6 gigatonne (Gt).

This is significant not just because the figure comes from the IEA – a highly conservative, hydrocarbon-friendly organization, but also because the all-time high has been reached despite the world having just gone through the biggest economic recession and downturn in energy demand since the 1930s.

Top 10 countries as per [CO2 emissions per capita]-2007

Ranking	Name of Country	Per capita CO2 emission [metric ton]
1	Qatar	55.4
2	Netherlands	32.5
3	U.A.E.	31.1
4	Kuwait	30.2
5	Bahrain	29.6
6	Trinidad & Tobago	27.9
7	Aruba	23.0
8	Luxembourg	22.8
9	Brunei	19.8
10	Falkland islands	19.7

Source CDIAC of United States

GLOBAL TRENDS IN PER CAPITA EMISSION

Available time series data present a mixed but largely disturbing trend in global per capita emissions. Global per capita emission was merely 0.64 metric ton in 1950. From then on, for three decades it was a story of continuous and unabated increase till 1980, when the figure reached 1.20 metric ton. The period 1980 to 2002 registered a welcome reversal of the trend, attributable to the twin impact of world oil crisis driving efforts to harness clean and renewable energy sources as also a new ecological awareness brought by the first waves of the Green movement. But like many good things, the declining trend did not last long and the data during the years 2002 to 2008, show a steep increase in emission per unit of population than ever before. The following graphs clearly bring out the disconcerting setback on the emission front:

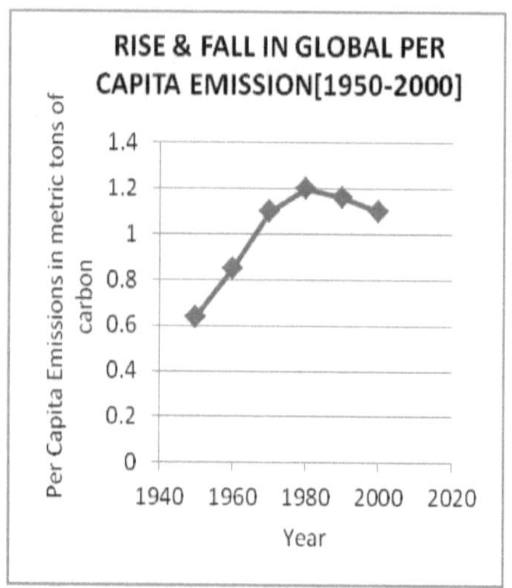

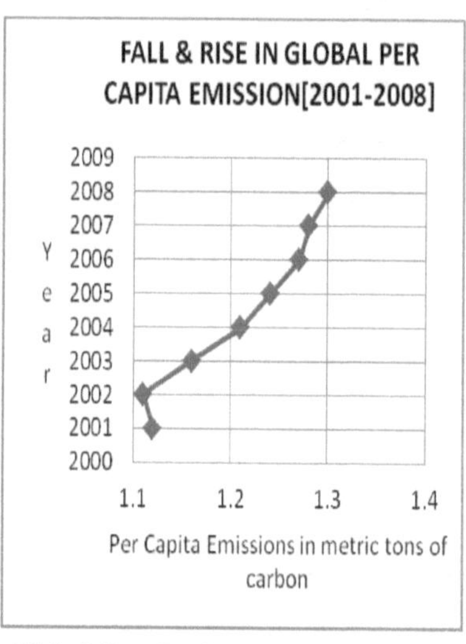

Source CDIAC   *Anomalous trends in Global Per Capita Emission [1950-2000 & 2001-2008]*

CARBON EMISSIONS OF MANKIND

After our micro-analysis of per capita emission figures, a macro-perspective would help in understanding the real nature and magnitude of the problem. Emission being a predominantly man-made crisis, a look at the cumulative total man-made emission over the first decade of the 21st century is revealing. The next columnar chart (left), tells us that the real villain in the story of human-induced pollution is our insatiable urge to tap energy from fossil sources and to create infrastructure with cement and concrete. Land use and wetland changes constitute a relatively minor, but still significant contributor to man-made emission.

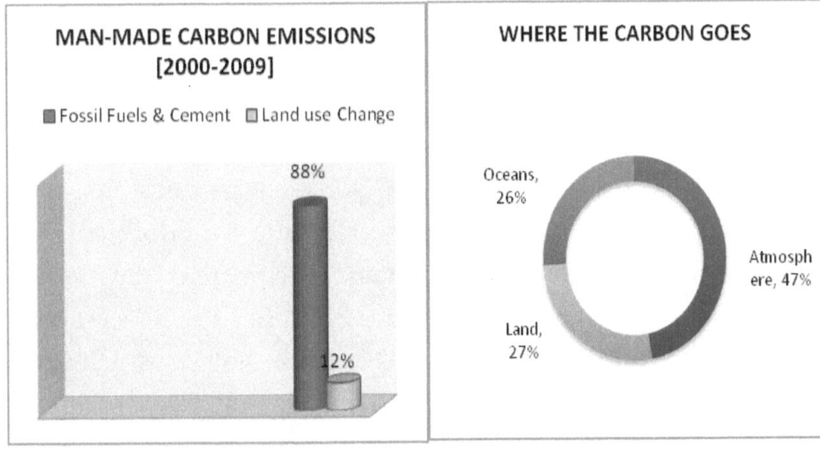

*Source Nature Geoscience and GlobalCarbonProject.org

*Per Capita Emission Sources &
Sinks of Mankind's Carbon Emission*

Where does all the Carbon go? Newtonian principle of 'what goes up must come down' does not strictly apply here. Almost half of the emitted carbon gets embedded in the atmosphere, the rest being deposited on land and oceans, as depicted in the ring chart above. The macro picture would not be complete without looking at the trend in year-wise carbon emissions in quantitative terms. The position over a four-year data band is shown below.

Year-wise Global Carbon Emissions

Year	Carbon Emissions (Fossil fuels, cement, land-use
2006	9.22 billion metric ton
2007	9.31 billion metric ton
2008	9.45 billion metric ton
2009	9.28 billion metric ton

Annual global emissions, as indicated above, seem to be straddling a high plateau, meaning a relentless increase in cumulative emissions. In effect, these emissions have put the world back on its complacent 'business as usual' course that the Intergovernmental Panel on Climate Change had previously warned would mean a 50% chance of a dramatic rise in global average temperatures of more than 4°C by 2100. But a firm global consensus still seems a far cry, with different agencies pursuing different priorities. Thus, the IEA (International Energy Agency), assembled by western oil-consuming countries to counter OPEC after the 1973 oil crisis, believes the world needs to be at 32Gt (CO2 emissions) in 2020 to avoid colossal economic and social disruption.

What with such energy hunger we are extremely close to the brink, as 80% of electricity power stations likely to be in use at the end of the 2011-2020 decade are using hydrocarbon fuel and emitting out more than 11Gt of CO2 annually.

Meanwhile, Switzerland has also joined Germany in scrapping all its nuclear plants (comparatively low carbon sources). National financial bailouts in Europe are entailing cutbacks in subsidies to renewable. Tendentious debates are being mooted in countries such as the UK and US about whether we can 'afford' to pump in public money into green technology. Russia, Japan and Canada have echoed their sentiments in the recent G8 summit at Deauville that they would not sign up to a second round of carbon cuts under the Kyoto Protocol at UN talks. The US has also reiterated its position of remaining outside the ambit of the treaty.

Opponents of Kyoto Protocol say they want a completely new agreement that would bind developing countries such as India and China, but environmentalists are deeply worried that this is just a delaying tactic largely aimed at slowing down any kind of global deal.

The odds seem indeed to be stacked against the environment. EU Commissioner for Climate Action Connie Hedegaard also seems to have given up on pushing emission reduction targets from 20% by 2020 to 30%. It might not be realistic either, in the light of the latest numbers released by IEA of carbon dioxide. Britain has opted for the goal of a 35% reduction by 2022, but latest statistics from the UK's Department of Energy and Climate Change show nearly a 3% rise in 2010 alone. Norway, having proclaimed itself a leader in the carbon-cut race by virtue of imposing its own 30% reduction target by 2020, actually saw an increase of 5% in emissions last year, according to new figures.

Fatih Birol, Chief Economist & Director, IEA was quoted sometime back in 'Guardian': 'The significance of climate change in international policy debate is much less pronounced than it was a few years ago. It is difficult to say the wind is blowing in the right direction'. It is indeed ironic for a renewable industry struggling to make its voice heard above a more politically savvy hydrocarbon lobby, urging ministers worldwide to 'dash for gas'. Oil companies, in their turn, are eager to present liquefied natural gas or shale gas as the answer to high CO_2 emitting coal base thermals. The former two are indeed lower carbon alternatives to coal-fired power stations, but do not completely eliminate carbon contribution.

It is high time the entire world starts seeing the move to shift towards a low-carbon economy as a 'growth opportunity', not as a deterrent or impediment.

1.02 CLIMATE CHANGE

Ancient annals tell us of prominent civilizations having been destroyed in various epochs owing to dramatic climate changes. New scientific studies suggest that climate change and drought caused yhe destruction of the Mayan civilization'that stretched across much of what is now southern Mexico, Brazil and Guatemala. Researches also suggest climate change might have brought about the fall of the ancient Khmer civilization in Cambodia nearly six centuries ago. Researchers suspect that El Nino might have played an important role in drying up monsoon rains, causing droughts and ultimate collapse of the civilization. Since 1900, the average global temperature has increased by 0.74°C. Humans are further changing the climate by their actions, especially through emissions of greenhouse gases, particularly carbon dioxide (CO_2) which artificially warms the earth's atmosphere. The burning of fossil fuels is largely to blame. The rising pattern of CO_2 concentration in the atmosphere during the half century since 1959 is glaringly conspicuous from the linear chart depicted below.

Risisng CO_2 Concentration in the atmosphere since 1956

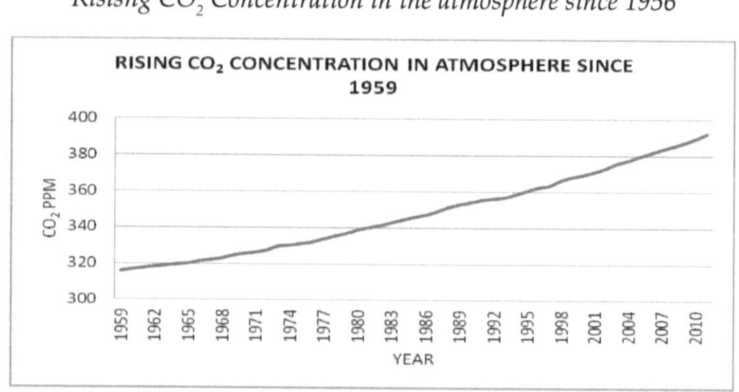

***Source** Scripps CO2 Program UCSD / Scripps Institution of Oceanography. Location: Mauna Loa Observatory, Hawaii

Correspondingly, there has been a consistent rise in the Annual Greenhouse Gas Index which is quite obvious from the line graph shown below. A whopping 27.5% rise has been recorded since 1990, which is taken as the base year with AGGI = 1:

Increasing Annual Greenhouse gas Index (AGGI) since 1990

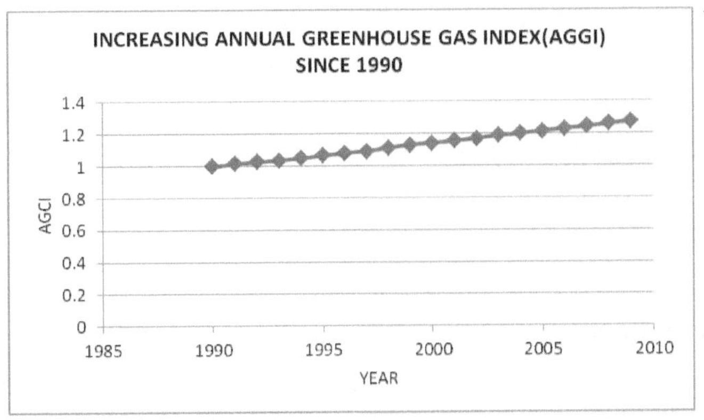

Climate change will increasingly cause storms, droughts, floods and fires and have a severe bearing on food production, water availability and ecosystems such as forests and wetlands. In particular, climate change has a strong potential for causing damage to agricultural production, leading to global food insecurity. Frequent occurrences of extreme natural calamities like flash floods; torrential rains and consequent inundation; cyclones and hurricanes; sudden cloud bursts and severe droughts would be the order of the future. A major concern is how rapidly climate change will intensify existing environmental stresses and contribute to food insecurity, conflict over resources, and loss of livelihood for millions of people.

Certain regions will be worse affected than others. India is one of the 12 countries that would be most severely affected by climate change. Warming is expected to be greatest over land and at high northern latitudes. The Arctic, Sub Saharan Africa, small islands and the big river deltas of Asia will be most seriously affected.

Those least responsible for global emissions, living on the periphery of the system – the poor and vulnerable in developing countries – are bearing the most grievous brunt of climate change impacts. For instance, Bangladesh could lose up to 20 percent of its land owing to sea level rise as a direct / indirect consequence of climate change. There are many other small and poor island countries that would lose considerable portions of their lands. Ensuing turmoil in these countries would be indispensably felt in their neighborhoods and in other parts of the globe. Developing and poor countries have fewer resources to acquire expensive environment-friendly technologies. It is a global responsibility to help these countries acquire and adapt mitigation technologies.

The world has before it a wide range of possible solutions that can help combat climate change. Protecting and better managing our natural resources is a cost-effective and efficient way to stabilize greenhouse gas emissions while we make the transition to a sustainable, low-carbon world in the coming decades. Natural resources can also help us adapt to the impacts of climate change we are already facing. It is an opportunity we cannot afford to lose. We should not soft pedal climate change concerns.

Climate Change & Water

During 1950-1970 there was a reasonably wet period, thereafter the trend reversed with declining precipitation. There is a high probability that many arid and semi-arid geographical areas, such as western United States, southern US, and northern Brazil, would be vulnerable to impact of climate change; these areas may also suffer decrease in water resources.

There are a number of attributes affecting 'Hydrological Cycle', notable among them being change in precipitation (rainfall). Change in precipitation has been apparent in some regions and would be more pronounced in some other regions. Changes in the frequency of floods and droughts would affect quality and quantity of water resources and may cause water pollution either directly or indirectly. In addition, food availability would be greatly affected, while there would be a certain impact on hydropower production as well.

As per IPCC, several gaps to knowledge exist in terms of observation and research related to climate change and water. Mitigation measures can reduce the magnitude of impact of global warming on 'water resources'. The following are some of the measures to counter the menace of Climate Change:

- Afforestation.
- Efficient energy use – both in residential and commercial buildings.
- CCS (Carbon dioxide capture and storage).
- Bio-energy crops.
- Enhanced use of Hydropower.
- Biomass electricity.
- Better land usage and change pattern: Land Use, Land-Use Change and Forestry (LULUCF)

Activities in the LULUCF sector provide a relatively cost-effective way of offsetting emissions, either by increasing the removals of greenhouse gases from the atmosphere (e.g. by planting trees or managing forests), or by reducing emissions (e.g. by curbing deforestation). However, there are drawbacks as it may often be difficult to estimate greenhouse gas removals and emissions resulting from activities of LULUCF. Moreover, greenhouse gases may get unintentionally released if a sink is damaged or destroyed through a forest fire or disease.

- Efficient management of crop water requirements (less water requiring crops and reduced tillage).
- Desalination.

Startling Facets of Climate Change

According to the IPCC, if global average temperature changes exceed 2°C there will be irreversible impacts on water, ecosystems, food, coastal zones and human health. We have a 50% chance of avoiding a 2°C warming if we stabilize greenhouse gases at 450 ppm CO_2 (parts per million carbon dioxide equivalent). Recent evidence suggests even more rapid change, which will greatly, and in some case irreversibly, affect not just people, but also species and ecosystems. This means we must start radically reducing emissions now and stay on a low emissions pathway to avoid increasing the amount of CO_2 in the atmosphere. The signs indeed are too ominous for us to neglect:

- ✓ Sea levels rose 20 cm in the preceding century.

- ✓ Glaciers, snow cover and sea ice have been all declining.

- ✓ We have been experiencing more heat-waves, droughts and extreme rainfall and more intense tropical cyclones.

- ✓ Global temperature could rise by as much as 6.4°C by the end of the century.

- ✓ Up to 30% of plant and animal species could become extinct if the global temperature increase exceeds 1.5-2.5°C.

- ✓ Arctic sea ice could disappear altogether during the summer by the second half of this century.

- ✓ Crop yields in tropical zones could significantly decrease with even a modest (1-2°C) temperature increase.

✓ One in six countries in the world faces food shortages each year because of severe droughts that could become semi-permanent with climate change.

✓ The overall costs and risks of climate change will be equivalent to losing up to 20% of global GDP each year, while the costs of action now can be limited to around 1% of global GDP each year.

✓ July 2011 is the 7th warmest July on record since 1880. Neither 'El Nino' nor 'La Nina' conditions were present during July 2011

Role of El Nino

El Nino has been associated with increased risk of floods and droughts. The strong El Nino event in 1982-3 was associated with economic losses of up to US$14 billion worldwide, and up to US$2 billion just in Peru due to the devastating effects on fish stocks. The El Nino is the main driver of short term climate variability in Latin America, and has large impacts on the economy and the well-being of people. Scientists believe that climate change will increase the frequency and severity of El Nino events. Climate change will have a significant impact on the sustainability of water supplies in the coming decades. A new analysis, done by one consulting firm for the ' Natural Resources Defense Council' (NRDC), examined the effects of global warming on water supply and demand in the contiguous United States. The study found that one-third of all counties will face higher risks of water shortages by mid-century as the result of global warming. Many of these counties would face extremely high risks of water scarcity.

1.03   GLOBAL WARMING

It bears repeating that human existence today faces the clear and present danger of disorder and destruction – a danger posed by the ugly duo of Global Warming and Climate Change. The world is at last waking up to the peril. Organizations have sprung up and Governments are spending billions on closely monitoring and watching the twin-monster that now stalks Mother Nature. What makes the matter worse is that the two deadly adversaries to ecology present a chicken-or-egg conundrum – because in tandem they make a whole vicious cycle, with global warming affecting climate and climatic factors causing temperature anomaly. But one thing is certain – making some progress in controlling atmospheric warming would be the best way to make a salubrious impact on world climate.

In the characteristic idiom of an environmentalist, 'global warming' signifies the unusually rapid increase in earth's average temperature particularly witnessed over the past century. The average facade temperature of the globe has augmented more than one degree Fahrenheit since 1900 and since 1970 the rate of warming has almost become three times the century long average.

Skepticism also abounds regarding global warming. We would give adequate space to skeptics' view point as well but a little later; before that we need to understand a few more terms in order to understand the phenomenon of global warming.

Temperature Anomaly is one parameter that helps greatly in understanding warming of the earth. The term signifies a deviation or departure in recorded temperature from a reference value or long-term average. A positive anomaly indicates that the observed temperature was warmer than the reference value, while a negative anomaly suggests that the observed temperature was cooler than the long-term average. It thus provides an overview of average global temperatures compared to a reference value.

Fortunately, enough reliable temperature data are available since 1880 to enable a scientific analysis of long term trends in temperature anomaly on a global scale. The 'anomaly' is expressed in units of 0.01°C, and the base period is taken as 1951 – 1990, the average temperature anomaly during which is assigned the base value of zero. Tabulation of the time series data before and after this base period reveals a pronouncedly high trend of temperature rise in the first decade of the twenty-first century in relation to not only the old historical data of the nineteenth century, but to the more recent base period (1951 – 1990) as well.

YEAR	1881	1891	1900	2001	2010
TEMPERATURE ANOMALY IN 0.01°C	-20	-27	-8	47	63

* **Source** Goddard Institute for Space Studies) *Temperature Anomaly in 0.01 C*
[Base Period 1951-90]

When put graphically, the picture of variation becomes more striking, as depicted in the liner chart shown below.

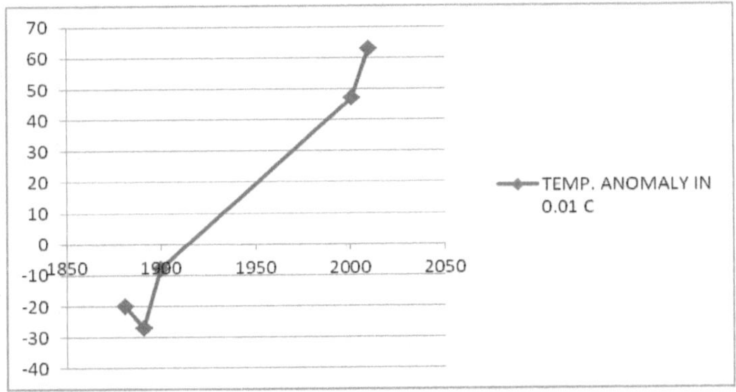

* **Source** GISS   *Temperature Anomaly since 1881*

It is evident that while increase in temperature is consistent and sharp during the period 1891-2000, the rise is still steeper and much more palpable beyond 2000. Quite obviously, the world now is getting hotter by the day, and the sharp gradient of temperature increase bodes ill for the future. The importance of studying long-term temperature trends in a variance analysis of the type shown above would be apparent when we consider that mere statistical averages over a long period cannot throw up any cognizable trend. For instance, the following table and its accompanying graph relating to the pattern of mean monthly temperatures over the entire twentieth century do not tell us anything about the awesome trend of inexorable global warming; on the contrary, all we get is a deceptively complacent picture of semi-sinusoidal symmetry in the trend of monthly average temperatures. That is why analysis of yearly anomalies is so important in understanding the real impact of global warming.

GLOBAL COMBINED (LAND & SEA SURFACE) MEAN MONTHLY TEMPERATURE ESTIMATES [BASE PERIOD 1901-2000] *source NOAA

Combined Mean Temp.	J	F	M	A	M	J	J	A	S	O	N	D	Annual
1901 to 2000 (°C)	12	12.1	12.7	13.7	14.8	15.5	15.8	15.6	15	14	12.9	12.2	13.9
1901 to 2000 (°F)	53.6	53.9	54.9	56.7	58.6	59.9	60.4	60.1	59	57.1	55.2	54	57

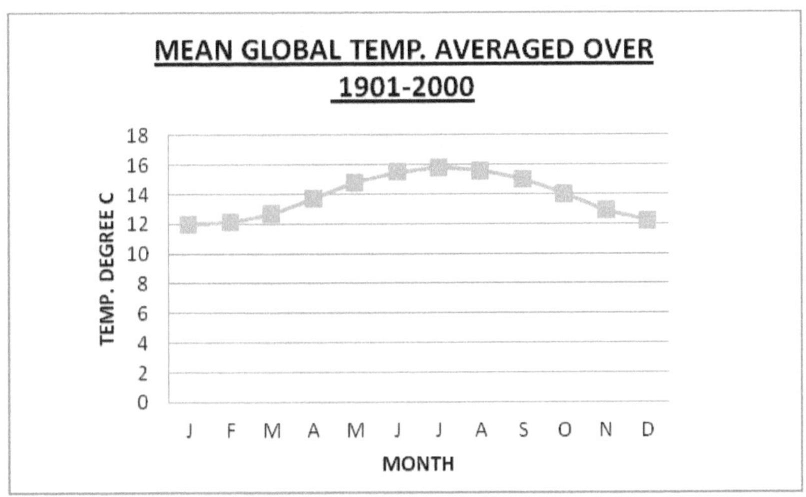

Mean Global Temp. Averaged over 1901-2000

CAUSES OF GLOBAL WARMING: GREENHOUSE GASES

The major cause of global warming is the emission of greenhouse gases like carbon dioxide, methane; nitrous oxide etc. into the atmosphere. The major sources of carbon dioxide (by far the biggest constituent of greenhouse gas) are the power plants. These plants belch out large amounts of carbon dioxide produced from burning of fossil fuels for the purpose of electricity generation. About twenty percent of carbon dioxide emitted in the atmosphere comes from burning of gasoline in the engines of vehicles. The combustion of oil across the global board (including both developed and developing countries) contributes 37% of total CO_2 emissions.

The relative causal impact of the four main greenhouse gases (CO_2, methane, chlorofluorocarbons and nitrous oxide) on global warming would be apparent from the following chart.

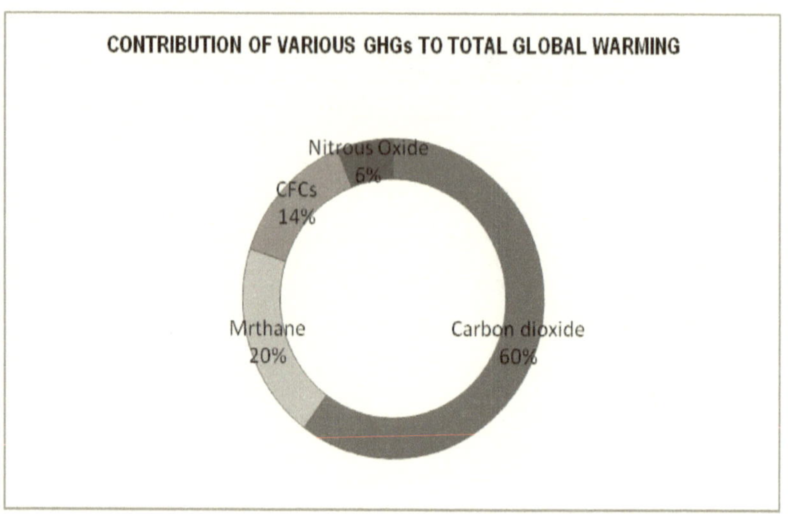

Contribution of Various GHGs to Total Global Warming

CONSTRUCTION OF BUILDINGS & OTHER STRUCTURES

Construction activity is also a great source of CO_2 emissions. In particular, making of buildings, both commercial and residential, represents a large sectoral contributor to global warming. Building of these structures requires a lot of fuel to be burnt, which emits a large amount of carbon dioxide in the atmosphere.

PRODUCTION OF CEMENT

Cement is a large contributing factor in enhancement of CO_2. Global carbon dioxide (CO_2) emissions from cement production were approximately 829 million metric ton of CO_2 (MMTCO2) in 2000 and have considerably increased by now. Globally, over 150 countries produce cement and/or clinker, the primary input to cement. Three largest producers of cement in world are China followed by India and USA.

Methane Emissions & Other Causes

Methane is more than 20 times as effectual as CO_2 in entrapping heat in the atmosphere. Methane is released from resources such as rice paddies, bovine flatulence, bacteria in bogs and fossil fuel accumulation. When fields are flooded, an anaerobic situation gets built up and the organic matter in the soil decays, releasing methane to the atmosphere. The main sources of nitrous oxide include nylon and nitric acid production; cars with catalytic converters; use of fertilizers in agriculture; and the burning of organic matter. Another cause of global warming is deforestation that is caused by cutting and burning of forests for the purpose of residence and industrialization. Also the warming can be due to variation in cloud cover, which in turn impacts on terrestrial temperatures. Temperature variations may also result from cosmic ray flux that is modulated by the solar magnetic cycles.

Multidimensional Ramifications of Global Warming

Scientists all over the world are making predictions about the ill effects of global warming and construing some of the events that have taken place in the past few decades as an alarm signal of global warming. The effect of global warming is increasing the average temperature of the earth. A rise in earth's temperatures can in turn lead to other alterations in the ecology, including a rising sea level and changes in the quantum and pattern of rainfall. These changes may boost the occurrence and impact of severe climate events, such as floods, famines, heat waves, tornados, and twisters. Other consequences may comprise of higher or lower agricultural outputs, glacier melting, lesser summer stream flows, genus extinctions and rise in the ranges of disease vectors.

As an effect of global warming species like the golden toad and the harlequin frog of Costa Rica have already become extinct. There are many other species that are now confronted with the serious threat of disappearing soon as an effect of global warming.

As an effect of global warming various new diseases have now raised their hydra heads. These diseases are occurring more frequently than ever before due to the increase in earth's average temperature, since the bacteria can survive better in elevated temperatures and can even multiply faster when conditions are favorable. Global warming is also causing proliferation of mosquitoes due to the increase in humidity levels and rapid growth of mosquitoes in warmer atmosphere. Various diseases due to the ebola, hanta and machupo virus are expected in the microbe-friendly warmer climates. Marine life is also highly sensitive to increases in temperatures. The effect of global warming would be particularly pronounced on some of the aquatic species. A survey has been carried out in which the marine life reacted significantly to changes in water temperatures. It is expected that many species will die off or become extinct in the warmer waters, whereas various other marine species, which prefer the very same ambience of warmth, will increase tremendously. Perhaps the most disturbing impact would be on the coral reefs, which are expected to die off as an effect of global warming. Global warming is expected to cause irreversible changes in the ecosystem and in the behavior of animals.

SKEPTICS' VIEWPOINT

But global warming skeptics are of the view that it is a natural phenomenon and should not be interfered with. According to them, one benefit to accrue from global warming will be increased humidity in the tropical deserts; also, higher levels of carbon dioxide in the atmosphere trigger plant growth. As predicted, due to global warming, sea levels will rise; but this can arguably be factored in through planned precautionary steps and rehabilitation measures. Another argument advanced by supporters of global warming is that the earth, in its long history, had been warmer than today. The point sought to be made is that global warming just takes us back to a more natural set of environment that prevailed in the past, when animals and plants appeared to do just fine in the warm bosom of Mother Earth. It must also be said that these ecology optimists also have an important role to play in the ongoing debate on environment inasmuch as making points and counterpoints is an essential element of informed debate. The world today has many problems and let us not add environmental bigotry to that list. At the same time, however, to summarily dismiss all the stark ecological symptoms and diagnostics presented in the foregoing sections relating to the malaise of global warming would be to take refuge in an ostrich-like delusion of wishing away a danger by not looking at it.

1.04   WATER POLLUTION & SCARCITY

For centuries, fecal waste and other pollutants were dumped in rivers. Major rivers of the world are now badly polluted. Apart from this, human well-being and ecosystem health in many places are being seriously undermined by changes in the global water cycle, caused largely by human pressures.

Today, the rivers of the world are afflicted with the dual scourge of water pollution and negative climatic changes. Water pollution has indeed become a matter of grave concern. Effluents, garbage, sewage and other liquid and solid wastes are being deliberately pumped into river systems, thereby rendering the river waters highly toxic and also killing precious aquatic life. In future, availability of fresh, potable and wholesome water would be severely compromised owing to widespread and rampant water pollution. It will create widespread shortage as the water flow of the major rivers of the world is declining fast, while at the same time the hitherto available water is grossly being polluted and defiled by mindless human action. The causes of pollution are more of anthropogenic than natural roots.

Though multi-million dollar schemes have been launched to rehabilitate the rivers world over yet, the situation still continues to be alarming. Some of the highly polluted rivers of world include Nile (Africa), Citarum (Indonesia), Yangtze (China), King River Murray Darling (Australia), Sarno (Italy), Ganges, Yamuna, Indus (India) Rio Grande (USA/Mexico) etc. They need urgent attention and to be saved from further contamination by concrete and time bound programmes and rehabilitation schemes

Water quality degradation from human activities continues to harm human and ecosystem health. Three million people die from water-borne diseases each year in developing countries, the majority of whom are children under the age of five. Pollutants of primary concern include microbial pathogens and excessive nutrient loads. Water contaminated by microbes remains the greatest single cause of human illness and death on a global scale. High nutrient loads lead to eutrophication of downstream and coastal waters, and loss of beneficial human uses. Pollution from diffused land sources, particularly agriculture and urban run-off, needs urgent action by governments and the agricultural sector. Pesticide pollution, endocrine-disrupting substances and suspended sediments are also hard to control. There indeed is a tremendous scarcity of fresh water which is reflected by the following illustrations.

GLOBAL SCARCITY OF FRESH WATER

The following three charts would lucidly explain the rarity of fresh water the world over. The scarcity is accentuated by the fact that the bulk of world's water is actually locked in oceans and glaciers.

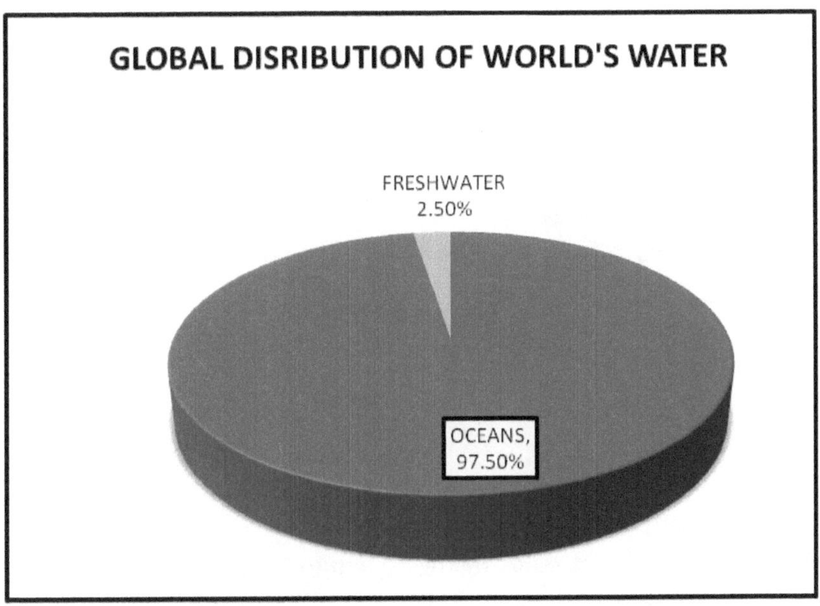

* **Source** GEO4 UNEP   *Global Distribution of World's Water*

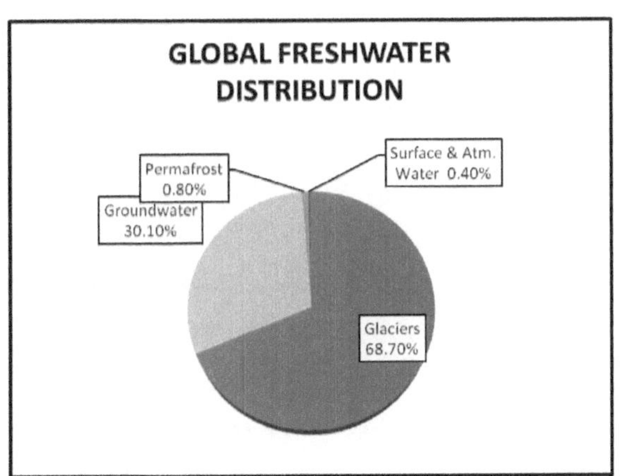

*Source** GEO 4 UNEP   *Global Freshwater Dsitribution*

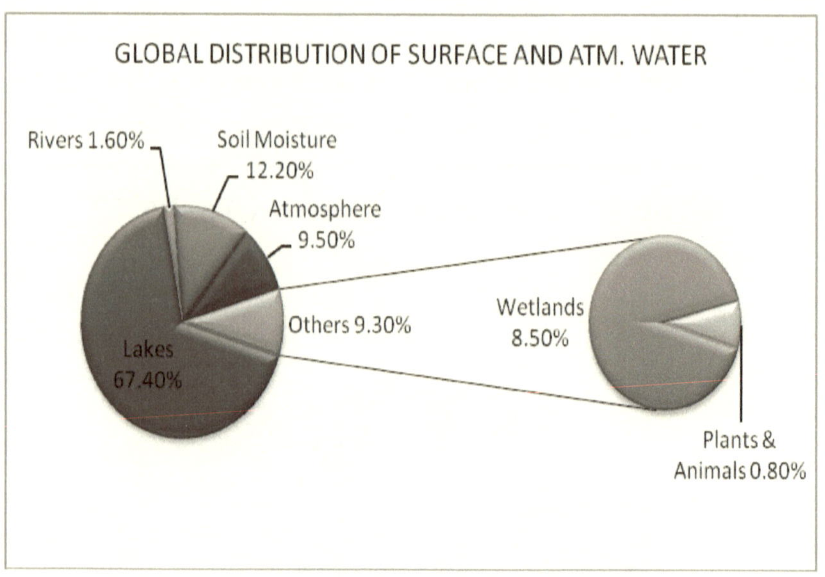

Global Distribution of Surface & ATM Water

WATER POLLUTION

Water Pollution is a state resulting when substances are released into a body of water, where they become dissolved or suspended in the water or deposited at the bottom, accumulating to the extent that they overwhelm its capacity to absorb, break down, or recycle them, and thus interfering with the functioning of aquatic ecosystems.

CONTAMINANTS IN WATER

Water pollution could be caused by combination of several contaminants, including substances drawn from the air; acid rain; silt from soil erosion; chemical fertilizers and pesticides; runoff from septic tanks; outflow from livestock feedlots; chemical wastes (toxic or otherwise) from industries; and sewage and other urban wastes from cities and towns. Various generic classes of contaminants are shown in the following pictorial diagram.

Contributors to Water Pollution

There are myriad contaminants that pollute water and newer contaminants continue to be discovered in different geographical locations. The subject in fact calls for a detailed analytical coverage that may not be possible within the scope of this study. Yet an effort has been made here to present the more important of them under 11 groups (broadly conforming to the above graphic) tabulated hereunder.

Classification of Contaminants of Water

	Contaminant Group	Contaminants	Remarks
1	Suspended Particles	Silt Pipe work Debris Colloids (organic/inorganic)	Colloids give rise to turbidity or haze in the water and can foul R O membrane.
2	Dissolved Organics	Detergents Fats Oils Solvents Residues of pesticides & herbicides Compounds leached from pipe works Humic & Pulvic acid (from decay of vegetable matter)	Organic impurities in water arise from decay of vegetable matters or from farming, domestic & industrial waste.
3	Volatile Organic Contaminants [VOC's]	Benzene Carbon Tetrachloride Chlorobenzene o-Dichlorobenzene p-Dichlorobenzene 1, 1-Dichloroethylene Cis-1, 2-Dichloroethylene trans-1, 2-Dicholoroethylene Dichloromethane 1, 2-Dichloroethane 1, 2-Dichloropropane Ethyl benzene Styrene	

		Tetrachloroethylene	
		1, 2, 4-Trichlorobenzene	
		1, 1, 1,-Trichloroethane	
		1, 1, 2-Trichloroethane	
		Trichloroethylene	
		Toluene	
		Vinyl Chloride	
		Xylenes	
4	Dissolved Inorganic Salts	Calcium bicarbonate & Magnesium carbonate	Amount of Dissolved Inorganic Salts (DIS) can be measured with reference to Total Dissolved Solids (TDS). The same can be estimated also by multiplying the conductivity of water (caused by dissolved inorganic ions) in µS/cm at 250C by 0.7.
		Sulphates & Chlorides	
		Sodium Salts	
		Silicates leached from sandy river beds	
		Ferrous & ferric ion compounds [from rusty iron pipes]	
		Chlorides from saline intrusion	
		Phosphates from detergents	
		Nitrates from fertilizers	
5	Inorganic Contaminants	Antimony	
		Asbestos	
		Barium	
		Beryllium	
		Cadmium	
		Chromium	
		Copper	
		Cyanide	
		Lead	

		Mercury	
		Nitrate/Nitrite	
		Selenium	
		Thallium	
6	Dissolved Gases	CO2	
		Oxygen	
7	Micro Organisms	Amoebae	* It causes Giardiasis which is a major diarrheal disease found throughout the world. It is the most commonly identified intestinal parasite in the United States and the most common protozoal intestinal parasite isolated worldwide. Infection is more common in children than in adults.
		Bacteria [Coliforms/Fecal Coliforms/E-Coliforms]	
		Paramecia	
		Rotifers	
		Diatoms	
		Algae	
		Cryptosporidium [Parasite causes 'Cryptosporidiosis' a mild gastrointestinal diseases]	
		Giardia lamblia [Causes diarrhea, vomiting & cramps]*	
8	Pyrogens		These are cellular fragments responsible for rise in temperature of mammals. They also have undesirable effects on tissue culture experimentation.
9	Radio Nuclides	Alpha emitters	* A gas which accumulates in underground water sources such as wells can present a risk of developing cancer
		Beta emitters [Photon emitters]	
		Combined Radium 226/228	
		Radon*	

10	Trace Metals	Mercury (Hg)	These 9 trace metals are being monitored in India
		Arsenic (As)	
		Chromium (Cr)	
		Cadmium (Cd)	
		Lead (Pb)	
		Copper (Cu)	
		Nickel (Ni)	
		Zinc (Zn)	
		Iron (Fe)	
11	Pesticides	Alpha BHC	These 15 pesticides are also monitored at select locations in India.
		Beta BHC	
		Gama BHC (Lindane)	
		OP DDT	
		PP DDT	
		Alpha Endosul-phan	
		Beta Endosulphan	
		Dieldrin	
		Aldrin	
		Carboryl (Carbamat)	
		2-4 D	
		Malathion	
		Methyl parathion	
		Anilophos	
		Choropyriphos	

HUMAN & ENVIRONMENTAL HEALTH EFFECTS

Fertilizer, animal manure, and effluent from waste-treatment plant all contain nutrients that stimulate excessive plant and algal growth in freshwater bodies. When the plants die and decompose, dissolved oxygen is depleted, causing die-offs of fish and other species living in the water. Effects of surfeit or deficiency of a few contaminants / nutrients on humans are indicated below.

A. **Fluoride**

Optimum Limit: 0.5 to 1.0 mg/l [As per WHO 1994].

Deficiency effects: Dental Cavities.

Excess effects: Bone diseases, pain and tenderness of bones, Dental fluorosis, brown straining, pitting of teeth, Skeletal fluorosis, spotting and discoloration of teeth.

Over fluoridation: May result in fluoride poising. Symptoms include nausea, vomiting and diarrhea.

* Children under 9 should not drink water that has more than 2 mg/l of fluoride.

B. **Arsenic**

Excess may result in skin damage, problem with circulatory system and increases risk of cancer. Every day, more than 140 million people in southern Asia drink groundwater contaminated with arsenic. Areas most affected are some regions in Bangladesh, Cambodia, India, Myanmar and Vietnam, where thousands die of cancer each year from chronic exposure to arsenic, according to the World Health Organization. Some health experts call it the biggest mass poisoning in history.

C. **Nitrate**

Excess may result in Mathemoglobinemia (also called blue baby disease). Children suffering from this disease may vomit; their skin color may become dark and they may die in extreme cases.

Optimum Limit: - Maximum limits 45 ppm.

D. **Methyl Mercury**

Excess may result in Minamata disease which is neurological.

Symptoms: -   Ataxia, numbness in hands and feet, general muscle weakness, narrowing of the field vision and damage to hearing and speech.

E. **Dissolved Oxygen**

The max. and min. limits of DO in water should be as under

Maximum: 110% of saturation

Min: 4 mg/l

Depletion of DO results in death of certain species of fish.

DIMINISHING RENEWABLE INTERNAL FRESHWATER RESOURCES

Renewable internal freshwater resources include the internal river flows and groundwater from rainfall in the country. Renewable internal freshwater resources per capita are calculated using the World Bank's population estimates. Global Per Capita availability of freshwater resources was 7889 cubic meters in 1992 and since then it has been declining. It has come down to 6509 cubic meters in 2007.The following bar chart depicts the diminishing per capita avilabilty in different reporting years.

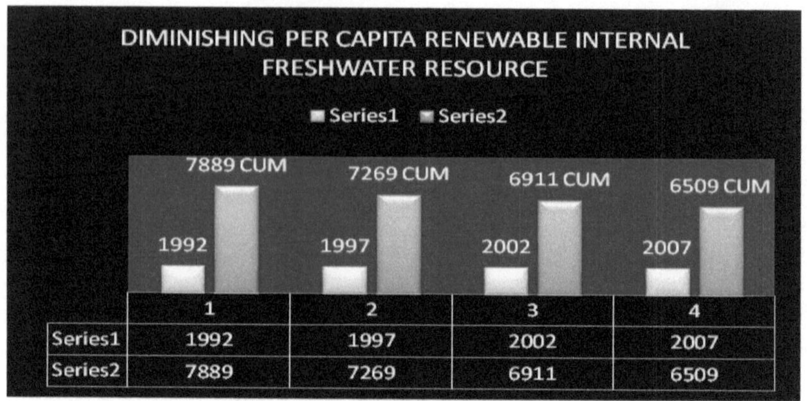

	1	2	3	4
Series1	1992	1997	2002	2007
Series2	7889	7269	6911	6509

* **Source** World Bank Diminishing Renewable Internal Freshwater
(global per capita average)

POLLUTION SCENARIO IN INDIA

The table below presents the profile of water quality in several river basins of India in terms of three key parameters, viz. pH value (indicative of acidity or alkalinity); Dissolved Oxygen; and Biochemical Oxygen Demand. The precarious state of pollution hovering near or beyond tolerance limits in some of these basins is a sad commentary on the quality of freshwaters in the country.

Water Quality in River Basins of India

Basin	pH (7= Neutral <7= Acidic >7= Alkaline)		DO (Dissolved Oxygen)		BOD (Biochemical Oxygen Demand)	
T L (Tolerance Limit)	6.5-8.5		Min-4		Max-3.0 mg/l	
	Min	Max	Min	Max	Min	Max
Mahanadi	6.7	8.48	5.96	8.82	0.4	7.0
Brahmani	7.1	8.1	5.4	8.39	0.37	1.1
Godavari	6.5	8.5	3.5	8	0.4	2.4
Krishna	7.14	8.62	3.9	8.1	0.1	4.4
Cauvery	7.2	8.66	5.4	7.1	0.1	3.7
Tapi	7.8	8.6	*	*	0.2	1.7
Narmada	7.8	8.52	*	*	0.1	1.1
Pennar	NA	NA	NA	NA	NA	NA
Sabarmati	NA	NA	NA	NA	NA	NA
Mahi	7.6	8.5	*	*	0.2	1.6

***Source** Central Pollution Control Board

The water quality monitoring results derived from Water Quality Monitoring Network during 1995 to 2006, indicate that organic and bacterial contaminations continue to be critical. The discharge of domestic wastewater, mostly in untreated form from the urban centres of the country, has been identified as the prime source for this contamination. The municipal corporations at large are not able to treat the increasing load of municipal sewage flowing into waterbodies and it is often discharged without treatment. Further, the receiving water bodies do not have adequate water for dilution. Therefore, the oxygen demand and bacterial pollution is on increase, which is mainly responsible for water borne diseases.

Analysis indicates that the number of observations having BOD and coliform density has increased between 1995-2006. Columnar depictions of the two important parameters TC (Total Coliforms) and BOD (Bio-chemical Oxygen Demand) are shown below.

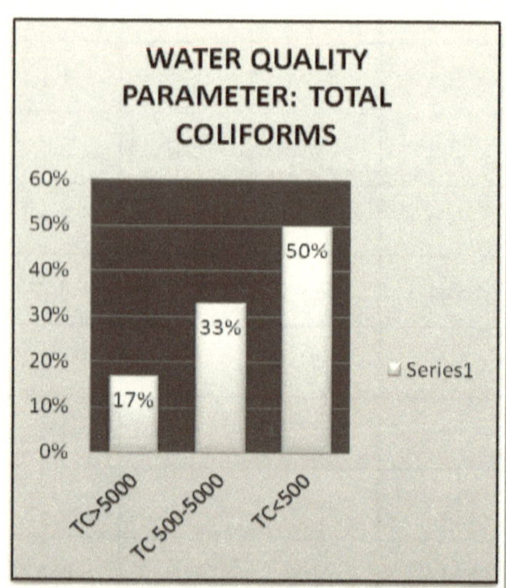

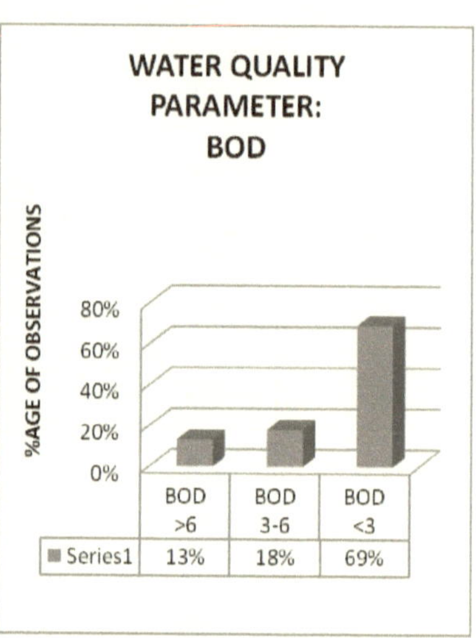

***Source** CPCB INDIA *Water Quality in Terms of PC & BOD in India (2007)*

1.05   DWINDLING FORESTS

WORLD SCENARIO

Forests harbor nearly 80 percent of land-based biodiversity and store more than 1 trillion ton of carbon. Deforestation is of dire concern because Greenhouse Gas Emissions (GHGe) from deforestation account for more than those by the world's entire transportation sector.

The world's total forest area covers just over 4 billion hectares, which corresponds to an average of 0.6 ha per capita. The five most forest-rich countries (the Russian Federation, Brazil, Canada, the United States of America and China) account for more than half of the total forest area. Ten countries or areas have no forest at all and an additional 54 have forest on less than 10 percent of their total land area.

Deforestation, mainly the conversion of tropical forest to agricultural land, shows signs of decreasing in several countries but continues at a high rate in others. About 13 million hectares of forest were converted to other uses or lost through natural causes each year in the last decade compared with 16 million hectares per year in the 1990s. Both Brazil and Indonesia, which had the highest net loss of forest in the1990s, have significantly reduced their rates of loss, while in Australia, severe drought and forest fires have exacerbated the loss of forest since 2000. But globally the big worry is, we are still losing around 5.2 million hectares per year which tantamount to about the size of Costa Rica!

Of course, Asia has been leading the afforestation drive in the world with a significant contribution from India which is adding 300,000 hectares of forest every year. According to the 'State of the World's Forests' report, published by the Food and Agricultural Organization, five countries – India, China, Australia, Indonesia and Myanmar – had the largest forested area in Asia and Pacific region. These countries accounted for 74 per cent of the forest in the region with China and Australia alone accounting for almost half the forest area of the region. In Asia and Pacific region, forest area decreased at a whopping rate of 0.7 million hectares per year in the 1990s but it grew by 1.4 million hectares per year over the period 2000–2010, the report said.

This was primarily due to large-scale afforestation efforts in China, where the forest area increased by 2 million hectares per year in the 1990s and by an average of 3 million hectares per year since 2000. India, Philippines and Vietnam also increased forest area in the past ten years. While according to report, China plans a 50 million hectare increase in the area of its planted forests by 2020, with the aim of covering 23 per cent of the total land area with forests, a target which may be reached by 2015 if current planting rates continue. However, Sri Lanka, Myanmar, East Timor and Bangladesh have not seen improvements in their forest cover in the past decade.

Forest cover was slightly less than one-third of the total land area of Asia and Pacific. The region's forested area was 740 million hectares in 2010, accounting for about 18 per cent of the global forest area, according to FRA. UN, which has declared 2011 as the 'International Year of Forests,' found that the net global deforestation has declined by 37 per cent, but there still exists a billion hectare of degraded forest land. Global extent of forest cover is depicted in the table given below, based on Global Forest Resources Assessment Report 2010 (*Source Global Forest Resources Assessment Report 2010)

	Global Extent of Forest 2010	Forest 1000 ha	% of Land Area
1	Eastern and Southern Africa	267517	27
2	Northern Africa	78814	8
3	Western and Central Africa	328088	32
4	Africa	674419	23
5	East Asia	254626	22
6	Western and Central Asia	43513	4
7	Asia	592512	19
8	Europe	1005001	45
9	Caribbean	6933	30
10	Central America	19499	38
11	North America	678961	33
12	North and Central America	705393	33
13	Oceania	191384	23
14	South America	864351	49
	World	4033060	31

Indian Scenario

Heavy destruction and razing of forests occurred in India in the later part of the 18th century and early part of the 19th century. The teak forests of Malabar Coast were over-exploited to meet the requirements of British navy, whereas sandalwood trees were felled to feed the European markets.

The first sincere effort to protect India's sylvan territory came in the form of the *Indian Forest act 1865*. Though the act of 1865 was applicable only to the forests in control of the government and did not cover private forests, yet it could be considered a good beginning. The Act of 1865 was replaced by a more comprehensive *Indian Forest Act of 1878* by which forests were divided into reserve forests, protected forests and village forests. Later, the *Indian Forest Act of 1927* replaced the earlier Act of 1878. This act embodied all the major provisions of the earlier act, while extending it to include those relating to the duty on timber.

After independence, The *Forest Conservation Act 1980* was indeed a landmark legislation which comprehensively dealt with issues like release of forest lands for non-forestry purposes and steps to be taken for compensating the loss of forest lands were also enumerated. A series of sustained and consistent efforts have since resulted in the stabilization of forests by arresting the pace of deforestation in India. At present 16 types of forest can be seen in India with a diversity ranging from the rainforests of Kerala to the evergreen forests of the north-east.

The following table and the corresponding bar chart depict the forest cover in different years, wherefrom it can be seen that the coverage has remained in the range of 19.5% to 21 % in the last two and a half decades or so.

Forest Cover in Different Years in India

Year of Assess-ment	1987	1989	1991	1993	1995	1997	1999	2001	2003	2004	2007
Forest cover (sq. km)	640819	638804	639364	639386	638879	633397	637293	675538	678333	677090	690900
Percent	19.49	19.43	19.45	19.45	19.43	19.27	19.39	20.55	20.64	20.59	21.02

***Source** Different SFR Reports, GOI & Global Forest Resources Assessment Report, FAO

YEAR-WISE FOREST COVER in INDIA

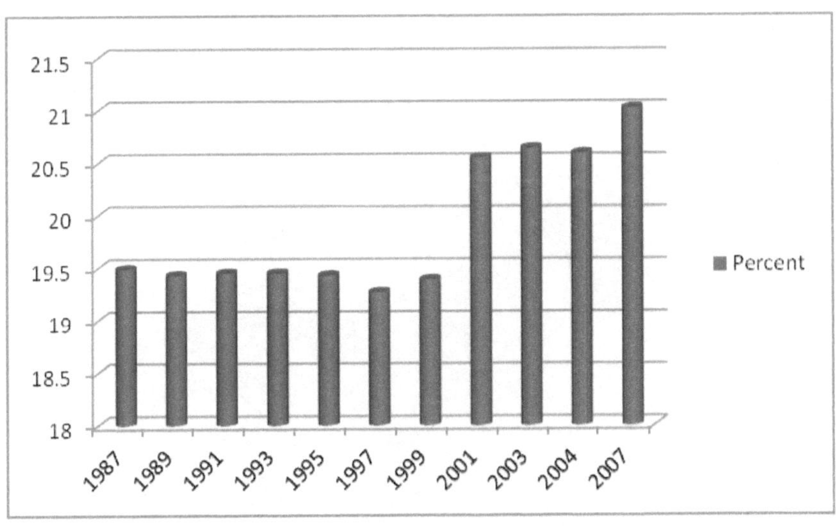

***Source** Different SFR Reports, GOI & Global Forest Resources Assessment Report, FAO

1.06   OZONE DEPLETION

The Ozone Problem, given its anomalous behavior and specific importance, has been dealt with comprehensively and exclusively in the chapter III of this book.

1.07   GROWING NOISE POLLUTION

'Just because we cannot see noise pollution doesn't mean we can turn a blind eye to it. This new report, building on the WHO's own work, makes it clear that the Environmental Noise Directive needs updating right away,' Louise Duprez of EEB (European Environmental Bureau) 6 June, 2011. The above statement eloquently reflects the severity of noise pollution and the same is second in magnitude only to the menace of air pollution (as per data of Europe); one in every three people experiences annoyance during the daytime and one in five has disturbed sleep at night because of noise emanating from roads, railways and airplanes. The main sources of noise have been depicted below.

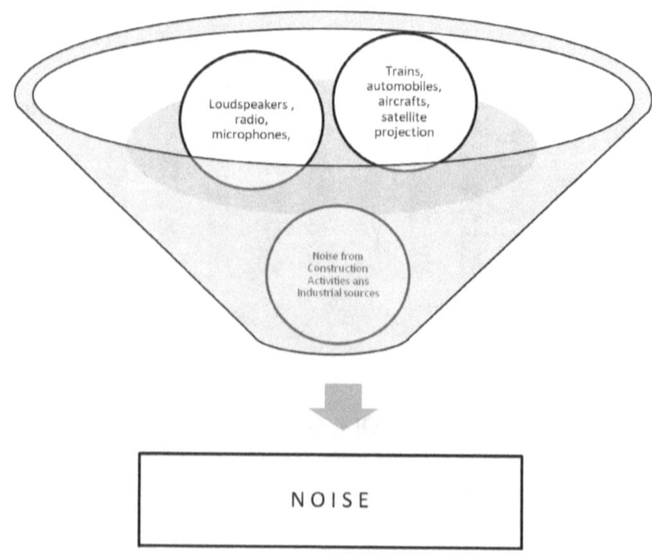

All transportation systems create noise pollution. Noise can also come from factory appliances, power tools and audio entertainment systems. In case of buildings located in the vicinity of factories, the residents experience noise pollution and its many adverse effects. Various academic definitions are there of noise pollution. Some of these are reproduced below for better understanding of the subsequent review:

'Noise is unwarranted sound without agreeable music quality'. In a more direct manner, the Encyclopedia Americana defines it as 'unwanted sound'. Another vivid definition says that 'noise is unwanted sound dumped into the atmosphere notwithstanding the adverse effects it may have on living and non-living things'.

In whatever way one may define noise, it is annoying for sure and wreaks havoc in the lives of people living in urban and downtown areas. When unwanted sound created by human beings hits our ears and disturbs the environment, noise pollution is created. Chiefly, noise pollution comes from barking dogs, loud music, vehicles, aircraft and rail transport, air-conditioners, factories, amplified music and construction work. Environmental Noise arising from transport and industry is an inevitable consequence of a mature and vibrant society, but it is regarded by the majority of people to be an unwelcome feature of everyday life.

Noise is subjective and different people react to it in different ways. What can cause annoyance to some people may be barely noticeable by others. As the noise level increases it can interrupt conversation, disturb sleep and, in extreme conditions, cause physical damage to those affected (although exposure to environmental noise is rarely at such a level as to cause this effect). Indeed, noise pollution can have wide-ranging effects, including physiological effects, behavioral effects, as also effects on animals and even non-living things.

In general, noise can be classified into some fairly broad categories. These include: occupational noise, which is experienced at work; neighbor and neighborhood noise; and environmental (ambient) noise. In another categorization, noise pollution may be caused from industrial or non-industrial sources.

NOISE MEASUREMENT: SPL & DECIBEL

Noise measurements are expressed by the term 'sound pressure level' (SPL) which is a logarithmic ratio of the sound pressure to a reference pressure and is expressed as a dimensionless unit of power, the decibel (dB). Various activities have varied dB levels, e.g. conventional human speech has SPL of 60 dB, light trucks at 20 feet distance creates 80 dB, a loud motorcycle at 20 feet makes a raucous 110 dB, a Rock & Roll band 120 dB and a Jet plane on the ground at a distance of 20 ft. may have SPL as high as 140 dB.

European Initiative: Environmental Noise Directives (END) The Environmental Noise Directive requires European Member States to establish through the process of noise mapping the number of people exposed to noise levels above 55 dB(A) Lden and 50 dB(A) Lnight from major roads, major railways, major airports and in large urban agglomerations.

The scope of END covers noise from road, rail and air traffic and from industry. It focuses on the impact of such noise on individuals, complementing existing EU legislation which sets standards for noise emissions from specific sources. END requires:

- Determination of exposure to environmental noise, through noise mapping;

- Provision of information on environmental noise and its effects on the public;

- Adoption of action plans, based upon noise mapping results, which should be designed to manage noise issues and effects, including noise reduction if necessary;

- Preservation by the member states of environmental noise quality where it is good.

NOISE MAPPING IN ENGLAND

England has come out with a novel solution for addressing the noise menace, which is known as 'Noise Mapping'. Noise maps provide an overview of the ambient noise environment in large urban areas and from major transport sources in England. These maps allow the determination of the number of people affected by different levels of ambient noise, the source of that noise (i.e. road, rail, air or industry) and the locations of the people affected.

ROLLING NOISE ACTION PLANS

The Environmental Noise (England) Regulations 2006, require noise action plans to be developed on a five year rolling programme. Action plans have to be developed for the major noise sources and areas for which maps have been produced. The action plans will seek to manage noise issues and effects including noise reduction if necessary, based on the results obtained through the mapping process.

Other countries should also follow suit and devise their own noise action plans as per their specific needs. Most of the Indian cities are in dire need of such 'noise mapping' and 'Rolling Noise Action Plans'.

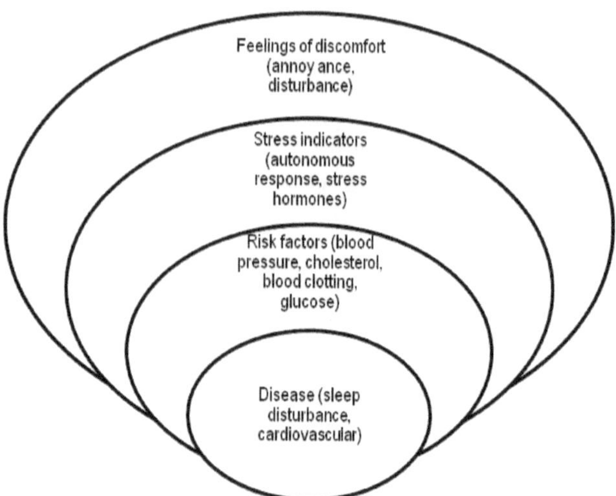

Health Effects of Noise

EFFECTS OF NOISE POLLUTION

Human health: Noise pollution disturbs our health and behavior in a number of ways including deafness causing lack of sleep, irritability, indigestion, heartburn, high blood pressure, ulcers, and heart disease. Just one noise explosion from a passing truck can drastically alter the endocrinal, neurological, and cardiovascular functions in many individuals. If the noise is prolonged or frequent, the physiological disturbances become chronic and contribute to mental illness.

Annoyance: Sometimes, even low levels of noise are irritating and can be frustrating, and high volumes can be annoying. Natural sounds are less irritating than those of artificial or mechanical origin. Thus, intermittent sounds such as a tap dripping water can be more irritating than the sound of falling rain.

Audio interference: Noise at more than 50dB can be very difficult to hear and interpret and cause problems such as partial deafness.

Sleep interference: High levels of noise can wake people from their sleep with a jerk and keep them awake or disturb their sleep pattern. This could make them irritable and tired the next day.

Decreased work performance: Increased noise levels give rise to lack of concentration and accuracy at work, and reduce one's productivity and performance. Difficult tasks can be impaired, and instructions or warnings difficult to be heard and interpreted, causing accidents.

Ways to Avoid Noise Pollution

Minimizing use of firecrackers: In India firecrackers are employed on various auspicious occasions. During a recent study, tests were conducted on firecrackers exceeding 100 dB, including the so called light based crackers. Some noise producing crackers such as 'Rassi Bombs' measured up to 145 dB, exceeding the maximum permissible limit of 125 dB. Use of such firecrackers should be minimized or abandoned altogether.

Staying away from heavy traffic: It is not desirable to live or work beside major intersections, noisy markets, shopping centres and sports facilities. Valleys and falls are noisier than flat roads.

Minding barking dogs: As a dog owner, one should take care to see that one's dog does not cause undue annoyance to neighbors with its barking and yowling.

Avoiding proximity to aircraft: Before buying a home, it should be ensured that it is not in close proximity of the local airport.

Being a considerate and thoughtful neighbour: Our responsibility as good neighbours is not to annoy those who live next door with irritating noise producing activities like playing loud music or lawn mowing with an old mower. Many noise problems can be prevented by considering others in a spirit of good-neighbourly cooperation.

NOISE LEGISLATION & REGULATION

In India, the Noise Rules 2000 under the Environment Protection Act 1986 were notified as per WHO recommendations. They were subsequently amended in 2010. Every aware citizen should be conversant with the provisions contained therein, as Appendices 1[A] & 1 [B] to the said rules.

In Europe, as already mentioned, Environmental Noise Directives (END) are there for member countries to frame policy and laws pertaining to noise. In the United States there are federal standards for highway and aircraft noise; states and local governments typically have very specific statutes on building codes, urban planning and roadway development. In Canada and the EU there are few national, provincial, or state laws that deal with noise.

Noise laws and ordinances vary widely among municipalities and indeed do not even exist in some cities. An ordinance may contain a general prohibition against making noise that is a nuisance, or it may set out specific guidelines for the level of noise allowable at certain times of the day and for certain activities.

In 1975, Dr. Paul Herman wrote the first comprehensive noise codes for Portland, Oregon. It was funded by the Environmental Protection Agency (EPA) and HUD (Housing and Urban Development). The Portland Noise Code became the basis for other ordinances in U.S. and Canadian metropolitan regions.

Most city ordinances prohibit sound above threshold intensity in respect of alarms for trespassing over property line at night, and during the day restrict the same to a higher sound level; however, enforcement is uneven. Many municipalities do not follow up on complaints. Even where a municipality has an enforcement office, it may only be willing to issue warnings, since taking offenders to court is expensive. The notable exception to this rule is the City of Portland Oregon which has instituted an aggressive protection for its citizens with fines reaching as high at $5000 per infringement.

Conflicts over noise pollution are often handled by negotiation between the emitter and the receiver. Procedures vary country by country, and may include action in conjunction with local authorities, in particular the police. Noise pollution often persists because only five to ten percent of people affected by noise would lodge a formal complaint. Many people are not aware of their legal right to quiet and do not know how to register a complaint.

Taking on the Menace of Noise Pollution

There are many strategies, ways and method to alleviate and mitigate noise emanating from myriad sources. Some of them are listed here.

- Noise Barriers
- The Sound Tube (used successfully in Melbourne, Australia)
- Limitation of vehicle speed and regulation of vehicular traffic
- Alteration of roadway surface texture
- Quieter jet engine design
- Redesign of industrial equipment
- Shock mounting assemblies
- Physical Barriers in workplace

- Computer modelling for roadway noise
- Residential insulation
- Review and reconsideration of Flight operations
- Strict enforcement of noise ordinance/rules.

Noise Barriers have been successfully deployed to mitigate vehicular Noise Pollution. They are generally installed along the major roads and have been used in many big cities of the world

1.08   RETREATING GLACIERS

Glaciers are large masses of snow, ice and rock debris that accumulate in great quantities and begin to flow outwards and downwards under the pressure of their own weight. They are formed when yearly snowfall in a region far exceeds the amount of snow and ice that melts in a given summer time. Recently NASA researchers discovered Greenland's Jakobshavn retreated 1.5 KM in a single day owing to breaking of a 7 sq. km section. Although glaciers have been retreating since 1850, the phenomenon has been more pronounced since 1980. Mid-latitude glaciers of the Himalayas, Southern Andes, Rocky Mountains, Alps, and Cascade Range all have been showing larger melting. Whitechuck glacier has retreated 1.9 km between 1973 to 2006; Argentiere, 1.15 km; Mont Blanc, 1.14 km (since 1870); Bossn glacier (Chamonix, France) has retreated 1.2 km, whereas Gangotri (India) has recorded 34 m per year retreat between 1970 to 1996. Swiss glaciers are not too far behind; in a study carried out in 2005, 84 out of 91 glaciers showed remarkable retreat. The Polar ice cap has also been melting more rapidly than thought earlier, recent studies indicating that both Greenland and Antarctica are contributing 0.5 mm/year rise to global sea level.

Retreating Swiss Glaciers

According to one BBC review, 'Swiss glaciers are melting away at an accelerating rate and many will vanish this century if climate projections are correct'. One assessment found that some 10 cubic km of ice has been lost from 1,500 glaciers over the past one decade. Another study, based on a sample of 30 representative glaciers, indicates that the group's members are now losing a metre of thickness every year. The retreat is being driven largely by longer melting seasons. The other key factor in glacier health – the amount of winter snowfall to replace ice melt – shows no long-term changes.

It is to be noted that in Switzerland, glaciers play an important role as water reservoirs for hydro-power production (generating 50% of the country's electricity).They are also considered an important attraction for tourists. But much to Switzerland's and the world's dismay, a recent report of 25 March, 2011, released by the Swiss National Academy of Sciences, indicated that most of the Swiss glaciers continued to shrink in 2010 also. Out of 112 glaciers under observation, the academy evaluated the position of 91. Of those, 82 had retreated, six had barely moved and three had shown slight progression. Most glaciers which had retreated, measured movements of between one and 25 metres, but the Gauli glacier in canton Bern retreated 196 metres. The Trient glacier in canton Valais, reported a 14 metre advance but was tempered by its sharp retreat over recent years.

Consequences of Retreating Swiss Glaciers

The glaciers' retreat is symptomatic of the state of the world's climate. The melting and retracing glaciers are certainly conveying signs of climate change. If they are shrinking it means the climate is changing. And that means our entire environment and weather system would change, with possibly very severe consequences, such as increased storms and flooding. The consequences of shrinking glaciers could be more severe in Switzerland. If they carry on shrinking the way they have been retracting of late, water supply to the hydro-electric power stations would be seriously affected. As a result, hydropower production could be seriously jeopardized. Swiss tourism industry would also be badly hit.

Retreating Glaciers of Asia

The Himalayas and other mountain chains of Central Asia support large regions that are dominated by glaciers. These glaciers provide critical water supplies to arid or semi-arid territories such as Mongolia, western China, Pakistan, Afghanistan and India. As with other glaciers worldwide, the glaciers of Asia are experiencing a rapid decline in mass. The loss of these glaciers would have a tremendous impact on the whole ecosystem of the region.

In the Wakhan Corridor of Afghanistan, 28 of 30 glaciers examined retreated significantly during the 1976-2003 period, the average retreat reported being 11 metres per year. One of these glaciers, the Zemestan Glacier, has retreated 460 m during the same period.

A MOUNTAIN RANGE DEVOID OF ICE IN ENGELBERG

A PEAK OF MOUNT TITLIS SWITZERLAND

*The beautiful Alpine Glaciers of Switzerland
now face the peril of gradual meltdown.*

More than 300 glaciers in China (of 612 studied) retreated during the period 1950-1970. Even After 1990, 95% of these glaciers were found to be retreating, confirming the long term retreating trend.

Glaciers in the Mount Everest region of the Himalayas are also in retreating mode. The Songbook Glacier, draining the north side of Mount Everest into Tibet, has been retreating 66 ft. per year. In the Khumbu region of Nepal along the front of the main Himalayas, of 15 glaciers examined from 1976-2007 all retreated significantly, average retreat was 28 m per year. The most famous of these – the Khumbu Glacier – retreated at a rate of 18 m per year from 1976-2007. In India, the Gangotri Glacier retreated 112 ft. per year between 1970 and 1996, registering an average loss of 30 m per year since 2000. It has retreated 1000 metre in the last 30 years. In a recent joint study conducted by two premier agencies, GSI and ISRO of India, 79 % of Himalayan glaciers were found to be retracing, disturbingly corroborating the melt down story.

To the south of the Tien Shan, the Pamirs mountain range located primarily in Tajikistan has many thousands of glaciers, all of which are in a general state of retreat. During the 20th century, the glaciers of Tajikistan lost 20 km^3 of ice. The 70 km long Fedchenko Glacier, which is the largest in Tajikistan and the largest non-polar glacier on the Earth, lost 1.4% of its length and the glaciated area was reduced by 11 km^2 during the 20th century. Similarly, the neighboring Skogatch Glacier lost 8% of its total mass between 1969 and 1986. The country of Tajikistan and neighboring countries of the Pamir Range are highly dependent upon glacial runoff to ensure river flow during droughts and the dry seasons experienced every year. The continued demise of glacier ice would ultimately result in reduced glacial melt water flowing into streams. The Tibetan glaciers are retreating at a greater speed than in any other part of the world. In the short term, this will cause lakes to expand and bring floods and mudflows. In the long run, the glaciers are vital lifelines for Asian rivers, including the Indus and the Ganges. Once they vanish, water supplies in those regions would heavily diminish.

Dwindling Glaciers of Africa

Africa's glaciers gone by 2025 – was the stark warning issued in May 2006, by the American Geophysical Union. As one study by Department of Geography, University College London reveals, 'Recession of these tropical glaciers sends an unambiguous message of a changing climate in this region of the tropics. Considerable scientific debate exists, however, as to whether changes in temperature or precipitation are responsible for the shrinking of glaciers in the East African Highlands that also include Kilimanjaro [in Tanzania] and Mount Kenya'.

Africa is located in the tropical and subtropical climate zones; glaciers there are restricted to two isolated peaks and the Ruwenzori Range. Kilimanjaro, standing tall at 5895 metre, is the highest peak on the continent. Since 1912 the glacier cover on the summit of Kilimanjaro has apparently retreated 75%, and the volume of glacial ice is now 80% less than it was a century ago due to both retreat and thinning. One section of the glacier of this mountain receded 300 metre from 1984 to 1998. A study of 2002 proclaimed that if current conditions continue, the glaciers atop Kilimanjaro will disappear sometime between 2015 and 2020. Similarly one report of March 2005 indicated that there is almost no remaining glacial ice on the mountain, and it is the first time in 11,000 years that barren ground has been exposed on portions of the summit. Researchers have attributed Kilimanjaro's glacier retreat to a combination of increased sublimation and decreased snowfall.

RETREAT IN THE ANDES

The Northern Patagonian Ice Field lost 174 km² of glacier area during the period 1975-1996, which establishes that the rate of retreat is alarmingly high. This represents a loss of 8% of the ice field, with all glaciers experiencing significant retreat. The Southern Patagonian Ice Field has exhibited a general trend of recession in 42 glaciers; four glaciers showed equilibrium while two others advanced during the years between 1944 and 1986. The largest retreat was on O'Higgins Glacier, which recorded retracement of 14.6 km during the period 1896 to 1995.

SOUTH AMERICA

Data in respect of Chacaltaya Glacier show a loss of 67% of its volume and 40% of its thickness over the period 1992 to 1998. Chacaltaya Glacier has lost around 90% of its mass since 1940. The observations of the Chacaltaya Glacier in Bolivia and Antizana Glacier in Ecuador indicated ice loss of 0.6 m to 1.9 m per year during the observed period 1992 to 1998.

RETRACTION OF OUTLET GLACIERS IN GREENLAND

Outlet glaciers are of considerable importance in Greenland and glacier retreat has been observed notably in three glaciers Helheim, Jakobshavns and Kangerdlugssuaq. These three jointly drain more than 16% of the Greenland Ice Sheet. Jakobshavn in west Greenland is a major outlet glacier of Greenland. It had been moving continuously at speeds of over 24 metre per day with a stable terminus since at least 1950. In 2002 the 12 km long floating terminus of the glacier entered a phase of rapid retreat, with the ice front breaking up and the floating terminus disintegrating and accelerating to a retreat rate of over 30 m (98 ft.) per day. On a shorter timescale, portions of the main trunk of

Kangerdlugssuaq Glacier that were flowing at 15 m (49 ft.) per day from 1988 to 2001 were measured to be flowing at 40 metre per day in the summer of 2005. Not only has Kangerdlugssuaq retreated, it has also thinned by more than 100 metre.

The pace of rapid thinning, acceleration and retreat of Helheim, Jakobshavns and Kangerdlugssuaq glaciers in Greenland, all in close association with one another, suggest a common triggering mechanism such as augmented surface melting due to regional climate warming.

Chilling Impacts of Glacial Retreat

The consistent and seemingly inexorable retreat of global glaciers will have multifarious and multidimensional ramifications along with qualitative impacts. Continual retreat would eventually diminish or deplete the glacial ice resulting in substantial reduction or complete elimination of runoff emanating from them. Some of the perceived consequences are summarized below.

- Many species of freshwater and saltwater plants and animals are dependent on glacier-fed waters to ensure the cold water habitat to which they have adapted. Some species of freshwater fish need cold water to survive and to reproduce, and this is especially true with salmon and cutthroat trout. Reduced glacial runoff could lead to insufficient stream flow to allow these species to thrive.

- Alterations to the ocean currents, due to increased freshwater inputs from glacier melt, and the potential alterations to thermohaline circulation of the world's oceans, may adversely affect existing fisheries upon which humans depend as well.

- A reduction in runoff will affect the ability to irrigate crops and will reduce summer stream flows necessary to keep dams and reservoirs replenished

- Skiing Resort would lose their sheen.

- Retreat of Swiss glaciers would heavily jeopardize hydropower production.

- A great loss to tourism activity and ice sports.

- If all the ice on the polar ice caps were to melt away, the oceans of the world would rise an estimated 230 ft. Although previously it was thought that the polar ice caps were not contributing heavily to sea level rise (IPCC 2007), recent studies have confirmed that both Antarctica and Greenland are contributing 0.5 mm a year to the rise.

1.09   RAPIDLY GROWING URBANIZATION

As per one recent report by McKinsey Global Institute – 'The city 600 will be home to an estimated 310 million more people by 2025 and 2.0 billion people will live in 600 cities by 2025 [constituting 25% of the Global Population]'. The projection is mind-boggling indeed. One can hardly imagine the consequences of such densely mushrooming urban expansion when humans would live like packed sardines in cities world over! Today nearly 50% of the world population lives in the cities, which would be enhanced to 75% in the not-so-distant future.

Nearly 400 million people are going to migrate to the cities in the next four decades. Urbanization indeed is one of the biggest environmental threats faced by the mankind and life forms. The sad irony is that urbanization has traditionally been the yardstick of civilization's progress, which normally involved migration of population from small rural communities to towns and cities. Urbanization is actually defined by the United Nations as movement of people from rural to urban areas with population growth equating to urban migration. Now, with growing urbanization, the accompanying higher population density in cities and towns exacerbated disease and better systems of public works and sanitation had to be devised. Cities became the repositories of humanity's collective intelligence; libraries were created to store this record of knowledge. Banks were built to store the accumulated wealth, while armories and stronger fortification were constructed to defend the cities against pirates and looters.

In 1950, 83% of the population of developing countries comprised rural inhabitants. By 1973, this had declined to 75% and by 1993 to only 60%. The number of major African cities grew from 2 to 37 between 1950 and 1993. In Cairo, the population was 5.4 million in 1970. By 1993, it had increased to 15 million, creating a massive increase in slums. African cities double in size every 12 years with some growing by 10% a year, the fastest rate of urbanization ever recorded. For the first time in history, more people live in cities than in the rural areas. The global proportion of urban population rose dramatically from 13% (220 million) in 1900, through 29% (732 million) in 1950, to 49% (3.2 billion) in 2005. It is believed that the figure is likely to rise to 60% (4.9 billion) by 2030. The UN predicts more people flocking to cities in the coming decades.

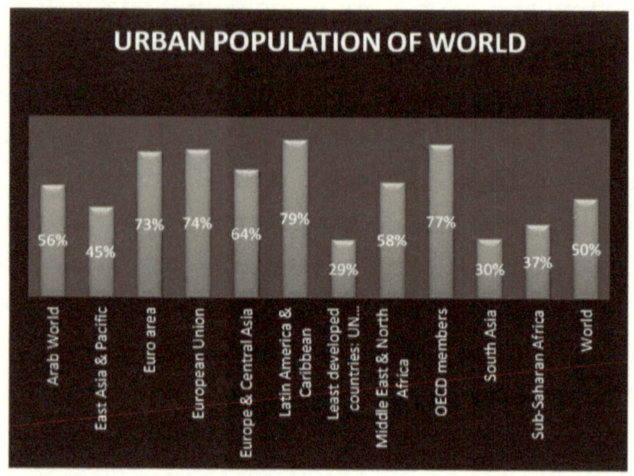

***Source** World Bank   *Worldwide Urban Population Pattern*

URBAN POPULATION IN DIFFERENT GEOGRAPHIES

Half of the world's population resides in urban areas. Latin America and the Caribbean Islands top the urban population (79%), followed by OECD Member countries and the European Union. LDCs (Least Developed Countries) as per UN Classification have the minimum urban population merely 29%.South Asia and Sub Saharan countries occupy the second and the third place respectively in the least urbanized geographies.

ENVIRONMENTAL IMPACTS OF URBANIZATION

Urbanization carries multiple effects some of which are still little understood. Impacts are many and varied. A few of them are:

1. Alteration in the chemistry of the atmosphere.
2. Urban area generally rendered hotter (1-6 degree C).
3. Gives rise to the phenomenon of photochemical smog.
4. Disfigurement of landscape.

5. Increased stress on water resources, both surface and subsurface.

6. Increased air pollution.

7. Contamination due to "Leachate" which comes from landfills of municipal solid waste or toxic wastes.

8. Alteration in the local circulation of air due to numerous tall obstructions haphazardly constructed.

9. Psychological stress caused by high density and fast paced life.

10. Overflow and recurrent flooding.

11. Deteriorated quality of run-off generated by urban space.

12. Growth of slums causing unhygienic living and environment.

13. Change in land use pattern.

14. Increased deforestation.

15. Intensified pressure on natural resources.

16. Increase in the incidence of water borne and other diseases like Malaria.

The diagram below lucidly displays the impacts of urbanization.

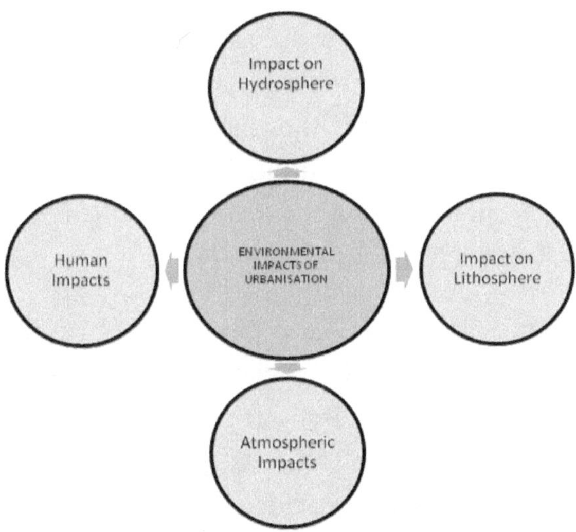

Environmental Impact of Urbanisation

Rapidly Rising Urban Population in India

India would be having 18 % of the world's population on 2.4 % percent of world's geographical area. As per the Provisional Population data of Census 2011, the total population of India was 1210.2 million. Of this, the urban population stands at 377.1 million. The urban population increased by 91.00 million in the last decade. Maharashtra has the highest urban population of 50.83 million (13.48% of country's urban population) in the country. The fierce pace of urbanization in India led to a whopping 91 million being added in just one decade registering 3.35 % decadal growth. It is phenomenal by all accounts, for a heavily populated country like India! Rise in some developing cities is still greater causing immense environmental burdens.

Indeed, the wave of urbanization in India continues to rise with no signs of let up. As per provisional figure of census of 2011 a whopping 31.16% of total population now lives in cities. Interestingly, it is the medium and small towns that are fuelling urbanization rather than the mega cities. In 2001, India had 35 cities / urban areas with a population of more than one million people. In total, some 108 million Indians, or 10.5 per cent of the national population, live in the country's 35 largest cities. Mumbai (Bombay) with a population of more than 16 million is now the world's fourth largest urban area followed by Kolkata (Calcutta) in fifth place.

According to provisional census figures of 2011, around 2774 new towns were created since 2001, registering an increase of 53.7% in ten years. In the absence of clear-cut planning, small and medium sized towns often tend to fall through policy gaps and as a result chart a haphazard growth trajectory. Urban slum areas are home to more than 40 million Indians or 22.6 per cent of India's urban population. More than 600 Indian towns and cities incorporate slum areas. The largest slum population in cities with a population of more than one million is found in Mumbai (48.9%).

How to tackle the menace of Rapid Urbanization

Here are some eco-friendly solutions by which we could reduce the pressure on our cities.

- ✓ Construction of more new eco-friendly green cities.

- ✓ Undertaking DSPs (De-urbanisation Satellite Projects) as explained in the chapter 8 of the book.

- ✓ Development of RGCs (Rural Growth Centres) in remote village areas

- ✓ Unfettered urbanisation needs restraining and reining in by appropriate regulatory mechanisms.

Benefits of Green Cities

The concept of a green city is relatively a new idea but gaining momentum the world over. Many such cities are being planned or are in the process of coming up. Some are: Sejong (South Korea), Dongtan, Huangbaiyu, Tianjin (China), Waitakere in New Zealand and Lavasa in India. These cities could provide some of the benefits enumerated below.

- Obviating landfill sites.
- Reduction in greenhouse gases.
- Reduction in Carbon footprints.
- Improvement in quality of life, living and lifestyle.
- Growth of biodiversity.
- Creation of new employment opportunities.

- Expansion in Tax Base.
- Generation of energy through renewable resources.
- Recycling sewage for irrigation and composting.
- Providing a way to Sustainable development.
- Small ecological footprints.
- Better management of both solid and liquid waste.
- An excellent solution to the problem of environmental degradation.

The Lavasa Eco-city: a project that holds much promise for the future.

1.10   THREATENED WETLANDS

Not So Wet & Wonderful Now!

Wetlands occur in all ecological regions throughout the world except Antarctica. Many of us have heard the term *Wetland,* which evokes the memory of an idyllic picnic spot. One can also vaguely remember names of some wetlands in the vicinity of one's dwellings. Some of them may not, however, belong to the standard normative category of wetland. An earnest attempt was made at Ramsar (an Iranian city where Ramsar convention was convened in Feb 1971) to clearly define and categorize wetlands. As per 'Ramsar convention' the wetland is defined as follows: 'Wetlands are areas of marsh, fen, peatland or water, whether natural or artificial, permanent or temporary, with water that is static or flowing, fresh, brackish or salt, including areas of marine water the depth of which at low tide does not exceed six metres. Wetlands may incorporate riparian and coastal zones adjacent to the wetlands, and islands or bodies of marine water deeper than six metres at low tide lying within the wetlands.'

Other Definitions

In the United States, wetlands are defined as 'those areas that are inundated or saturated by surface or groundwater at a frequency and duration sufficient to support, and that under normal circumstances do support, a prevalence of vegetation typically adapted for life in saturated soil conditions. Wetlands are also described as ecotones, providing a transition between dry land and water bodies'.

Wetlands are habitats that fall somewhere on the environmental spectrum between land and water. Since wetlands lie at the interface of terrestrial and aquatic habitats, they possess a unique mixture of species, conditions, and interactions. As a result, wetlands are among our planet's most diverse and varied habitats. They are important both for mankind and nature. Amphibians, migratory birds, insects, plants, and trees they all survive in these ecotones. But unfortunately, they are now threatened owing to variety of reasons prominent among them being 'encroaching populations'.

TYPES OF WETLAND

There are many types and categories of wetland, some of which are listed here. There are many types and categories of wetland, some of which are listed here.

1. Swamp
2. Slough
3. Flooded grasslands
4. Riparian zone
5. Freshwater swamp forest
6. Coniferous swamp
7. Marsh
8. Salt marsh
9. Bog
10. Peat swamp forest

Some wetlands are common to particular regions of the country:

*   Tanoe Swamps of Ivory Coast
*   Ruoergai marshes of Tibetan Plateau
*   Vembanad Kayal of Kerala India

In the USA, the following are the important wetlands.

*   Bogs and fens of the north-eastern and north-central states and Alaska
*   Wet meadows or wet prairies in the Midwest
*   Inland saline and alkaline marshes and riparian wetlands of the arid and semiarid west
*   Prairie potholes of Iowa, Minnesota and the Dakotas
*   Alpine meadows of the west
*   Playa lakes of the southwest and Great Plains
*   Bottomland hardwood swamps of the south
*   Pocosins and Carolina Bays of the southeast coastal states
*   Tundra wetlands of Alaska.

Importance & Need for the Conservation of Wetlands

Wetlands are highly productive communities and provide habitat and food resources for a wide range of species. They are extremely vital ecosystems that provide livelihoods for the millions of people who live in and around them. Wetlands have a high level of nutrients coupled with the availability of water. They provide ideal habitats for fish, amphibians, shellfish, and insects. Also, many birds and mammals rely on wetlands for food, water and breeding grounds. The Millennium Development Goals (MDGs) called upon different sectors to join forces to secure wetland environments in the context of sustainable development and improving human wellbeing. A three-year project carried out by Wetlands International in partnership with the International Water Management Institute found that it is possible to conserve wetlands while improving the livelihoods and living conditions of local people. Wetlands have historically been the victim of large-scale draining efforts for real estate development, or flooding for use as recreational lakes. By 1993 half the world's wetlands had been drained. More focus has, however, been put on preserving wetlands for their natural function since the 1970s. Wetlands provide a valuable flood control function. Wetlands are very effective at filtering and cleaning water pollution, often from agricultural runoff from the farms that replaced the wetlands in the first place.

Presently Threatened Wetlands

All over the world wetlands have been facing continuous threats. Depending on the type of wetland the threats vary; from converting a mangrove forest into shrimp farms to drainage and burning of peatlands for palm oil plantations. In India alone, there are more than 100 wetlands that need protection from pollution, development and other forms of misuse. Main reasons for continuing wetland degradation are economic development and inconsistencies in government policies in many countries. This results in drainage for agriculture, settlements and urbanization, pollution and hunting. Here is a list of vulnerable wetlands, which of course is not exhaustive but covers the more prominent areas.

1. Chilika Lake, Orissa, India
2. Loktak Lake, north east India
3. Jhelum & Wular Lake, J & K, India
4. Tanoe Swamp Forest, Ivory Coast
5. Ruoregai Marshes, Tibet
6. Vemband Kayal, Kerala, India
7. Aceh's Swamp Forests
8. Tropical Peatlands, South-East Asia
9. Peat Swamps Forests, Sarawak, Malaysia
10. Wakkarstroom Wetlands
11. Coastal area, Gulf of Mexico, affected by BP oil spillage [very recent]

Many of these wetlands are direly threatened, some of them being on the verge of extinction, while others are degenerating at a fast pace. The matter needs immediate attention. Though all is not lost yet governments, non-profit NGOs and green groups around the world should join the battle unflinchingly to preserve this precious ecosystem.

1. 11 ASTRONOMICALLY SOARING AIR POLLUTION

Air pollution is the contamination of air by the discharge of harmful substances. Air pollution can cause health problems and it can also damage the environment and property. It has caused thinning of the protective ozone layer of the atmosphere, which is leading to climate change. Industries, vehicles, increase in the population, and urbanization are some of the major factors responsible for air pollution. Air pollution results from a variety of causes, not all of which are within human control. Dust storms in desert areas and smoke from forest fires and grass fires contribute to chemical and particulate pollution of the air.

Global Scenario

Human and environmental exposure to air pollution is a major challenge, and an issue of global concern for public health. The World Health Organization (WHO) estimated that about 2.4 million people die prematurely every year due to fine particles (WHO 2002, WHO 2006c). This includes about 800,000 deaths due to outdoor urban particulate matter (PM10) and 1.6 million due to indoor PM10. There is evidence that the health of over 900 million urban people around the world is deteriorating daily because of high levels of ambient air pollutants. The toxicology of air pollution is a highly complex discipline that needs careful study and coordinated initiatives at both the state level as also at the individual level.

Though the air quality of some cities, notably in the richer nations, has improved dramatically over the last 20 years, yet the air quality of many cities in developing nations has deteriorated to extremely poor levels. Even in richer countries, in recent years, improvements in levels of particulate matter and tropospheric ozone have stagnated, and further measures are needed.

Regional air pollution problems of acidification have been reduced in Europe and North America, but are now a growing policy focus in parts of Asia, where acidic deposition has increased. Tropospheric (ground-level) ozone pollution causes significant reductions in crop yield and quality. The transfer of pollutants, especially tropospheric ozone, across the northern hemisphere, is becoming an increasingly important issue. Despite efforts to tackle air pollution since 1987, emissions of various air pollutants to the atmosphere are still having telling impacts on human health, economies and livelihoods, as well as on ecosystem integrity and productivity.

Atmospheric environment issues are complex. Different primary and secondary pollutants formed in the atmosphere, have very different residence times, and are transported to varying distances, and this characteristic affects the scale at which their impact is felt. Those substances that have short residence times affect indoor and local air quality. Substances with residence times of days to weeks give rise to local and regional problems; those with residence times of weeks to months give rise to continental and hemispheric problems; and those with residence times of years give rise to global problems. Some greenhouse gases last up to 50,000 years. The following diagram highlights the differences in residence time and spread of various chemical air pollutants.

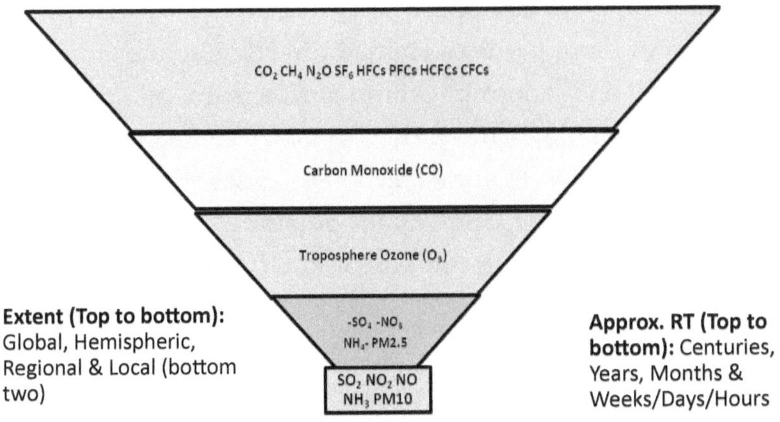

Air pollutants, their Extent & RT (Residence Time)

PARTICULATE MATTER

Particulate Matter (PM), arises from natural sources and processes, for example, soil and wind-blown dust, fires, and sea-salt aerosol. Other particles are by-products of various combustion or industrial activities. Still others enter the ambient air through condensation and other processes. PM air pollution includes several types of particles with different chemical compositions. Epidemiological studies indicate that small particulate matter air pollution is related to the increase in mortality, especially in people older than 60 years, who have existing cardiopulmonary diseases and in infants (up to 10 / 12 years). It is also associated with health problems including aggravation of asthma, especially in children, and other chronic lung diseases, impacts on lung function, and increased susceptibility to infectious illnesses. PM10 particles (the fraction of particulates in air of very small size, <10μm aerodynamic diameter) can potentially pose significant health risks, as they are small enough to penetrate deep into the lungs. Larger particles are not readily inhaled.

PM10 pollutants are comprised of two components. The primary component of those particles emitted directly into the atmosphere from natural and anthropogenic sources such as road traffic, industry or wind-blown dust. The secondary component is formed in the atmosphere by chemical reactions of gases, particularly sulfur dioxide, nitrogen oxides and volatile organic compounds. Concern about the potential health impacts of PM10 has increased rapidly in recent years.

COUNTRIES HAVING PM10 CONCENTRATION EXCEEDING 100PPM

COUNTRY	PM10 Concentration in [PPM]	Ranking
Uruguay	160	I
Sudan	159	II
Iraq	138	III
Bangladesh	134	IV
Mali	112	V
Mangolia	111	VI
Pakistan	109	VII
Saudi Arabia	104	VIII

***Source** World Development Indicators, WORLD BANK

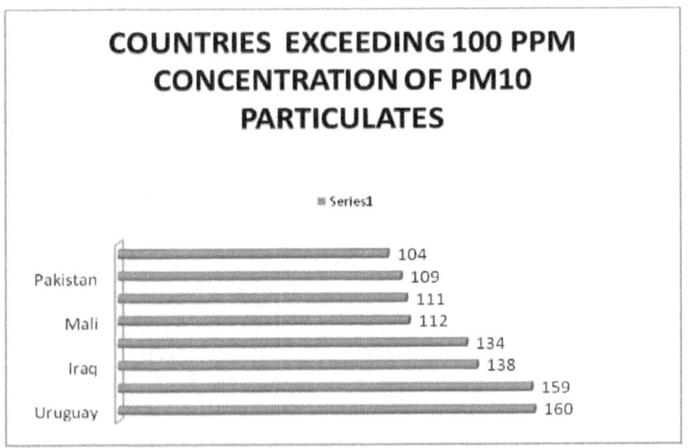

* **Source** World Bank   *Countries Exceeding 100PPM Concentrations of PM10 Particulates*

Key Air Pollution Issues around the World

The key issues have significant regional variations. In Asia and Pacific, Africa, West Asia, Latin America and the Caribbean, the issue with the highest priority is the effect of indoor and outdoor particulates on human health, especially for women and young children exposed to indoor smoke when cooking. The widespread use of poor quality fuels for industrial processes and transport represent a critical outdoor urban air pollution issue for the regions' policy-makers, especially in Asia and the Pacific. Food security issues caused by growing levels of tropospheric ozone also represent future challenges for parts of the regions.

The risks of acidic deposition are not yet well understood, but acidification already is a policy focus in parts of Asia and the Pacific. Europe and North America the priority issues for these regions are impacts of fine particulates and tropospheric ozone on human health and agricultural productivity, and the effects of nitrogen deposition on natural ecosystems. The effects of SO_2 and coarse particles emissions, and acidic deposition are well understood in these regions. They have been generally successfully addressed and are of decreasing importance.

Major Air Pollutants

Fine particles (PM2.5): Particles less than 2.5 micrometers in diameter are called "fine" particles. These particles are so small they can be detected only with an electron microscope. Sources of fine particles include all types of combustion, including motor vehicles, power plants, residential wood burning, forest fires, agricultural burning, and some industrial processes.

Particulate Matter (PM10): Particles less than 10 micrometers in diameter are called PM10. They are so small that they can get into the lungs, potentially causing serious health problems. Ten micrometers is smaller than the width of a single human hair. Particles between 2.5 and 10 micrometers in diameter are also referred to as 'coarse particles'. Sources of coarse particles include crushing or grinding operations, and dust stirred up by vehicles travelling on roads.

Carbon monoxide (CO) is a colorless, odorless gas that is produced by the incomplete burning of carbon-based fuels including petrol, diesel, and wood. It is also produced from the combustion of natural and synthetic products such as cigarettes. It lowers the amount of oxygen that enters our blood. It can slow our reflexes and make us confused and sleepy.

Carbon dioxide (CO$_2$) is the principle greenhouse gas emitted as a result of human activities such as the burning of coal, oil, and natural gases. It is also one of the key gases responsible for the global warming.

Chlorofluorocarbons (CFC) are gases that are released mainly from air-conditioning systems and refrigeration. When released into the air, CFCs rise to the stratosphere, where they come in contact with few other gases, which lead to a reduction of the ozone layer that protects the earth from the harmful ultraviolet rays of the sun.

Lead is present in petrol, diesel, lead batteries, paints, hair dye products, etc. Lead affects children in particular. It can cause nervous system damage and digestive problems and, in some cases, cause cancer.

Ozone occurs naturally in the upper layers of the atmosphere. This important gas shields the earth from the harmful ultraviolet rays of the sun. However, at the ground level, it is a pollutant with highly toxic effects. Vehicles and industries are the major source of ground-level ozone emissions. Ozone makes our eyes itch, burn, and water. It lowers our resistance to colds and pneumonia.

Nitrogen oxides (NOx) cause smog and acid rain. Produced from burning fuels including petrol, diesel, and coal, Nitrogen oxides can make children susceptible to respiratory diseases in winter.

Sulphur dioxide (SO_2) is a gas produced from burning coal, mainly in thermal power plants. Some industrial processes, such as production of paper and smelting of metals, produce sulphur dioxide. It is a major contributor to smog and acid rain. Sulphur dioxide can lead to lung diseases.

Air Pollution in India

In India, air pollution is proving to be an issue of enormous concern, especially in urban areas. India's ongoing population explosion along with rapid urbanization and industrialization has placed significant pressure on its infrastructure and natural resources. While industrial development has contributed significantly to economic growth in India, it has done so at considerable cost to the environment. Air pollution and its resultant impacts can be attributed to emissions from vehicular, industrial and domestic activities. The air quality has therefore been an issue of social concern in the backdrop of various developmental activities.

The metropolitan cities of India suffer from extremely high levels of urban air pollution, particularly in the form of suspended particulate matter. Region-wise, urban air pollution is estimated to cause over 2,50,000 deaths and billions of cases of respiratory illnesses every year. Air quality data suggest that the pollutant of the gravest concern from the point of view of environmental health risk is the airborne particulate matter.

In cities like Mumbai, Faridabad, Lucknow, Bangalore and Delhi the PM10 annual average levels have appreciably increased in 2007 over 2002. NOx (measured as NO_2) is emerging as the new national challenge and a growing problem. The NO_2 levels during 2007 at seven monitoring stations exceeded the annual average standard in residential areas and NO_2 level at one monitoring station in industrial area exceeded the annual average standard.

Indian cities are reeling under heavy particulate pollution with 52 percent of cities (63 cities) hitting critical levels (exceeding 1.5 times the standard), 36 cities with high levels (1 – 1.5 times the annual standard) and merely 19 cities are at moderate levels, which are 50 per cent below the standard.

Costs to society arising from urban air pollution include damage to human health, buildings, and vegetation, lowered visibility and heightened greenhouse gas emissions. Of these, increased premature mortality and morbidity are generally considered to be the most serious consequences of air pollution.

There has been unbalanced industrial growth, unplanned urbanization and deforestation. According to reports, India's urban air quality ranks amongst the world's worst. Of the three million premature deaths in the world that occur each year due to outdoor and indoor air pollution, the highest numbers are assessed to occur in India. Some cities in India have witnessed decline in air pollution levels due to various measures taken by the Governments. In fact, according to a World Bank study, Delhi, Mumbai, Kolkata, Ahmadabad and Hyderabad have seen about 13,000 less premature deaths from air pollution related diseases.

Population & Vehicular Growth: Key drivers of Air Pollution in Indian Cities

Population growth, rise in income due to burgeoning middle class and consequent augmentation in cars, two wheelers and commercial vehicles are the factors largely contributing to the air pollution in Indian cities. India has witnessed an explosive growth of population (from 0.3 billion in the year 1950 to 1.2 billion in the year 2011) accompanied by unplanned urbanization over the last five-six decades. The total population of India is expected to exceed 1.6 billion by the year 2050 (Oldenburg 2005).

The population growth has mainly centered on cities with large scale migration of rural population in search of livelihoods. In 2001, India had 35 cities / urban areas with a population of more than one million people. In total, some 108 million Indians, or 10.5

per cent of the national population, live in the country's 35 largest cities. Mumbai (Bombay) with a population of more than 16 million is now the world's fourth-largest urban area followed by Kolkata (Calcutta) in fifth place. Apart from this, high population growth rates especially in the Indo-Gangetic (IG) basin has resulted in unbalanced human concentration. The result is that IG basin is one of the most densely populated regions in the world. This rapidly expanding population, especially in urban areas, is one of the main reasons for environmental concerns in the country. Air quality is deteriorating especially in many metropolitan cities, mainly due to vehicular emissions.

10 Simple Tips to Minimise Air Pollution

As a layman one can do the following to thwart or at least reduce air pollution.

- Ensuring timely tuning up of car every 30,000 mile and replacement of spark plugs, oil filter and PCV (Positive Crankshaft Ventilation) valve.
- Switching over to low emission / bio-mass cook stove.
- Desisting from burning garbage especially plastic in the open.
- Changing air filter of vehicle from time to time.
- Cycling or simply walking to cover shorter distances.
- Resorting to carpools.
- Trying to live nearer to workplace.
- Minimizing use of Air Conditioners.
- Trees are air purifiers, hence planting them wherever possible.

TRAFFIC JAM A SCENE FROM ONE HIGHWAY OF SWITZERLAND	TRAFFIC GRIDLOCK : A SCENE FROM THE BUSY ROAD IN MUMBAI INDIA

*Growth in vehicular traffic is a major source of noise
and air pollution globally, as also in India.*

1.12 DEPLETION OF BIODIVERSITY & GENETIC RESOURCES

Over 100 species are becoming extinct every day. In the preceding 500 million years in the annals of this planet, five great episodes of extinction have occurred. If thoughtful conservation measures are not undertaken soon, we would witness a time wherein 50-150 species would be disappearing every day! Two thousand species of animals and 60,000 species of plants are already on the verge of extinction. All this portends a bleak future, and the very existence of human civilization seems to be at stake. But all is still not lost; we could avert the cataclysm provided we calibrate our actions to suit Mother Nature and start imbibing green habits right now.

Biological Diversity

Biological diversity or simply 'Biodiversity' is the term given to the variety of life on earth and the natural patterns it forms. The biodiversity we see today is the fruit of billions of years of evolution, shaped by natural processes and increasingly by the influence of humans. It forms the web of life of which we are an integral part and upon which we are heavily dependent for sustenance and support.

This diversity is often understood in terms of the wide variety of plants, animals and microorganisms. So far, about 1.75 million species have been identified, mostly small creatures such as insects. Some scientists reckon that there are actually about 13 million species, while other estimates range from three to one hundred million. There is, however, no consensual figure universally agreed upon and estimates tend to vary enormously.

Biodiversity also includes genetic differences within each species – for example, between varieties of crops and breeds of livestock. Chromosomes, genes, and DNA – the building blocks of life – determine the uniqueness of each individual and each species.

Yet another aspect of biodiversity is the variety of ecosystems such as those that occur in deserts, forests, wetlands, mountains, lakes, rivers, and pastoral lands. In each ecosystem, living creatures, including humans, form a community, interacting with one another and with the air, water, and soil around them. The variety of life on Earth, its biological diversity is commonly referred to as biodiversity. The number of species of plants, animals, and microorganisms, the enormous diversity of genes in these species, the different ecosystems on the planet, bogs, marshes, swamps, deserts, rainforests and coral reefs are all part of the great biodiversity that animates our 'living planet'.

It is the combination of life forms and their interactions with each other and with the rest of the environment that has made earth a uniquely habitable place for humans. In terms of existential economics, biodiversity provides a large number of goods and services that sustain our lives.

Convention on Biological Diversity

At the 1992 Earth Summit in Rio de Janeiro, world leaders agreed on a comprehensive strategy for 'sustainable development' -- meeting our needs while ensuring that we leave a healthy and viable world for future generations. One of the key agreements adopted at Rio was the Convention on Biological Diversity. This pact among the vast majority of the world's governments sets out commitments for maintaining the world's ecological underpinnings as we go about the business of economic development. The Convention enshrines three main goals:

> - The conservation of biological diversity.
> - The sustainable use of its components.
> - The fair and equitable sharing of the benefits from use of genetic resources.

Biodiversity Conservation

Appropriate conservation and sustainable development strategies are integral to any approach to preserving biodiversity. Almost all cultures have their roots in biological diversity in some way or other. Healthy biodiversity provides a number of natural services for everyone. Hence declining biodiversity is a matter of paramount concern for all stakeholders in nature. Keeping this in view, the UN declared year 2010 as International year of Biodiversity with the slogan, 'Biodiversity is Life: Biodiversity is Our Life'; the iconographic logo for the year includes fish; waves; a flamingo; an adult with child; and a tree.

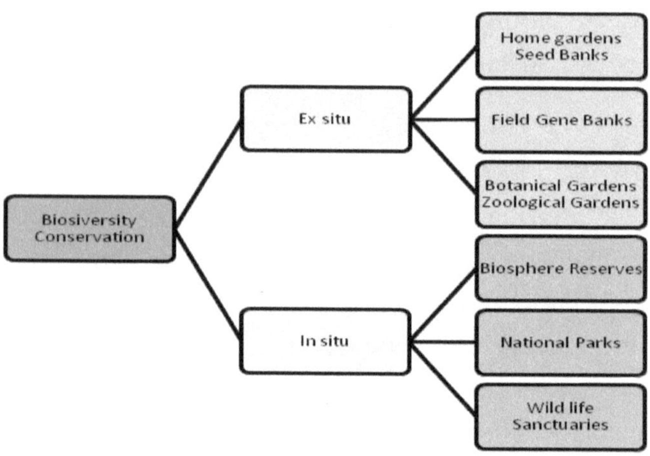

Biodiversity Conservation

SERVICES OFFERED BY BIODIVERSITY

Ecosystem Services

i. Regulation of Hydrological cycle
ii. Contribution to climate regulation and stability
iii. Maintaining the perfect balance of ecosystems
iv. Nutrient storage and recycling
v. Pollution breakdown and absorption
vi. Protection of water resources
vii. Recovery from unpredictable events
viii. Soil formation and protection from erosion

Treasure of Biological Resources
  i.   Breeding stocks
  ii.   population reservoirs
  iii. Diversity in genes, species and ecosystems
  iv.   Food
  v.   Medicinal resources and pharmaceutical drugs
  vi.   Ornamental flowers and plants
  vii. Timber products

Socio-Economic Benefits
  i.   Inviting research, education and monitoring
  ii.   Offering magnificent scope for natural recreation
  iii. Fostering Global Tourism
  iv.   Sustaining Cultural values

And we get all these invaluable services almost free of cost; but more importantly, the cost of losing these would be disastrous to us all. It therefore makes economic and developmental sense to move towards sustainability. A report from the Nature magazine also makes the point that genetic diversity has been proven to prevent chances of extinction in the wild. To avert the well-known and well documented problems of genetic defects caused by in-breeding, species need a variety of genes to ensure successful survival. Without this, the chances of extinction increase, and as we start destroying, reducing and isolating habitats, we effectively undermine the scope for interaction with species from a large gene pool.

Threats to biodiversity

The approximate overall number of species upon this planet is estimated at around 5-50 million. However, only about 1.8 million species have been identified and described. Our thoughtless actions have rendered many species extinct and some are on the verge of extinction. Biodiversity the world over is in peril because the habitats are threatened due to such development programmes as creation of reservoirs, mining, forest clearing, laying of transport and communication networks, etc. It is estimated that in the world-wide perspective, over 1000 animal species and sub-species are threatened with an extinction rate of one per year, while 20,000 flowering plants are thought to be at risk. The rate of species loss is rapidly increasing, thus posing a grave threat to biodiversity and genetic pool. Some of the manifold threats are listed here.

1. World over 14000-40000 species are being lost every year and rate of extinction is still increasing.
2. Disappearance of genes and consequent reduction of gene pool and 'genetic erosion'.
3. Habit of thinking in terms of monoculture.
4. Habitat loss and fragmentation.
5. Intensive Agriculture.
6. Introduction of exotic species.
7. Invasion of alien species.
8. Maximum loss occurred in the 20th century which witnessed a loss of 75% of the genetic diversity of crops.
9. Out of 3000 food plant species only 150 have been commercialized. Now, agriculture is dominated by only 12 species out of which four (Rice, wheat, Maize and Potato) yield more than 50% of the total.
10. Over exploitation of natural resources.
11. Since 2000, six million hectares of forest have been lost each year.
12. Soil, water and atmospheric pollution.

PROMINENT AGENCIES WORKING TOWARDS PROTECTION OF BIOLOGICAL DIVERSITY

Here is a list of some of the prominent agencies working for biological diversity. One can contact them in case of specific need.

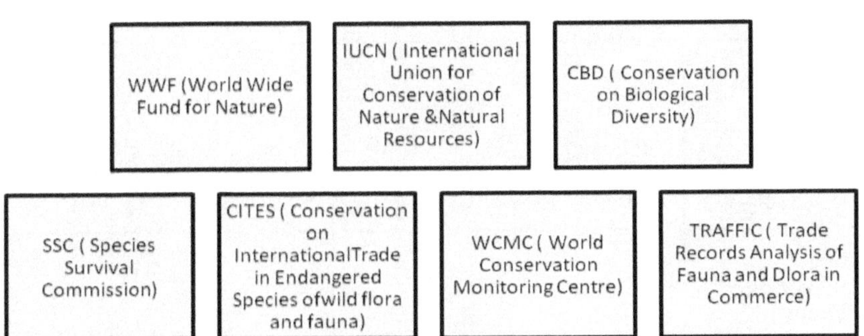

INDIA AS A MEGA BIODIVERSITY COUNTRY

India is one of 12 mega biodiversity countries of the world. From about 70% of the total geographical area surveyed so far, 46,000 plant species and 81,000 animal species representing about 7% of the world's flora and 6.5% fauna respectively, have been described. Of the 12 biodiversity hot spots in the world, India has two: one is the north-east and the other is the Western Ghats.

NUMBER & STATUS OF PLANT SPECIES IN INDIA

Type	No. of known species in the world	No. of known species in India	Percentage of Occurrence in India	No. of species endemic	No. of Species endangered	No. of species Extinct
2	3	4	5	6	7	8
Flowering Plants						
Gymnosperm	650	48	7.38	8	7	Not known
Angiosperm	250000	17672	7.00	5725	1700	28
Non-flowering Plants						
Fern & Fernallics	10000	1135	11.35	193	113	Not known
Algae	40000	6500	16.25	1100	120	Not known
Fungi	70000	14500	20.71	3500	140	Not known
Lichens	13500	2021	14.97	417	400	Not known
Liverworts	7500	852	11.26	260	100	Not known
Mosses	7000	2000	28.60	608	115	Not known

Source: Botanical Survey of India, Kolkata and Compendium of Environment Statistics India (9th Issue)

Rare & Threatened Species of Vertebrates in India

No.	Category	Approximate Number				
		Mammalia	Aves	Reptilia	Amphibia	Total
1	2	3	4	5	6	7
1	Rare		2			2
2	Vulnerable	23	22	4		54
3	Endangered	29	21	16	1	67
4	Critical	3*	8**			11
5	Extinct	1†	2††			3
6	Insufficiently Known	16				16
Total		77	55	20	1	153

***Data Source** Zoological Survey of India and compendium of environment statics India (9th Issue)*

*Mammal-Brow: Antlered Deer, Yak, Hispid Hare

**Aves: Christmas Island Frigate Bird, Mrs. Hume's Bar Tailed Pheasant, Burmese Peafowl, Black necked Crane, Hooded Crane, Masked Finfoot, Jerdon's Courser, Forest Spotted Owlet

†Mammal: Cheetah

††Aves: Pink headed Duck, Mountain Quail

1. 13   E-WASTE GALORE

The world is heading for a potentially devastating deluge of electronic waste as many nations struggle to keep the sheer volumes under control, a UN Study has warned.

UNDERSTANDING E-WASTE

E-waste is a popular, informal name for electronic products nearing the end of their useful life. Computers, televisions, VCRs, stereos, copiers, and fax machines are common electronic products. Electronic waste, e-waste, e-scrap, or Waste Electrical and Electronic Equipment (WEEE) all describe discarded electrical /electronic devices. There is a lack of consensus as to whether the term should apply to resale, reuse, and refurbishing industries, or only to product that cannot be used for its intended purpose.

The appellation 'electronic waste' may also be applied for discarded computers, office electronic equipment, entertainment device electronics, mobile phones, television sets and refrigerators. This definition includes used electronics which are destined for reuse, resale, salvage, recycling or disposal. Many of these products can be reused, refurbished, or recycled. Although e-waste is a general term, it can further be extended to cover almost any household or business item with circuitry or electrical components with power or battery supply. Unfortunately, electronic discards is one of the fastest growing segments of world's waste stream. Possible sources and items contributing to e-waste are shown in the next diagram.

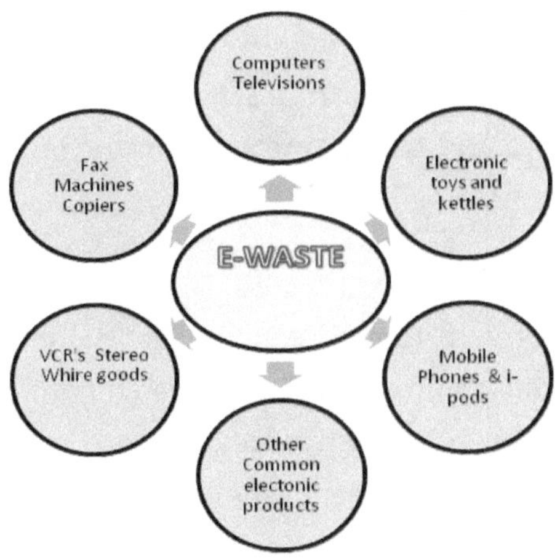

Items contributing to E-Waste

BASEL CONVENTION ON HAZARDOUS WASTE

The Basel Convention on the Control of Trans Boundary Movements of Hazardous Wastes and their Disposal was adopted in Basel, Switzerland on 22 March 1989. The Convention was initiated in response to numerous international scandals relating to trafficking in hazardous waste that began to occur in the late 1980s. The Convention came into force on 5 May 1992 and today has its Secretariat in Geneva, Switzerland.

UN REPORT ON SOARING E-WASTE

The United Nations in its report dated Feb2, 2010 expressed serious concern over mounting e-waste. In the report, the UN called for new recycling technologies and regulations to safeguard both public health and the environment in the context of 'the mountains of hazardous waste from electronic products growing exponentially in developing countries, sometimes by as much as 500 per cent'. An alarm was also sounded that the so-called e-waste from products such as old computers, printers, mobile phones, pagers, digital photo and music devices, refrigerators, toys and televisions, are set to rise sharply in tandem with growth in sales in countries like China and India and in Africa and Latin America over the next 10 years.

Estimated E-Waste Generation

A UNEP Report of 2010, titled 'Recycling from E-waste to Resources' has indicated the approximate e-waste generation. The report used data from 11 representative developing countries to estimate current and future e-waste generation. Broken down by types, the report estimates e-waste generation today as follows:

- *China*: 500,000 tonnes from refrigerators, 1.3 million tonnes from TVs, 300,000 tonnes from personal computers.

- *India*: over 100,000 tonnes from refrigerators, 275,000 tonnes from TVs, 56,300 tonnes from personal computers, 4,700 tonnes from printers and 1,700 tonnes from mobile phones.

- *Colombia*: about 9,000 tonnes from refrigerators, over 18,000 tonnes from TVs, 6,500 tonnes from personal computers, 1,300 tonnes from printers, 1,200 tonnes from mobile phones.

- *Kenya*: 11,400 tonnes from refrigerators, 2,800 tonnes from TVs, 2,500 tonnes from personal computers, 500 tonnes from printers, 150 tonnes from mobile phones.

Mammoth E-Waste will be Generated in Coming Decades

The said study, Recycling – from E-Waste to Resources, which was launched at a meeting of hazardous wastes experts in Bali, Indonesia, predicts that by 2020 e-waste from old computers will have jumped by 500 per cent from 2007 levels in India, and by

200 to 400 per cent in South Africa and China, while that from old mobile phones will be 7 times higher in China and 18 times higher in India. Growth on such a scale will create intractable problems for people's health and the environment as the waste, much of it containing toxic material, decays.

Mind-Boggling Nature of the E-Waste Menace

The amount of electronic products discarded globally has skyrocketed recently, with 20-50 million tons being generated every year. The problem indeed is of such terrifying nature that if the estimated amount of e-waste generated every year could be loaded into hypothetical railway containers, the train would make one whole serpentine circle around the world!

Electronic waste now makes up five percent of all municipal solid waste worldwide, nearly the same amount as all plastic packaging, but it is much more hazardous. As already mentioned, the problem is global. Not only developed countries generate e-waste; Asia discards an estimated 12 million tons each year.

E-waste is now the fastest growing component of the municipal solid waste stream because people are upgrading their mobile phones, computers, televisions, audio equipment and printers more frequently than ever before. Mobile phones and computers are the biggest problem because they are replaced most often.

E-Waste in India

Currently, an estimated 380,000 tonnes of e-waste is generated annually in India, of which 19,000 tonnes are recycled. India faces a mounting challenge to dispose of an estimated 420,000 tonnes of electronic waste a year that it generates domestically and imports from abroad. India has only six regular recycling units with an annual capacity of 27,000 tonnes.

Computers and electronic equipment which have completed their life cycle and are obsolete in the West have started arriving in India and the entire South Asian market in huge quantities. These 'cheap' machines are almost totally made out of phased-out parts like CPUs (central processing units), memory chips, hard disk drives and others extracted from cheap and obsolete personal computers and electronic equipment that are no longer in use on the other side of the Atlantic are being indiscriminately dumped in India.

Imports of obsolete electronic equipment that have been discarded for recycling in the developed world have become a lucrative business in developing countries like India. India is rapidly turning into a deadly dumping ground of toxic organic compounds and poisonous metals. One report by Toxics Link claims that the country generates 150,000 tons of waste electrical and electronic equipment (WEEE) a year, including computers, TVs, refrigerators and washing machines. This does not include clandestine imports from the developed world shipped into the country under the guise of scrap or second hand goods.

The growth of e-waste has significant environmental, economic and social impact. The increase of electrical and electronic products, consumption rates and higher obsolescence rates lead to higher generation of e-waste. The increasing obsolescence rate of electronic products also adds to the huge import of used electronics products. The e-waste inventory based on the obsolescence rate in India for the year 2005 has been estimated to be 146180 tonnes, and is expected to surpass 800000 tonnes by 2012. There is no large scale organized e-waste recycling facility in India, whereas there are two small e-waste dismantling facilities functioning in Chennai and Bangalore, while most of the e-waste recycling units are operating in the un-organized sector.

Meagre & Deficient E-Waste Recycling Facilities

Owing to enormous lack of appropriate and befitting recycling facilities for e-waste, much of it ends up in local recycling yards. The recycling is highly dangerous in India, with all the operation and the procedure being still very primitive and rudimentary; people are recycling just with their bare hands, they have no protection at all. Environmental organizations say that Delhi's e-scrap yards alone employ more than 20,000 laborers who handle 20,000 tons of e-waste every year. A substantial percentage of total e-waste processing activity in the country takes place in the highly unorganized recycling and backyard scrap-trading outfits.

Children are affected most by the e-waste poison. According to one survey, 53 percent of children under 12 in India's cities engaged in this business are lead-poisoned, and so running the risk of permanent brain damage.

Lucrative Business

Computers and other hardware discarded as obsolete are imported from rich countries, because the recycling is much costlier in those countries. Some traders export the waste to a poor, developing country in Africa, China or India, and make money off that waste. International treaties prohibit the export of obsolete computer hardware from developed to developing countries. But there are loopholes. In India, livelihood becomes a priority over environment. Cathode ray tubes laden with toxic components are rebuilt by Ash Recyclers instead of crushed. Many are turned into television sets, sold far more cheaply than new ones to rural customers who could not otherwise afford them. Some Ash Recyclers started a foundation that provides rebuilt machines to area schools. Computers may get obsolete quickly in Bangalore's I.T. companies, but for most others there is solid demand for used or repaired machines. So electronic waste is now being carefully stocked in an inventory of spare parts.

Rules for E-Waste Management in India

The Government of India had prepared the draft rules for managing, dismantling or recycling e-waste namely 'The E-waste (Management and Handling) Rules, 2010'. The rules ask the producer to ensure all electrical and electronic equipment are provided with a unique serial number or individual identification code for tracking their products in the e-waste management system. These rules define e-waste as waste electrical and electronic equipment scraps or rejects from their manufacturing process, which is intended to be discarded.

E-Waste policy included Extended Producer Responsibility (EPR). EPR means that the brand owners such as Apple, Dell and Hewlett Packard will be required to take financial responsibility for recycling their products. It is an important milestone that India is trying to get a handle on this issue and make sure the manufacturers are held responsible. The Indian EPR law also requires electronic manufacturers to partner with Indian recyclers, including the informal sector, in setting up collection centers. This is the first time in Indian history the informal sector participation has been written into the law.

The Way to Electronic Perdition

Finally, here goes the list of six hard facts depicting the generation of huge quantum of existing e-waste and potential for the future generation of the same. Sales growth of various electronic gadgets is witnessing a phenomenal rise. One shudders even to think of the colossal deadweight of future e-waste generation, once these items have run their useful life, become obsolete and scrapped in course of time. That, unless we act quickly, could be the way to turn our good earth into a raging inferno.

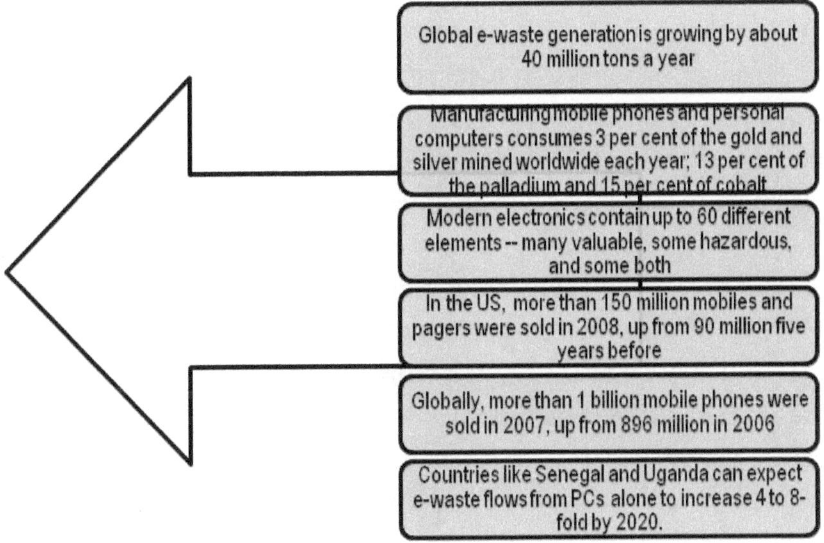

Sixfold Pointer Depicting Potential E-Waste

1.14 Ocean Acidification, Pollution & Warming

A new and relatively lesser known problem is now catching scientists' attention the world over. A recent report by Europe's leading scientists indicates that the oceans are absorbing dangerous levels of carbon dioxide as a direct result of human activity. This absorption is causing heavy damage to the survival prospects of numerous marine species.

The world's oceans are turning acidic at a rate faster than at any time in the last 50 million years. The consequences of this 'Ocean Acidification' (OA) may be as grave as the effects of global warming. A really threatening disaster looms before us, sending advance alarms for marine life, for aquatic food supply and for the very existence of the pristine oceans.

Acidity in sea has increased 30% since the later half of the 18th century. Many of the effects of acidification are irreversible and the process is expected to accelerate further. In fact, ocean surface pH is estimated to have decreased from about 8.25 to 8.14 since the beginning of the industrial era, and it is estimated that it will drop by a further 0.3–0.4 units by 2100 as the oceans absorb more anthropogenic carbon dioxide. Normally, the conditions for calcium carbonate production are stable (being in a state of chemical equilibrium) in surface waters since the carbonate ions therein are at supersaturating concentrations. However, as ocean pH falls, so does the concentration of this ion, and when carbonate becomes under-saturated, structures made of calcium carbonate are vulnerable to dissolution. Research has already revealed that corals experience reduced calcification or enhanced dissolution when exposed to elevated CO_2 presence.

Cause of Ocean Acidification

Ocean acidification results from increases in the atmospheric carbon dioxide, which in turn increases the amount of carbon dioxide dissolved in the oceans. The dissolved carbon dioxide gas reacts with the water to form carbonic acid, and thus acidifies the ocean. The resultant decrease in ocean surface pH is another long-term concern for the survival of coral reefs.

Deep Sea Bamboo Coral: An Indicator of Ocean Acidification

Bamboo coral is a deep sea coral which produces growth rings similar to a tree. The growth rings demonstrate how growth rates change as deep sea conditions change over time, and can also record changes due to ocean acidification. This coral type is especially long-lived. Coral specimens as old as 4,000 years old have given scientists 4,000 years of information about what has been going on in the deep ocean interior.

Survival of many Marine Species in Peril

One report published by a European project on ocean acidification reveals that survival of a number of marine species is affected or threatened in many ways. The species include:

i. Brittle star
ii. Whales
iii. Dolphins
iv. Tiny algae such as *calcidiscus leptoporus*
v. Clownfish

Seas most affected by pronounced levels of acidification are the
1. North Atlantic
2. North Pacific
3. Arctic Sea.

Ocean Pollution due to Oil Spills

According to estimates of the NRC (National Research Council) of US, on an average 700 million gallons of oil pollutants enter the oceans every year. The big oil spills account for only 5%, rather the largest contribution comes from the drains and urban street run-offs which constitute 51% of the oil injected into the oceans world over every year. Routine maintenance including boat bilge discharge and other ship operations contribute 19% whereas 13% is attributed to air pollution. Natural seepage from the seafloor accounts for 9% of the annual oil discharged into the oceans.

Effects of Oil Spills on the Ecosystem

Oil spills severely affect the aquatic life and the whole marine ecosystem. A few of the ill effects are listed here:

a. Animals living on the surface get coated with the oil; this thwarts their flying ability as well as the ability to keep themselves warm enough.

b. Ingested toxin could result in death of some aquatic fauna.

c. The animals that do not die immediately run the risk of developing reproductive and liver diseases.

d. Oil spills often kill marine larvae.

e. Waste emanating from oil spill poisons the substrate, interrupting the food chain of fish and other aquatic animals. It largely impacts the fishing industry.

f. The contamination can lead to altered coastal weather conditions.

Methods to Counter Oil Spills in Oceans

Adoption of any of the several methods depends upon several variables like weather, waves, water current, time constraint, marine population density, distance off the coast etc. The commonly deployed methods are enumerated below.

a. Skirt fitted Booms: Containment of the spill is done by using long skirt fitted booms. The booms float on the surface and skirts keep the oil from spreading further.

b. 'Sponge Sorbents' are also used for absorbing oil slicks.

c. Another method makes use of chemical 'Dispersants'. Though these chemicals break down the oil, yet they may pose danger to marine life.

d. Oil spills can be treated with 'Biological Agents' which are spread over the spill area. They result in the growth of 'oil-eating' microorganisms, thus speeding up the breaking down of hydrocarbons.

Ocean Warming

Some climate models predict that augmented sea temperatures caused by global climate change will lead to more frequent and more severe hurricane activities. Sea surface temperature anomaly data retrieved from NOAA [National Oceanic and Atmospheric Administration] clearly reflects a warming trend similar to that of land surface. Here is the reproduction of the data choosing important milestones.

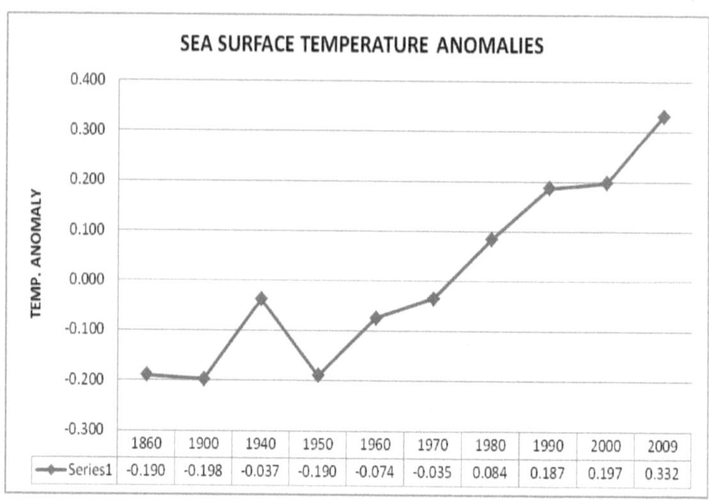

	1860	1900	1940	1950	1960	1970	1980	1990	2000	2009
Series1	-0.190	-0.198	-0.037	-0.190	-0.074	-0.035	0.084	0.187	0.197	0.332

*Data retrieved from NOAA *US Sea Surface temperature Anomalies [Relative to 1961-1990]*

It is evident from the linear chart that the rising pattern started from the closing decades of the 19th century. The trend is more palpable and pronounced since the middle of the 20th century.

DIRE CONSEQUENCES

Warmer sea temperatures are also associated with the spread of invasive species and marine diseases. If an ecosystem becomes warmer, it can create an opportunity where outside species or bacteria can suddenly thrive where they were once excluded. This can lead to forced migrations and even species extinctions. Warmer seas may result in melting of polar ice shelves from bottom, jeopardizing their structural integrity and leading to dramatic shelf collapses. Scientists also worry that warmer water could interfere with the so-called ocean conveyor belt, the system of global currents that is largely responsible for regulating Earth's temperature. Its collapse could trigger catastrophic ramifications.

But scientific research is finding that marine ecosystems can be far more sensitive to even the most modest temperature change. Global warming caused by human activities that emit heat-trapping carbon dioxide has raised the average global temperature by about 1°F (0.6°C) over the past century. In the oceans, this change has only been about 0.18°F (0.1°C). This warming has occurred from the surface to a depth of about 2,300 feet (700 meters), where most marine life thrives.

Damage to Coral Reefs

Perhaps the ocean organism most vulnerable to temperature change is coral. Reefs will bleach (eject their symbiotic algae), at even small, persistent temperature rise. Bleaching slows growth, makes it susceptible to disease, and leads to reef destruction.

Effect on other Organisms

Other organisms affected by temperature change include krill, an extremely important link at the base of the food chain. Krill spawn in smaller numbers when ocean temperatures rise. This can disrupt the lifecycle of krill eaters, such as penguins and seals, which in turn would cause food shortages for higher predators.

Solution Ahead!

The only way to reduce ocean temperatures is to minimize and dramatically rein in our emission of greenhouse gases. However, even if we could immediately drop carbon dioxide emissions to zero, the gases we have already injected would take several decades or longer to dissipate.

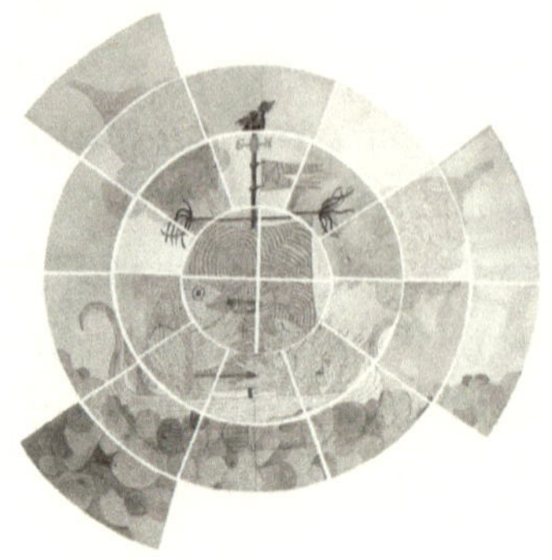

II
WATER — ELIXIR OF LIFE

About 1.20 billion people the world over have to struggle to meet their day-to-day water requirements.

o   *One of every six people does not get even the bare minimum of 50 litres of water per day.*

o   *47% of the world's population will be living in water-stressed areas by the end of 2003.*

We were monumentally wrong in nurturing the notion 'Water-An Infinite Resource'! We used it, abused it and polluted it the way we wanted! Now of course we know water is a lot more precious in the rapidly unfolding scenario of climate change which is imposing long-term droughts and recurrent flooding across the entire expanse of earth. Those unwise allocations of old have drained primeval aquifers, and much of the water people have necessarily to drink today is polluted by things nobody really wants to know about. It indeed is high time to rethink and redefine our entire approach to water. This is yet another necessary modification in humanity's relationship with nature that must encompass the countryside, the urban living place as also the downtown, with motivated individuals acting as agents of change in inculcating sustainable water habits among the people at large. Water is a scarce and vital resource and management of it has assumed paramount importance by now. Effective management of water resources is critical to ecology, public health, social balance, economic development, and the long-term health of the environment. Greater focus is required on delivering and managing sustainable water and wastewater solutions. Many of the country's problems seem to centre on water; and just as problems are myriad so are the required solutions. Here is an itemized summary of the identified issues which need to be addressed, and addressed soon, to avert an irretrievable crisis on the water front.

- *Lack of Awareness:* There is tremendous lack in awareness among the public about optimal use of water. Water as a resource is taken for granted, with nary a thought on its conservation, economic use and proper harvesting.

- *Constrained availability of utilizable water:* Of the total precipitation, including snowfall, of about 4000 billion cubic metres in the country, available surface and replenishable ground water is just 1869 billion cubic metres. Due to topographical/other constraints, only 60% of this, comprising 690 billion cubic metres from surface water and 432 billion cubic metres from ground water can be put to beneficial use.

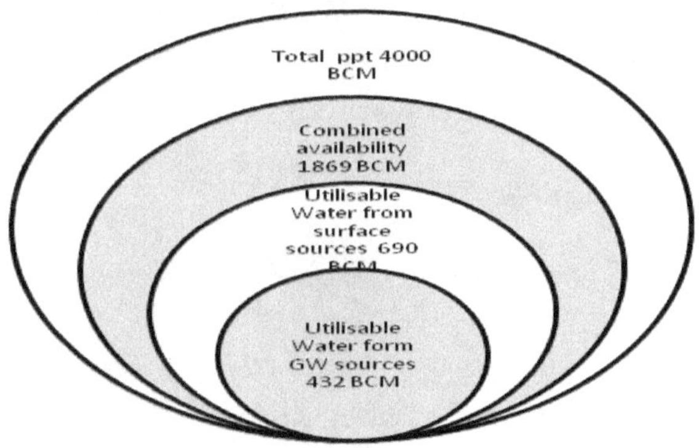

Constrained Availability of Utilizable Water

Mismanagement of water: Mismanagement is owing to:

> ➤ Over-irrigation by farmers
> ➤ Open points without tap
> ➤ Taps left running
> ➤ Leaking/ damaged service lines

Wanton Mismanagement of Water

- *Wastage of water by evaporation:* As per one recent report of IHP (International Hydrological Programme) evaporation rate, which at present is 2.5%, would double in the next 15 years due to global warming.

- *Losses due to floods.*

- *Degradation of surface and ground water quality.*

- *Erroneous design of Water Retaining Structures:* Failure of hydraulic structures often due to erroneous hydrology.

- *Widespread prevalence of water borne diseases* due to contamination of water.

- *Lack of Organized Water Supply:* Only 70.5 % of households in Urban Area (U. A.) and 8.7% in Rural Area (R. A.) receive organized water supply.

- *Delay in planning and implementation* of water resource projects.

- *Recurring floods and droughts:* One sixth of the country is drought prone. About 40 million hectare area is flood prone. Nearly 7.5 million hectare is affected by flood year after year.

- *Lack of Management of Drought & Flood:* There is a conspicuous lack of drought and flood management.

- A large area has to be brought under irrigation and water demand would likely to increase for this sector. [Absence of realistic data].

- *Precarious Rainfall:* Erratic and uneven distribution of rainfall.

- *Oceans are turning acidic:* Due to ocean pollution and acidification, Poikilothermics are experiencing phonological changes such as spawning.

- *Pollution of Lakes:* Day by day lakes are being polluted and some are on the verge of extinction.

- *Less availability of water in rivers:* Reduced inflow in the major rivers of the world has been established. The National Centre for Atmospheric Research, Colorado, USA, carried out studies on the waterflow of 900 rivers over 50 years up to 2004. Prominent rivers like the Ganga, Niger and Yellow River, showed signs of reduced flow.

- *Rising Temperature of Seas:* The sea surface temperature (SST) has increased by 0.2 degree to 0.3 degree Celsius over the last 45 years and likely to increase further by 2 – 3.5 degree Celsius by the next 90 years.

- *Possible slowing down of ocean current system*, the Great Ocean Conveyor, would alter the season pattern, affecting rain, agriculture, living organisms and industries.

- *Diminishing Dew:* Dew precipitation is decreasing in northern rain fed regions.

- *Water Pollution in Umpteen Ways:* Eutrophication is increasing world over. Giving rise to Algal bloom, red tides, and Toxification of water.

- *Depleting Ground Water:* As per one recent survey, the amount of water being used in India is approximately 45% more than what nature's system or artificial recharge can replenish. Hence ground water is depleting very fast.

- *Reduced Water Availability:* PCA(Per Capita Availability) of water has been diminishing: The figures for India:

  - 1951: 5177 cubic metre/year
  - 1991: 2200   -----"-----
  - 2001: 1869   -----"-----
  - 2025: 1341   ------"-----[Predicted]
  - 2050: 1140   ------"-----[Predicted]

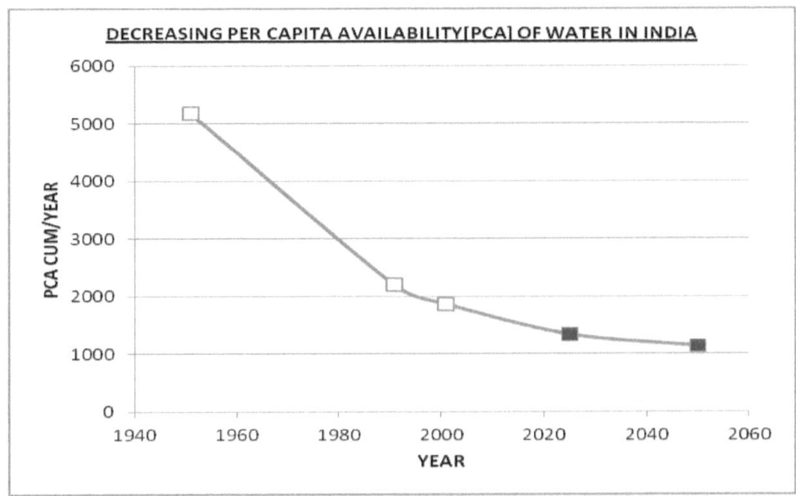

*Future PCA figures of 2025 & 2050 are projected figure based on estimation
Decreasing per Capita Availability (PCA) of Water in India

- *Water Scarcity in Future:* We are hurtling towards water scarcity from water-stress conditions. Tapi, Pennar and Mahi Basins (India), are already under water-stress conditions.

- *Increase in water requirements* due to increase in population and living standards.

- Easily *available sources of water already tapped.*

- *Delay in project initiation* time due to rising social and environmental concerns.

- *Industrial development.*

- *Decreasing Capacity of Reservoirs:* Erosion of fertile soil leading to land degradation & sedimentation in reservoirs.

- *River Water Contamination:* Today major rivers of India and world (some countries like Switzerland being worthy exceptions) have been fighting with the double scourge of water pollution and negative climatic change. Water pollution has turned into a matter of grave concern. Effluents, garbage, sewage and other liquid and solid wastes are being deliberately pumped into river systems which in turn rendering the river waters toxic and also killing the precious aquatic life. In future, availability of fresh, potable and wholesome water in rivers could be severely compromised owing to widespread and rampant water pollution. It will create a sorry picture as the water flow of the major rivers of the world is declining fast and at the same time the hitherto available water is grossly being polluted and defiled by human misdemeanor!. The causes of pollution are more of anthropogenic than natural.

- *Rapidly Depleting Ground Water Table:* Ground water level is depleting rapidly across the country. India is witnessing a depletion of around 3 ft. per year whereas Rajasthan registers a lowering of 6 ft. per year.

- *Global Increase in Ground Water Loss:* The rate at which ground water stocks are shrinking world over has more than doubled in the past four decades, increasing the ground water lost in a year from 126 cubic km to 283 cubic km. More and more exploitation of Ground Water will destabilize the natural balance of the Hydrological Cycle.

- *Change in Rainfall Pattern:* Periodicity and intensity of rainfall is altering.

- *Non-Sustainable Ground Water Withdrawals:* Recently CGWA (Central Ground Water Authority, India) has notified 134 districts in which ground water abstractions are more than average replenishments. A whopping 23 are from Rajasthan alone.

- People who do not have easy access to water have to spend a considerable time in fetching water for daily use. This results in lesser availability for pursuing other economic activities.

Though majority of the problems and issues enumerated above are India-centric yet many of them hold good for numerous other counties of the world; as a matter of fact, the problems now pertain to the entire globe. Problems like decreasing PCA, contamination of surface and ground water and depletion of the latter are much pronounced and ubiquitous across the globe. Considerate use of water and its meticulous management are the only way to counter the problems. For effective and economical management of our water resources, the frontiers of knowledge need to be pushed forward in several directions by intensifying research efforts in several disciplines. There should be separate post graduate level courses to open the door for higher studies in the following streams.

- Advanced soils and material research
- Advanced water management practices and improvements in operational technology
- Assessment of water resources
- Best rehabilitation practices
- Best water conservation practices
- Climate change and different crop water requirements
- Crops and cropping systems
- Economical and viable designs for water resource projects
- EIA and development of EMP
- Equitable distribution of water
- Essentials of water quality

- Evaporation and seepage losses
- Five R's for water resources
- Hydrometeorology
- New Era construction materials & technology
- Prevention of salinity ingress
- Prevention of water logging and soil salinity
- Reclamation of water logged and saline lands
- Recycling and re-use
- Remote sensing techniques for micro watersheds.
- Risk analysis and disaster management
- River morphology and hydraulics
- Sedimentation of reservoirs
- Seismology and seismic design of structures
- Snow and lake hydrology
- Surface and ground water hydrology
- The safety and longevity of water-related structures
- Use of sea water resources
- Use of static ground water resource as a crisis management
- Water and Saline Alkaline and Sodic soil
- Water and Ecology
- Water application methods
- Water harvesting and ground water recharge

Suggestions, Solutions, Remedial Measures & Some Innovative Ideas

The following suggestions and remedial measures have been arrived at based on insight gained through prolonged professional experience of over two decades. Some problems call for an innovative approach. The issues and their possible solutions are enumerated below.

1. *Continuous Basin Planning:* The process of Basin Planning should be a continuous and sustained one by the respective states to contend with changing parameters of rainfall, ground water, surface water and incessant construction of secondary and tertiary riparian structures.

2. *Environment Directorate for each state:* Each state of the country should have an Environment Directorate within its irrigation/water resources department. Alternatively a separate 'Climate Change Department' could be constituted. The state of Gujarat in India has constituted one such department. In fact, Gujarat is the first state not only in India but also in entire Asia to set up a dedicated department for climate change. Across the world, only six countries have so far put up separate ministries for climate change. The other states should also follow suit. The prime focus of such an organization ought to be on research work regarding availability of water in the face of rapidly changing climate scenario, possible future migration owing to reduced availability of water, and region-specific crops tolerant to extreme temperatures and requiring less water.

3. *Environmental considerations should guide projects:* In the planning, implementation and operation of a project, the preservation of the quality of environment and the ecological balance should be a primary consideration

4. *Restructuring of RBO's (River Basin Organizations):* RBOs can be identified with various names like JWC (Joint Water Committee/Commission), JOA (Joint Operating Authority), JPTC (Joint Permanent Technical Committee), TBTC (Trans-boundary Technical Committee), River Basin Commission, and so on and so forth. They are specifically created bodies for addressing numerous issues often involved between two or more basins,

states and nations. They might be created for single river basin as well. The purpose generally assigned is joint management of fishing, border issues, water quality and quantity, hydro-power/ hydro-electricity, irrigation, navigation control, flood relief, economic development, technical assistance and cooperation, infrastructure development etc.

Water in each river basin including rainfall, groundwater, and surface water stored in various structures, wetlands, etc. can be used many times over for various purposes if planned, developed, operated and managed in an integrated manner. For this it is imperative to set up a river basin organization in each state. For an inter-state river these river basin organizations (RBOs) can be set up jointly by the concerned states by agreement among themselves.. These would be advisory and could act on the authority delegated by the states. An RBO should have two wings:

a. An *RBA (River Basin Assembly)*, consisting of representatives from each state starting from the lowest watershed with a federated system; and

b. *MTC (Multidisciplinary Technical Committee)*, consisting of a multidisciplinary team of professionals taken from various departments of each state and fresh recruits in disciplines such as social science, economics, geology, water resources, environmental science etc.

The RBA representatives should represent all interests like: Watershed Associations; Water Users Associations(WUAs) in irrigated areas; Associations of forest users and pastoral people; Resident Welfare Association(RWA) representatives as users of drinking and/or domestic water including those from urban areas; Large industries; Small and tiny industries; and Other users such as fishermen, washer men, potters etc. Where interstate disputes are not resolved by themselves or by RBO, these could be referred by states to a single or a panel of arbitrators to give the verdict, which should be accepted by all under a legal provision. This system would lead to quicker decision and help to reduce the politicization of the issue and avoid time-consuming judicial process.

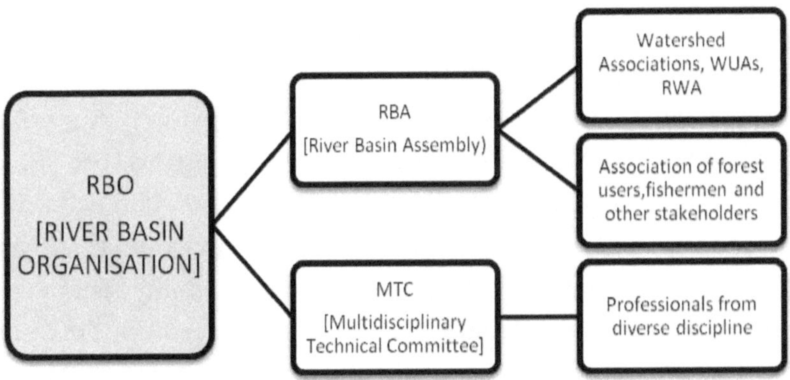

Schematic Structure of an River Basin Organiszation (RBO)

5. *Watershed Projects: for the People by the People*: A total land area of around 140 mha in India has to be covered under this monumental venture. There is no precise record/information with regard to the land area taken up and completed under various watershed management schemes taken up by various agencies. However, it is estimated that about 40-50 mha has been covered by different government agencies and NGOs through outside financial help; thus the balance 90-100 mha has still to be managed by various agencies. The Planning Commission has drawn up a programme of covering 63 mha.

There is no adequate arrangement for the maintenance and management of the watershed work already done by the government agencies, as the people were not fully involved in carrying out this work. Such works might need repair/maintenance or even need redoing through community level organizations.

At present various departments and ministries like rural development, forest and agriculture etc. are looking after this programme through special programmes enacted by the centre, which are not always suitable for local conditions. A nodal agency like the Rural Development ministry needs to co-ordinate and monitor the work and release funds with necessary flexibility to choose the technology as per local conditions with full involvement of the Gram Sabha from the planning stage itself, so that maintenance and operation can be done by them with authority and responsibility. There are several land-based programmes being serviced by different ministries of the Government of India. The important land-based programmes are: Drought Prone Area Programme (DPAP), Desert Development Programme (DDP), National Watershed Development Project for Rain fed Areas (NWDPRA), Integrated Watershed Development Programme (IWDP), soil conservation in the catchments of river valley projects and flood prone rivers. However, despite vigorous efforts made in the past, progress has not met expectations. The MoA has restructured NWDPRA providing for decentralization for procedures, flexibility in choice of technology and provision for active involvement of the watershed community in the planning, implementation and evaluation of the programme so that it becomes sustainable. The states of Karnataka, Maharashtra, Orissa and Rajasthan have already established a separate nodal department for implementing all the GOI and the state government watershed and soil conservation programmes.

6. *Discovering Viable Pricing Mechanism:* The energy pricing should be done at market rates for electricity and diesel (used for groundwater exploitation) and the surface water rates should be competitive so that it induces conservation of water and creates a sense of value of water. For the state of UP, the Uttar Pradesh Water Sector Restructuring Project, the World Bank and the Government of Uttar Pradesh have entered into an agreement to set up an autonomous regulatory body to fix service charges for all types of uses of water. This kind of regulatory body to fix tariffs for different uses of water should be set up in all states.

7. *Separate Pipelines:* Wherever possible, two separate pipeline networks, one for sewage and one for kitchen and bath water should be provided so as to reduce treatment costs and to be able to recycle the water. Rooftop rainwater should also be stored separately for use or for groundwater recharge.

8. *Concept of CBO's (Community Based Organizations):* The concept of CBO's has been evolving gradually over the past few years. The CBOs should have a legal status and should be recognized fully by the concerned administrative authorities. Government officials/NGOs may help to set up Community Based Organizations but should not themselves be members of the CBO. They may advise the CBO from the outside and may even be present in their meetings, but should not have voting/decision-making rights. NGOs with the requisite competence should be asked to come forward, motivate and train the potential leaders and competent individuals from the community or smaller NGOs. To facilitate and support the work of NGOs, the concerned nodal departments/ministries

(Ministry of Rural Areas for WMAs, Irrigation department/ Water Resources Department for WUAs, Forest department for JFM (Joint Forest Management) committees, Ministry of Urban Areas for RWAs/ Neighborhood User Groups) can play a suitable role. Since each area has its own local problems and priorities, there should be no restriction through a centralized scheme for the type of project to be prepared. Only broad guidelines should be indicated by the government within which community based-organization can prepare projects.

The following important points should form the checklist for a CBO project:

i. Potential leaders (5-6 candidates) in each unit should be identified and trained further for leadership roles, care being taken not to include contractors.

ii. Technical NGOs and government departments should help the CBOs in preparing required projects aimed at the integrated management of land, water and biomass and eking out of livelihood.

iii. Contribution to the creation of physical assets, in the form of labor, material or cash, should be at least 15-25% in the initial stages and should gradually, over the years, be increased to 70%.After project approval and funding, the work should be implemented only by the CBO. For this purpose a committee should be formed to supervise the project implementation.

iv. OMM (Operation, maintenance and management) should be done by the CBO concerned, for which the cost should be recovered from the beneficiaries or members.

v. Monitoring of works should also be done by fund providers and also by government to safeguard natural resources and ensure proper use of funds.

vi. Post-project auditing monitoring should also be done to ensure that the project benefits reach all members of the community and are not cornered by the powerful local elite or upper classes or castes.

9. *Multi-disciplinary Approach for Implementation of Water Projects:* There should be an integrated and multi-disciplinary approach to the planning, formulation, clearance and implementation of projects, including catchment area treatment and management, environmental and ecological aspects, the rehabilitation of affected people and command area development The drainage system should form an integral part of any irrigation project right from the planning stage The inadequate funding of projects should be obviated by an optimal allocation of resources on the basis of prioritization, having regard to the early completion of on-going projects as well as the need to reduce regional imbalances. The involvement and participation of beneficiaries and other stakeholders should be encouraged right from the project planning stage itself. There should be a periodical reassessment of the ground water potential on a scientific basis, taking into consideration the quality of the available water and economic viability of its extraction

10. *Appropriate Regulatory Mechanisms for Ground Water Exploitation:* Exploitation of ground water resources should be so regulated as not to exceed the recharging possibilities, as also to ensure social equity. Integrated and coordinated development of surface water and ground water resources and their conjunctive use should be adhered to.

11. *Judicious Allocation of Water:* Water allocation in an irrigation system should be done with due regard to equity and social justice. Disparities in the availability of water between head-reach and tail-end farms and between large and small farms should be obviated by adoption of a rotational water distribution system and supply of water on a volumetric basis subject to certain ceilings and rational pricing.

12. *CAD Approach to fully harness the potential of Projects:* Concerted efforts should be made to ensure that the irrigation potential created is fully utilized. For this purpose, the command area development approach should be adopted in all irrigation projects

13. *Scientific Water Management:* Irrigation being the largest consumer of fresh water, the aim should be to get optimal productivity per unit of water. Scientific water management, farm practices and sprinkler and drip system of irrigation should be adopted wherever feasible.

14. *Reclamation of Affected Soil:* Reclamation of water logged / saline affected land by scientific and cost-effective methods should form a part of command area development programme.

15. *Evolving R & R Policy:* States should evolve their own detailed resettlement and rehabilitation policies for the R & R (Rehabilitation and Resettlement) sector, taking into account the local conditions.

16. *Participatory Approach:* Management of the water resources for diverse uses should incorporate a participatory approach, by involving not only the various governmental agencies but also

the users and other stakeholders, in an effective and decisive manner, in various aspects of planning, design, development and management of the water resources schemes.

17. *Greater Involvement of Private Sector:* Private sector participation should be encouraged in planning, development and management of water resources projects for diverse uses, wherever feasible. Private sector participation may help in introducing innovative ideas, generating financial resources and introducing corporate management and improving service efficiency and accountability to users

18. *Water Quality Monitoring:* Both surface water and ground water should be regularly monitored for quality. A phased programme should be undertaken for improvements in water quality

19. *Effluent Discharge:* Effluents should be treated to acceptable levels and standards before discharging them into natural streams.

20. *Polluters should pay:* The principle of 'polluter pays' should be followed in management of polluted water.

21. *Water Zoning:* Economic development and activities including agricultural, industrial and urban development should be planned with due regard to the constraints imposed by the configuration of water availability. There should be water zoning of the country and the economic activities should be guided and regulated in accordance with such zoning.

22. *Water Conservation:* Efficiency of utilization in all the diverse uses of water should be optimized and an awareness of water as a

scarce resource should be fostered. Conservation consciousness should be promoted through education, regulation, incentives and disincentives. The resources should be conserved and their availability augmented by maximizing retention, eliminating pollution and minimizing losses. For this, measures like selective linings in the conveyance system, modernization and rehabilitation of existing systems including tanks, recycling and re-use of treated effluents and adoption of traditional techniques like mulching or pitcher irrigation and new techniques like drip and sprinkler may be promoted, wherever feasible.

23. *Masterplan for Flood Control:* There should be a master plan for flood control and management for each flood prone basin.

24. *Modernized Flood Forecasting:* The flood forecasting activities should be modernized, value added and extended to other uncovered areas. Inflow forecasting to reservoirs should be instituted for their effective regulation

25. *Checking of Land Erosion:* The erosion of land, whether by the sea in coastal areas or by river waters inland, should be minimized by suitable cost-effective measures

26. *Special heed to Drought Prone Areas:* Drought-prone areas should be made less vulnerable to drought-associated problems through soil moisture conservation measures, water harvesting practices, minimization of evaporation losses, development of the ground water potential including recharging and the transfer of surface water from surplus areas where feasible and appropriate. Pastures, forestry or other modes of development which are relatively less water demanding should be

encouraged. In planning water resource development projects, the needs of drought-prone areas should be given priority.

27. *Need to Review the Inter - State River Water Disputes Act 1956:* The Inter-State Water Disputes Act of 1956 may suitably be reviewed and amended for timely adjudication of water disputes referred to the Tribunal.

28. *Focus upon Created Infrastructure:* There is an urgent need of paradigm shift in the emphasis in the management of water resources sector. From the present emphasis on the creation and expansion of water resources infrastructures for diverse uses, there is now a need to give greater emphasis on the improvement of the performance of the existing water resources facilities.

29. *New Dam Safety Legislation:* A 'dam safety legislation' may be enacted to ensure proper inspection, maintenance and surveillance of existing dams and also to ensure proper planning, investigation, design and construction for safety of new dams.

30. *Advanced Technology for Material & Design*: New construction materials and technology (with particular reference to roller compacted concrete, fiber reinforced concrete, new methodologies in tunneling technologies, instrumentation, advanced numerical analysis in structures and back analysis).

31. *Intensive & Comprehensive Training:* A perspective plan for standardized training should be an integral part of water resource development. It should cover training in information systems, sectoral planning, project planning and formulation, project management, operation of projects and their physical

structures and systems and the management of the water distribution systems

32. *Thrust upon EOE:* The buzz word for future should be *EOE.* The planning and management of water resource and its EOE *(economical, optimal and equitable)* use should receive utmost priority and precedence.

33. *Database Integration:* A database integrating all states is required. This database should contain information on rainfall, ground water, surface water availability and also water use for different purposes along with its quality. Successful community action for water conservation and use as well as details of traditional water conservation and use systems should also be contained in the database, which should be constantly upgraded. The GIS format will be most appropriate for this database and for making it available in the public domain. It should be available in a user-friendly format and should be available for public access through the Internet.

34. *Uniform Standards for Nationwide Database:* Uniform standards for coding, classification, processing and methods/procedures for the whole slew of database should be adopted. Advances in information technology must be introduced to create a modern information system promoting free exchange of data among the various agencies like the Ministries of Water Resources (MoWR), Agriculture, Environment and Forests, Urban Development and Rural Development in GoI (Government of India) and similar departments at the State level. MoWR may be the nodal agency for this purpose. Similarly access to this information at district, panchayat and community level is also important. Special efforts should be made to develop and continuously upgrade the

capability to collect, process, and use and disseminate reliable data in the desired time frame. Apart from data regarding water availability and its use, the system should also include comprehensive and reliable projections of future demand, availability and its quality. The depth to which groundwater extraction is advisable / allowed along with quality in each watershed area should be publicly available. Both surface water and ground water should be regularly monitored for quality. A phased programme should be undertaken for improvement in Water Quality. The data generated by this exercise should be available in the public domain through the Internet.

35. *Mandatory Use of Water Saving Appliances/Devices:* Legislation should be enacted for mandatory use of domestic water saving devices Water meters on all consumers/ groups of consumers should be installed. Progressive water tariff structure is badly needed. Auditing of water balance on each distribution system should be resorted to. Sewage and other domestic use should be piped out separately.

36. *Progressive Water Tariff for Industries:* Industrial Sector also needs progressive water tariff. Water recycling facilities ought to made mandatory. Only treated urban sewage water for cooling and other processes should be allowed.

37. *Water Rates on Volumetric Basis:* Agriculture Sector reforms are paramount. Water rates on volumetric basis to WUAs should be fixed at an appropriate level with a scope for revision, in order to yield enough revenue for maintenance costs. Treated sewage water for non-edible crops ought to be encouraged. Farmers should be educated to use saline water for tolerant crops. There is an urgent need for Improvement in irrigation practices and

reduction of water losses. Pressure irrigation systems need to be introduced far and wide.

38. *Livestock Management:* Better livestock management and judicious use of Bio-pesticide is all the more warranted.

39. *Restoration & Reclamation of Wetlands and Traditional Water Harvesting Systems:* Restoration and Reclamation of Wetlands and traditional water harvesting systems like Tankas, Yeri, Zabo, Dighis, Johads, Cheruvu, Virdas, Kundis, Kuis, Baolis, Zing, Jhalars, village ponds, etc. have been badly neglected in the last few decades. These structures should be restored, maintained and used properly and these water bodies should not be allowed to be encroached upon for any other land use.

40. *Prioritization of projects:* The prioritization of projects basin wise and state wise is needed. Due to the extreme paucity of funds, projects should be reprioritized in such a way that those on-going projects, where over 25 per cent of the project cost has already been incurred, should be completed first. In basins where most Water Resources available have already been developed, the emphasis should be on the modernizing and upgradation of existing systems in an integrated manner.

41. *Considerate Selection of Locations of Industries & Plants:* Most of the thermal power houses and industries involving heavy use of water should be located nearby coastal area or water stream/body. They should be encouraged to use sea water/desalinated water, adopt process with minimum use of water, recycle , reuse and thereafter discharge only treated and cooled water into the sea/water body to maintain perfect ecological balance.

42. *Community Participation in Ground Water Management:* The detrimental environmental consequences of over-exploitation of groundwater need to be effectively prevented by legislation and its enforcement by local government bodies, CBO's, RWAs and Gram Sabhas can play a vital role in this. To give teeth to their actions the Central and State governments should enact suitable legislation and notify the permissible water depths to which ground water depletion w permitted for each region/ block/ Gram Sabah/ watershed after identifying the special problems of each area. Groundwater recharge projects should be developed and implemented with community participation for augmenting the available supplies. There should be a reassessment of groundwater quantity and quality every two years.

43. *Moderation of Flood:* To get rid of excess water during monsoon season due to sudden heavy rainfall. If natural depressions, wetlands, tanks, lakes, ponds etc. are properly maintained and even created more to absorb water and retain it during wet season, water thus retained can be employed for various economic and recreational purposes. This way flood intensity could be moderated and water would not flow to the sea unused.

44. *Appointment of an Independent Agency to monitor R & R Activity:* Governments concerned should appoint an independent agency to monitor the R&R activities at regular intervals for the whole duration of the Water Resource development project. Representatives of local people/reputed NGOs should be inducted as a part of this agency to inspire confidence among the affected people. They should visit both upstream and downstream of the project for redressing grievances rather than wait for complaints and subsequent redressal.

| PRISTINE PURE WATER RESOURCES ENGELBERG | RHINE FALLS SWITZERLAND |

| A MEDIUM IRRIGATION PROJECT RAJASTHAN INDIA | A MEDIUM IRRIGATION PROJECT MAHARASHTRA INDIA |

1. *Water, water everywhere, because nature doles out its bounties free. But utilizable water is a precious resource to be conserved and saved from wastage and pollution.*
2. *Medium Dams cause lesser human displacement and submergence. Gestation period is also comparatively low.*

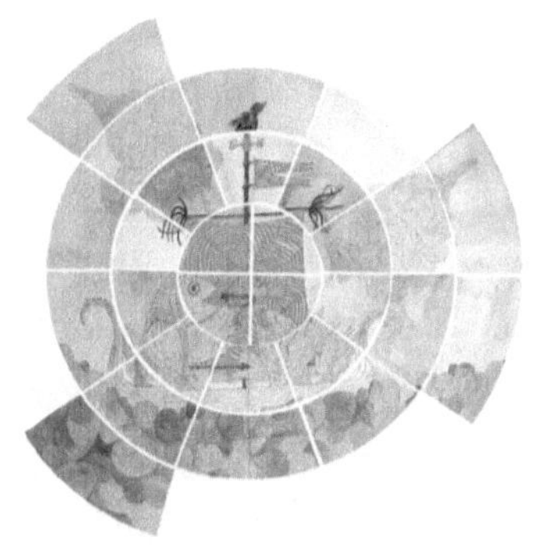

III
Ozone — Friend, Foe or Frenemy?

Ozone, the relatively scarce tri-atomic allotropic form (O_3) of oxygen, has of late been engaging the attention of environmentalists almost as much as carbon dioxide and other major determinants of global ecology. The International Day for the Preservation of the Ozone Layer is observed every year on September 16. The date was chosen for the celebration of World Ozone Day because the Montreal Protocol was signed on that day in 1987 by many countries that were apprehensive about the depletion of the Ozone Layer. This commemoration around the world offers an opportunity to focus attention and action at the global, regional and national levels on the protection of the ozone layer. The global theme for the year 2011 celebration was: 'HCFC Phase-out: a Unique Opportunity'.

Come September, and the stratosphere (second layer of the atmosphere) of the South Pole is completely excluded and segregated from the rest of the world. The disconnect is aggravated further when the temperature drops below -78°C; then clouds consisting of a deadly concoction of water, sulphuric acid and nitric acid begin to form. On the surface of these clouds, known as PSCs –I (Polar Stratospheric Clouds), chemical reactions occur that transform passive and innocuous halogen compounds (e.g. HCl and HBr) into so-called active chlorine and bromine compounds (e.g. ClO and BrO). These active forms of chlorine and bromine cause rapid 'ozone loss' in sun-lit conditions through catalytic cycles where one molecule of ClO (chlorine monoxide) can destroy thousands of ozone molecules.

The 'ozone hole' is really a reduction in concentrations of ozone high above the earth in the stratosphere. The ozone hole is defined geographically as the area wherein the total ozone amount is less than 220 DU (Dobson Units). In Antarctica, the so-called ozone hole is an annually recurring winter/spring phenomenon due to the existence of extremely low temperatures in the stratosphere and the presence of ozone-depleting substances.

As per one recent Antarctica Ozone bulletin of WMO, despite international progress in cutting production and consumption of ozone-depleting chemicals, such chemicals have a long atmospheric lifetime and hence it would take several decades before their concentrations are back to pre-1980 levels.

The onset of ozone depletion varies considerably from one year to the next, depending on the position of the polar vortex and availability of daylight after the polar night. The Ozone hole area in the year 2011 (up to mid-August) remained normal compared to the preceding years, being larger than in 2008 and 2010, but smaller than in 2009. According to the WMO bulletin, as the sun returns to Antarctica after the polar night, it is expected that ozone destruction will speed up. The extent of ozone loss will to a large extent depend on meteorological conditions.

The situation with annually recurring Antarctic ozone holes is expected to continue as long as the stratosphere contains an excess of ozone depleting substances. Antarctic ozone holes will, it is believed, continue to form during the next couple of decades.

Distribution of Ozone

Distribution of ozone is quite interesting. Total concentration varies above the earth with time and latitudes. Seasonal variations are more pronounced. Total ozone is by and large lowest at the equator and highest near the poles. This is largely attributed to seasonal wind patterns in the stratosphere.

Early Story of Ozone Hole Detection

The initial decreases in Antarctica ozone were witnessed in the early 80s over research stations located on the Antarctica continent. The observations showed unusually low ozone during the late winter months of September, October and November. Total ozone was lower in these months compare with previous observations made in 50s. The first reports came from the British Antarctica Survey and the Japan Meteorological Agency. The results became more widely known in the international community after scientists of the BAS published them in the journal 'Nature' in 1985.

Anomalous Occurrence of 2002

A significant anomaly was observed in 2002.The warming in that year was unprecedented, as recorded in Antarctica meteorological observations, and as a possible consequence of this, the ozone hole of Antarctica showed features that surprised the scientific community the world over. However, the said hole had much less area as viewed from space and much less ozone depletion was observed simultaneously.

The hole broke apart into two separated depleted regions and unusual elongation was viewed. The anomalous depletion can be attributed to several factors, like specific atmospheric air motion of Polar Regions, augmented and early warming of the polar stratosphere, air disturbances originating in mid-latitudes etc.

MEASUREMENT OF OZONE

The first instrument for monitoring was developed by Gordon M B Dobson in the 1920s, which is now called Dobson Spectrophotometer. Because of stability and accuracy these are used to calibrate space based observations of total ozone. Various methods are employed to measure the ozone which could be on the ground or off the ground. Local measurements employ 'ozonesondes' which are lightweight ozone measuring modules suitable for launching on small balloons. Other local measuring instruments use optical and chemical detection schemes.

Most remote measurements of ozone rely on its unique absorption ability of UV (ultra violet) radiations. Altitudinal distribution of total ozone amounts can be obtained by remote measurement techniques. Lasers are routinely deployed at ground bases or on board aircrafts to detect ozone over a distance of many km along the laser light path.

WHY OZONE HOLES FREQUENTLY OCCUR ONLY OVER ANTARCTICA

We all hear and read about ozone holes over Antarctica but seldom try to find out why at Antarctica alone. Well, they occur there because of the 'special weather conditions' that exist there and nowhere else on the globe. As already mentioned, the very low temperatures of the Antarctic Circle create clouds called PSC (polar stratospheric clouds). The special conditions that prevail on PSCs and the relative isolation of polar stratospheric air allow special chlorine and bromine reactions to produce holes in the Antarctic.

Many are aware that ozone is a great friend of us but only a few might know that it is a deadly foe as well. It is well-known that ozone layer absorbs UV-rays that are responsible for skin cancer and cataract formation. Ozone also regulates temperature in the stratosphere. Despite all these benefits, ozone in lower atmosphere (troposphere) is responsible for formation of 'Photochemical Smog' which is an eye irritant to human beings and reduces visibility to a great extent. Recent studies corroborate that this smog has also the potential to damage lungs, cause stress to heart, damage to immune system, induce fatigue etc. In short, ozone in higher atmosphere is our friend, whereas in the lower atmosphere it is our sworn enemy. We shall deal with this contrariety in ozone's properties at some length, but before that let us clearly understand the phenomenon of ozone depletion which has such an important bearing on the environment of our planet.

Understanding the Process of Ozone Depletion

We all are too familiar with the phrase ozone layer depletion. How does it take place? The process actually begins with the emission of halogen source gases at the earth's surface and ends when reactive halogen gases are removed from the troposphere by precipitation (rain and snow) and get deposited on earth's surface. In the stratosphere these reactive halogen gases viz. ClO and BrO (chlorine monoxide and bromine monoxide) destroy ozone. The graphics given below explain the entire process step by step.

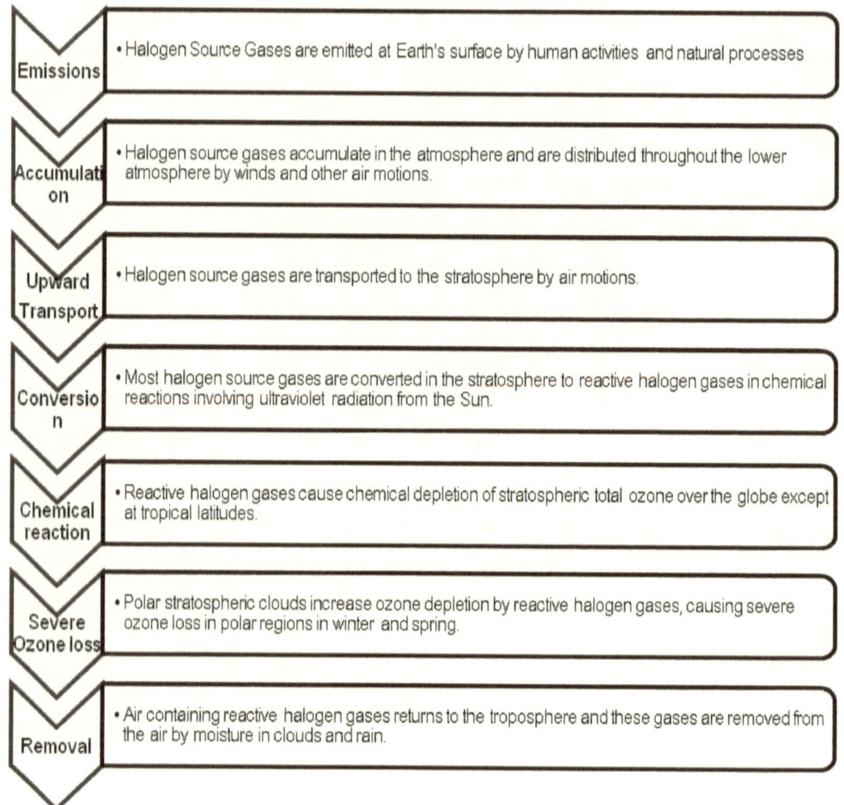

The Process of Ozone Depletion

Ozone — A Good Friend

Stratospheric ozone is considered a very good friend of humans and other life forms because it absorbs ultra-violet B radiations from the sun. The following are some of the harmful effects of ultra-violet B radiations.

❖ Increased risk of skin cancer

❖ Weakened immune system

❖ Increased risk of cataract

❖ Harm caused to terrestrial plant life, single cell organism and aquatic ecosystem.

The absorption of UV-B radiation by ozone is an exothermic process, and is thus a source of heat in the stratosphere. This helps in sustaining thermal stability in the atmosphere. In this fashion, ozone plays a key role in regulating the temperature structure of Earth's atmosphere.

Another advantage of ozone is in its use as a bactericide and algaecide. For example, ozone generated at low concentration levels is used in swimming pool disinfection plants, or in hotel rooms to remove odors.

Ozone — A Disguised Foe

Ozone is an important trace gas in the troposphere. It is not directly emitted into the troposphere, but is chemically produced by NOx, CO, and CH_4 and other hydrocarbons. These ozone precursors are emitted in large quantities by humans. Ozone in the troposphere plays various dubious roles, some of which are discussed below. The enhanced production of ozone in the summer can cause photochemical smog and it is deadly.

- It has the potential to damage lungs
- It causes stress to heart
- It tends to damage the human immune system
- Prolonged exposure induces fatigue

Excessive amounts of ozone near the surface are toxic to ecosystems, animals and man.

Ozone is a primary source of hydroxyl radicals, which are the detergents of the troposphere, initiating almost all oxidation processes. Ozone changes in the troposphere have a large impact on the tropospheric composition.

Ozone in the upper troposphere acts as a greenhouse gas by absorbing long-wave terrestrial radiation. Although ozone pollution is formed mainly in urban and suburban areas, it ends up in rural areas as well, carried by prevailing winds or resulting from cars and trucks that travel into rural areas. Significant levels of ozone pollution can be detected in rural areas as far as 250 miles downwind from urban industrial zones.

Ozone indeed is a double-edged sword. Ground-level ozone is the main ingredient in smog. Motor vehicle exhaust and industrial emissions, gasoline vapors, and chemical solvents as well as natural sources emit NOx and VOC (Volatile Organic Compounds) that help form ozone. Sunlight and hot weather cause ground-level ozone to form in harmful concentrations in the air. Ozone is also manufactured either purposely, or as a bi-product of another activity such as by electric discharges from arc welding or sparks from electric motors. These artificial sources can contribute to significant increases in ozone concentrations in the working and living environment.

The negative aspects of ozone relate to both its toxicity to man and its detrimental effect on a wide range of materials, including printing inks and textiles, as well as rubbers and plastics. This toxicity, primarily affecting the eyes and lungs, commences at levels of 0.1 ppm, with a variety of symptoms identifiable as ozone concentrations rise. For example, welders exposed to ozone at 9 ppm have suffered pulmonary Oedema (fluid accumulation in the lungs). Rubbers under strain are particularly vulnerable to attack from ozone. The rubber and automotive industries have long been aware of the potential damage to rubber components such as engine compartment hoses, from ozone. These are subject to high temperatures and strain, in addition to operating in an ozone-rich environment because of the electrical components found within the engine compartment. Over time, ozone can attack the rubber, causing surface cracks, which can then degenerate into a hose failure. It is probable that a number of failures across a wide range of rubber-based products have ozone as a hidden contributing factor.

Ozone Depletion Potential of Source Gases

Some Halogen source gases inherently possess longer lifespan and ozone depletion potential called ODP. These include the chlorofluorocarbons, CFC-12, CFC-113 and CFC-11, with lifespan 100, 85 and 45 years respectively. Similarly carbon tetrachloride (CCl_4) and bromotrifluoromethane (Halon-1301) possess 26 and 65 years of lifespan. Their ozone depletion potential is mind boggling. Having been injected recklessly into the atmosphere for several decades, their dissipation is likely to take considerable time. Sustained and consistent human efforts have brought about some fruitful results. Mention may be made of the couple of conferences pertaining to ODSs (Ozone Depleting Substances) that include, Montreal Protocol (1987), Helsinki declaration (1989), London Conference (1990), and Copenhagen Conference (1992) whereby phasing out of CFC, CCl_4 and hydrochlorofluorocarbon (HCFC) was laid down. Success of Montreal Protocol amply proves that if focused and synchronized efforts are made, the most tedious of environmental issues can be untangled and addressed to some logical end.

Ozone Depletion Potential
& Lifetime of Halogen Source Gases

HALOGEN SOURCE GAS	[†]ODP (OZONE DEPLETION POTENTIAL)	ATMOSPHERIC LIFETIME (YEARS)
CFC-12	1	100
CFC-113	1	85
CFC11	1	45
CCI_4	0.73	26
HCFCs	0.02-0.12	1-26
Methyl chloroform (CH_3CCl_3)	0.12	5
Methyl Chloride	0.02	1
Halon-1301	16	65
Halon-1211	7.1	16
Methyl bromide CH_3Br	0.51	0.7

†mass by mass

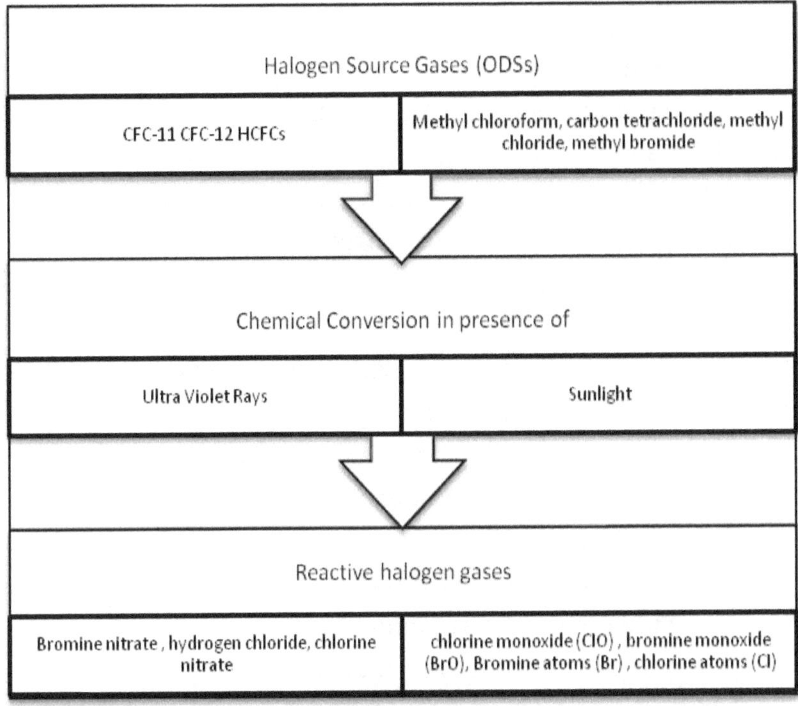

Reactive Halogen Gases

Ozone Protection: What We Can Do

There are a number of practical measures which can be taken at the individual level to contribute to the protection of the ozone layer. The basic objective is to strive to protect stratospheric ozone and minimize tropospheric ozone (ozone of lower atmospheric level). Listed here are a few simple Dos and Don'ts that all of us can observe to contribute our mite to the wellbeing of our planet.

- ✓ Always make use of ozone friendly substances.
- ✓ Recover and recycle the old CFCs (of Air conditioners / refrigerator) so they are not released into the atmosphere.

- ✓ Vehicle air conditioning units should intermittently be checked for leaks.
- ✓ Converting your car to a substitute refrigerant if the a/c system needs major repair.
- ✓ Help start a refrigerant recovery and recycling program in your area if none already exists.
- ✓ Suggest school activities to increase awareness of the problem.
- ✓ Instead of driving, share a ride, walk or bike.
- ✓ Take public transportation, wherever possible.
- ✓ Avoid excessive idling of engine and jackrabbit starts.
- ✓ Refueling of car and other vehicles should be done only after 7 p.m.
- ✓ Avoid using outboard motors, off-road vehicles, or other gasoline powered recreational vehicles.
- ✓ Defer mowing your lawn until late evening or the next day. Also avoid using gasoline-powered garden equipment.
- ✓ Postpone chores that use oil-based paints, solvents, or varnishes that produce fumes.
- ✓ If you are barbecuing, use an electric starter instead of charcoal lighter fluid.
- ✓ Limit or postpone your household chores that will involve the use of consumer products.
- ✓ Conserve energy in your home to reduce energy needs.

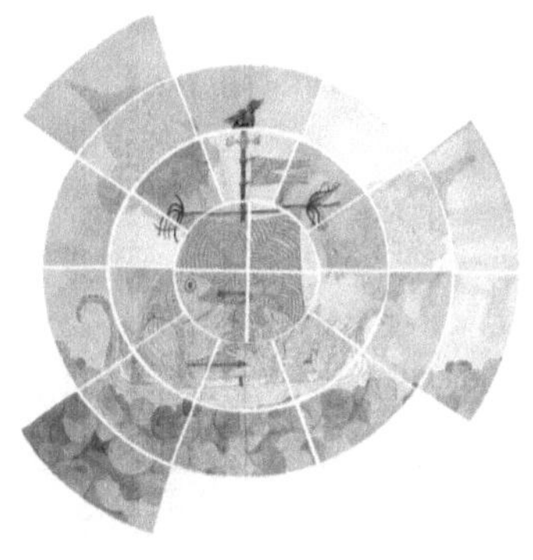

IV
Fog, Smog & E-Smog

Fog, by its very nature of dank opacity, evokes a sense of cold mystery in people's minds. Fog is a phenomenon associated with coldness, its occurrence being fairly common in chillier climate. Of late, even in temperate India, fog is often seen in the first week of November itself – something unheard of in the past, but now quite common, courtesy the advent of climate change.

Fog is actually a type of horizontally extending 'stratus' cloud, comprising a collection of water droplets or ice crystals suspended at or near the earth's surface. It is similar to normal clouds except that clouds do not touch the earth's surface as fog often does. Smog, on the other hand, is fog impregnated with smoky pollutants from industries, automobiles, thermal power plants etc.

In the winter time, a moist air mass, light wind, and cooling overnight can lead to dense fog. When after sunset in a cold day, the ground cools off further by thermal radiation, the contiguous air mass may cool to its dew point and condense into clouds. This type of fog is called radiation fog. There are several other types of fog, such as advection fog (caused by moist air passing over a cool surface); evaporation fog (resulting from passage of cold air over warmer sea water); valley fog (caused by heavier cold air settling into a valley), and so on.

ADVERSE EFFECTS OF FOG

Fog reduces visibility to varied length and area. Sometimes the extent is widespread, both in space and time, causing inconveniences to outdoor work, including transportation and sporting activities. Fog, in conjunction with cold, often aggravates asthma. It mainly happens due to the particulate matter in fog (or smog) which triggers asthma in individuals allergic to it. Fog might be delaying countless appointments, pushing up the nation's fuel bills and denying vital sunlight to winter crops. But it has also emerged as the most significant perceived weather change during winters in various parts of the world in recent times. With the fog persisting longer than before, scientists are scrambling to seek out clues to decipher this trend. But the answers that tumble out might be hard to digest. Weather scientists have been puzzled by the sharply growing number of days that dawn with dense fog during winter months. The blinding fog produces traffic snarls and elsewhere, super-fast trains move at a snail's pace as billowing fog hugs railway tracks. Dozens of flights and trains are either delayed or cancelled due to low visibility. Air services are severely affected, and most flights have to be rescheduled due to heavy fog. Hundreds of passengers remain stranded at airports, validating the patent realism depicted in the lyrics cited at the beginning of this chapter.

SMOG: DEADLY GREY-BROWN HAZE

Smog is a portmanteau term, involving an evocative fusion of the two more common words 'smoke' and 'fog'. Smog occurs globally in the big and small cities alike. Among the cities prone to suffer from smog are, Mumbai, Santiago, Tehran, Oslo (Norway), Utah, Los Angeles, Mexico city, Sao Palo etc. The most notorious smog occurred in London in 1952, wherein at least 4000 were killed; the root cause was burning of coal in households containing higher Sulphur content compounded by prevailing low temperatures in city. Smog of California is also well known because the weather conditions there often favor the formation of thermal inversion leading to smog.

Smog generally can be classified into two types: (i) Photo-chemical Smog and (ii) Coal induced Smog. Smog occurs at times when atmospheric conditions prompt 'thermal inversion'. Thermal inversion can be simply put as a phenomenon wherein the temperature increases as one goes up. Under normal circumstances, the temperature decreases with rise in altitude. The normal value is around 6.5^0 Centigrade per 1000 metres, which is also known as 'Normal Lapse Rate'. This normal depletion in temperature with altitude has many implications for weather. Decrease in temperature helps mix the air and disperse pollutants. If a pocket of air is warmer than the surrounding air, it is less dense and more buoyant and so develops a tendency to rise until it finds the air of same temperature and density. This helps disperse pollutants at the surface.

The thermal inversion might take place on a clear night when the earth's surface radiates heat away rapidly. If the air is clear, the air directly above it could be cooler than the air at higher altitude. This type of situation occurs during some wintry nights. Other types of inversions could be 'advectional inversion' and 'valley inversion' – both terms already referred in our foregoing discussion of typical fogs.

Photo-chemical Smog is generally a grey-brown miasmal haze that prevails in many cities of the world. The problem occurs specially in sunny warm regions where there is lot of traffic and attendant heavy smoke caused by burning large quantities of gasoline. The three main agents responsible for formation of smog are: Hydrocarbons, Nitrogen Oxides (NO_x) and UV rays (Ultraviolet rays) emitted from the sun. The actual process involves a series of chemical reactions. The steps are outlined.

The first reaction occurs between Nitrogen & Oxygen as gasoline is burnt:

$$N_2 + O_2 = 2NO \text{ (Nitric oxide)}$$

Nitric oxide (NO) combines further with molecular Oxygen to form Nitrogen dioxide:

$$2NO + O_2 = 2NO_2 \text{ (Nitrogen dioxide)}$$

Nitrogen dioxide splits (by absorbing light energy) into Nitric oxide and atomic Oxygen:

$$NO_2 = NO + O \text{ (Atomic Oxygen)}$$

The free Nascent Oxygen then combines with Oxygen gas (in presence of sunlight) to form Ozone:

$$O + O_2 = O_3 \text{ (Ozone)}$$

Ozone & Nitric oxide further react to form NO_2 and O_2 and this reaction could be in either direction:

$$O_3 + NO \leftrightarrow NO_2 + O_2 \text{ (Reversible reaction)}$$

NO and NO_2 react with hydrocarbons emitted out from traffic:

NO + Hydrocarbons = PAN + Other Compounds [PAN = Peroxyacyl Nitrate]

NO_2 + Hydrocarbons = PAN + Other Compounds

Thus, the concentration of ozone increases to damaging levels together with formation of PAN and other compounds, which collectively give rise to formation of Photochemical Smog. This smog affects humans as an eye-irritant and reduces visibility to a great extent. It has the potential to damage lungs, cause cardiac stress, inflict damage on immune system, induce fatigue etc.

Inversion also magnifies the 'green flash' occurring at sunset or sunrise. It also causes disturbance in radio transmission and sometimes FM radio may suffer signal degradation. Temperature inversion could also result in 'freezing rain' in cold climates.

Electronic Smog or E-Smog

Thou art ubiquitous! We have learnt about two types of smog, viz. 'photo-chemical smog' and 'coal induced smog'. Electronic Smog (ES) is however an entirely different phenomenon that has attracted much attention in recent years. Items responsible for producing electronic smog are the many aids that constitute the wherewithal of modern life: cell phones, hairdryers, shavers, laptops, pylons, power cables, wiring, computers, mobile towers, microwave ovens, T.V. and digital alarms. Electronic Smog has a mind-boggling range of electromagnetic spectrum with frequencies ranging from several seconds to $5X10^{19}$ Hertz. Being less than 80 times the thickness of a human hair, we breathe them in, virtually constantly all the time.

The World Health Organization reports that electronic smog affects up to three in every 100 people and is 'one of the most common and rapidly growing environmental influences'. The report further adds that 'everyone in the world' is exposed to it and that the 'levels will continue to increase as technology advances'.

Common Source of Radiation

As mentioned above, sources of radiation are myriad. Some of them are depicted hereunder:

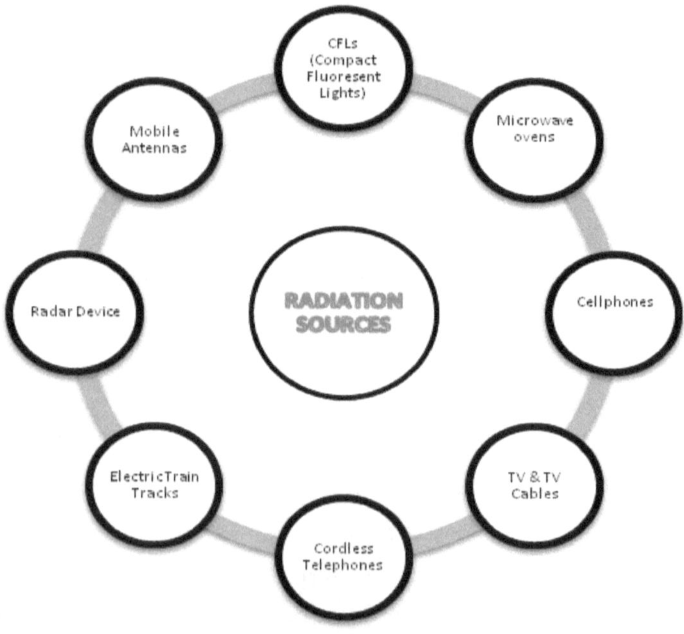

Sources of Electromagnetic Radiation (EMR)

Alarming Effects on Individuals

Scientists have convincingly shown that EMRs can be disruptive to the human body's own natural energy fields. Electromagnetic waves are not blocked or weakened by objects in their way and they enter human body and upset its cellular function and biological processes. EMR can cause headaches, tiredness and even immune system disorders. Appliances which have proximity to the human head, like electric hair dryers, shavers and bedside digital alarms, are more dangerous. This is the reason why sensitivity to a computer screen is common, as we sit near to them, but sensitivity to television sets is less common, as we are usually 6-8 feet away from them.

Our body goes through a lot of electric activity. It uses electric impulses to transmit signals between nerves. EM (electromagnetic) interferences can seriously affect these activities. Everyday electronic items such as computers, microwave ovens, televisions, cookers, lamps and even seemingly innocuous wiring (even when nothing is turned on), create a magnetic field around them and can affect human body. According to scientists, the electrical fields given off by such household items charge minuscule particles in the air such as viruses, bacteria, allergens and highly toxic pollutants. These minute particles are constantly in touch with us and ubiquitous in the surrounding environs. And the level of such invasive radiation will only increase further with advances in technology. Numerous ailments emanating from exposure to electronic smog are reflected in the next diagram.

Too much of exposure to EMR causes our body's electric field to become unbalanced, to slow down, to darken in spots, to stagnate, resulting in sickness and even premature death. Other health effects of EMR may involve dental pain, digestive problems, dryness of lips and mouth, abdominal pain, hair loss, impaired sense of smell, increased feeling of thirst, ovarian pain, altered sugar metabolism and many more. At least 28 ailments from exposure to EMR have been identified. The most common are joint pain, headache, depression, fatigue, muscle spasms etc.

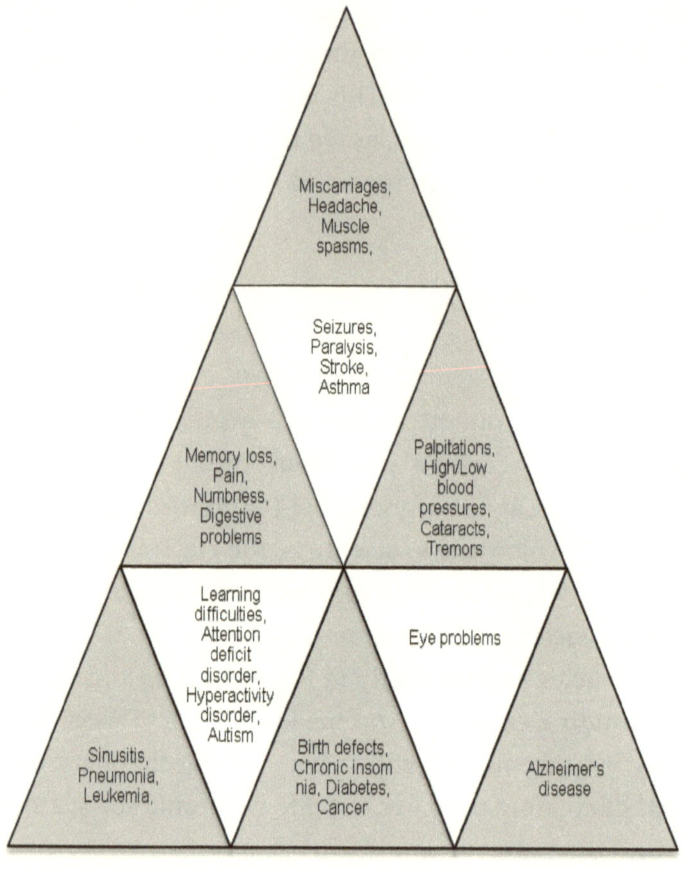

Aliments Emanating from Exposure to Electronic Smog

Electronic smog, as this all-pervading household radiation is called, covers a sweepingly wide range of the electromagnetic spectrum. At one end of the scale are fields with frequencies of several seconds, and at the other, frequencies of billions of times a second. Scientists estimate that our daily exposure to radiation is 100 million times higher than it was in our grandparents' time. Some people react to even very low levels of exposure, often even to specific items.

Deadly for Children

The International Agency for Research on Cancer, a segment of the WHO, has classified electronic smog as a 'possible human carcinogen' and the University of New York's School of Public Health is of the opinion that electronic smog can cause up to 30% of all childhood cancers. A study by the National Radiological Protection Board, UK, has also linked electronic smog to leukemia in children. The Health Protection Agency, Britain's top health protection watchdog, has warned against the ill effects of Wi-Fi networks on children as this system is increasingly being set up in British schools.

A study, commissioned by the National Radiological Protection Board (NRPB) concluded that one in 200 British children run double the risk of leukemia as they are exposed to high levels of electromagnetic radiation in the home. According to the study, radiations emitted by power cables, pylons and electrical appliances cause cancer in two children in Britain every year.

In the US disputes over possible links between electromagnetic fields and cancer goes back to the 1970s. However, worldwide a series of laboratory and epidemiological investigations across the globe had come up with contradictory and inconclusive findings. But with recent findings arguments have dramatically shifted in favor of this theory.

Cell Phone Radiation

According to a revealing Swedish study, because of intense usage of cell phones, the present generation of teenagers runs the risk of becoming senile by middle age. A study by Finnish scientists reported 40 percent increase in the risk of developing brain tumor for those using cell phones for over ten years. They are likely to be affected on that side of the head where they hold the phone to talk. Most scientists agree that children below the age of eight should not be allowed to use a cell phone.

Recent research has found a dangerous association between cell phone and a man's sperm quality. It has been found that the more hours a man spends on his cell phone leads to lower sperm count and greater percentage of abnormal sperm.

How can We Increase our Resistance to EMR damage?

- Increase intake of antioxidants, melatonin, vitamins B, C, E and folic acid as these are natural oxidative stress fighters.

- Fish, poultry, meat and tap water are main sources of heavy metal ingestion. Find out the source of these items before consumption. Eat fresh, chemical-free, organic fruits and vegetables.

- Get the test done for allergic responses if any.

- Avoid or minimize caffeine and alcoholic beverages, especially distilled liquor.

- Drink carbon filtered water possibly in glass or ceramic containers. Limit water in plastic bottles. Use recycled paper products for drinking and eating; avoid plastic or Styrofoam.

- Imbibe the habit of regular exercise as it tends to increases metabolism. Breathe slowly and deeply. Surround yourself with nature as often as possible.

- Replace bright and fluorescent light with subdued full-spectrum bulbs or candle light as much as possible. Increase melatonin naturally by sleeping in the darkest room possible.

- Try to get adequate sun exposure particularly at dawn as it contains nascent oxygen which is beneficial to our body in several ways.

How to Avoid Electronic Smog

- ✓ Minimize usage of cell phones, cordless phones, and Wi Fi devices.

- ✓ Do not keep cell phones near your head. Turn it off when you are not using it and keep sufficient feet gap between yourself and any part of your body. Never use it to play games, movies, etc.

- ✓ When using the cell phone wear air tube headsets

- ✓ Avoid keeping cell phone in pocket, purse, back or on hip all day. Close proximity to the hip may also affect fertility because the hip produces four-fifth of the body's red blood cells and is especially vulnerable to EMR damage.

- ✓ Pregnant women, women with a small child in arms, and those in adolescent age, should avoid cell phone use when in a vehicle (car, train, plane, subway) as radiation gets trapped and is higher in these closed metal zones. Cordless phone base emits high levels of EMR even when not in use.

So it is advised to replace them with wired, corded lines (phones, Internet, games, appliances, devices, etc.).

✓ Minimize use of computers, sit as far away from the screen as possible; preferably use flat screens. Use wired Internet connections, not Wi Fi – especially for laptops. Keep laptops off of the body and away from metal surfaces.

✓ Keep alarm clock away. Keep radio at least 3 feet from head or use battery power. It is recommended that you keep at least 6 feet distance from all electronic devices during sleep. Avoid waterbeds, electric blankets and metal bed frames. Futons/wood frames are better than metal-coiled mattresses and box-springs.

✓ When using electric stoves, cook on back burners instead of front, as much as possible. Keep away from metals as they attract EMR.

Due Recognition of the Malady Warranted

As electromagnetic sensitivity has not yet been recognized as a medical condition, those affected often receive little understanding or support from society or institutions including the medical profession. Sweden is the only country that has recognized electro-sensitivity as a physical impairment since 2000. About 300,000 Swedish men and women are sufferers. Those who are allergic to electrical energy receive support from the Swedish government to reduce exposure in their homes and workplace.

Precautions Against the Sea of Microwaves

We can't escape this 'sea' of microwaves that now pervades everyday life. TV, Oven, Washing M/C, Vacuum Cleaner, Laptop, AC, Cell Phone and hair dryer – all have electromagnetic field ranging from 1 milligauss to a few hundred milligauss. As per US EPA (Environment protection agency of US) one milligauss is the safe level. Therefore, we should:

1. Use of the above appliances as sparingly as possible, and with due care as already discussed.

2. Better use cell phone having SAR (specific absorption ratio) lees than 1.6.

3. Minimize the use of Cell Phone.

Hazards of E-Smog: A Summarized Reminder

1. Invisible 'smog', created by the electricity that invigorates our civilization, is giving our children cancer, causing miscarriages and suicides and making some of us allergic to modern life. This is amply attested by newer scientific evidences.

2. The evidence, which is being taken seriously by national and international bodies and authorities, suggests that almost everyone is being exposed to this new form of pollution from countless gadgets in daily use in every home.

3. The UN's World Health Organization (WHO) calls the electronic smog 'one of the most common and fastest growing environmental influences'. Taking the threat very seriously, WHO further adds that 'everyone in the world' is exposed to it and that the 'levels will continue to increase as technology advances'.

4. Seemingly innocuous wiring generates electrical fields, one component of the smog, even when nothing is turned on. And all electrical equipment from TVs to toasters tend to give off another one, magnetic fields. The fields rapidly decrease with distance but appliances such as hair dryers and electric shavers, used in close proximity, can give high exposures. Electronic clocks and radios near beds produce even higher doses of exposure because people are exposed to them for many hours while sleeping.

5. According to WHO, the smog could interfere with the tiny natural electrical currents that help to drive the human body. Nerves relay signals by transmitting electric impulses, for example, while the use of electrocardiograms testifies to the electrical activity of the heart.

6. A study conducted by the official National Radiological Protection Board concluded that children living close to electric train lines are more likely to get leukemia, and municipalities are considering whether to stop any more homes being built near them. The discovery is causing a large-scale reappraisal of the hazards of the smog.

7. The International Agency for Research on Cancer – a part of the WHO and the leading international organization on the disease – classes the smog as a 'possible human carcinogen'. A report by the California Health Department concludes that it is also likely to cause adult leukemia, brain cancers and possibly breast cancer and could be responsible for a tenth of all miscarriages.

8. Professor Denis Henshaw, an expert on human radiation effects at Bristol University, says that 'a huge and substantive

body of evidence indicates a range of adverse health effects' of EMR. He revealed that the smog causes thousands of cases of depression.

9. Perhaps strangest of all, there is increasing evidence that the smog causes some people to become allergic to electricity, leading to nausea, pain, dizziness, depression and difficulties in sleeping and concentrating when they use electrical appliances or go near mobile phone masts. Some are so badly affected that they have to change their lifestyles. While not yet certain how it is caused, both the WHO and the HPA (Health Protection Agency, United Kingdom) accept that the condition exists, and the UN body estimates that up to three in every 100 people are affected by it.

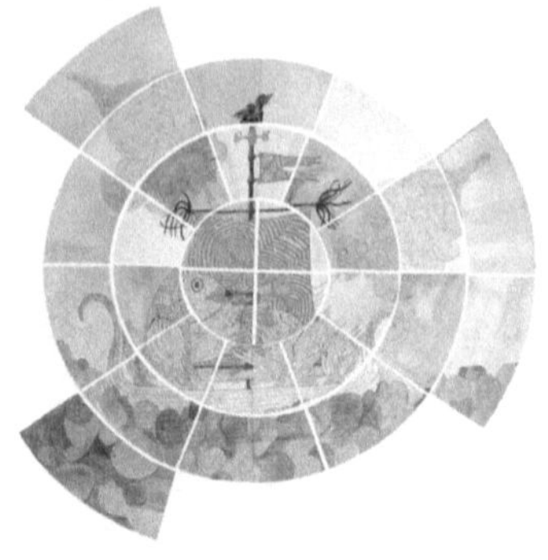

V
When Time Ran Out — A Sad Chronicle of Disasters

Disasters have been known to mankind since the days of the Antediluvian patriarch Noah. But apart from the annals of Biblical cosmology, and throughout the multi-millennial spread of geological ages, disasters had wreaked havoc and left behind a trail of cataclysmic devastations. The 10,000 odd years of Holocene were, however, a period of relative calm and stability on Earth, when temperatures and sea levels were relatively stable. Hence the interglacial warmth of the Holocene also fostered the growth and all-pervading impacts of the human civilisation, including all its written history, its path-breaking transition toward urban living, and its giant strides in art and science. Given these significant features, and given the tell-tale lithospheric indicators, as also the more recent atmospheric evidence of human impacts on the Earth and its ecosystems, the latest geological epoch has quite appropriately been given the new appellation, 'Anthropocene'.

Indeed, today we live in a world and environment remade by man, man who is merrily oblivious of the havoc wrought by his emissions of greenhouse gases. We have messed with the 'planetary energy balance', there being now far more energy in our atmosphere than there ever used to be. And that energy expresses itself in myriad ways: ice meltdown, glacial retreat, cloudburst, heat waves and the like. As a matter of fact, the year 2010 was the warmest year on record ever since temperature records are available.

Reverting to the specific topic of environmental disasters, these can broadly be classified into two categories. Some disasters are 'anthropogenic', arising out of dereliction, judgmental error and nonfeasance, while others are 'natural', like influenza, plague, earthquake, tsunami, hurricane, storm and volcanic eruption. Both types of disaster tend to impart some lessons. Anthropogenic disasters remind us of our follies, neglect, greed and human misdemeanour. They also convey a warning to rectify our faults for future. On the other hand, the more frequently recurring natural disasters have been sending us alert signals regarding the urgent need for a review, retrospection and recalibration of our actions toward nature and the whole ecosystem.

A factual account of the salient features of some of the major disasters experienced by mankind is given in the ensuing pages. The sequencing here does not imply that one particular disaster listed higher is worse or more severe than one appearing lower in the list. Due care has, however, been exercised in selection of the disasters based upon a number of critical parameters such as death toll, injuries, loss, damage, media exposure and public attention a particular disaster received at the time of occurrence and thereafter. But first let us look at the bare shortlist of the disasters under the two typical categories as is listed here.

	Anthropogenic Disasters		**Natural Disasters**
1	Bhopal MIC gas leak tragedy	1	The Plague of 14th century (Black Death)
2	Chernobyl nuclear power plant explosion	2	Spanish Flu (Great Influenza Epidemic)
3	Crippling of Fukushima nuclear plant in Japan	3	The Dutch Flood Disaster 1953
4	BP oil spill of Gulf of Mexico	4	Mount Pinatubo volcanic eruption Philippines 1991
5	London Smog Crisis of 1952	5	Turkish Earthquake of1999 [IZMIT Earthquake]
6	The European BSE Crisis	6	Indian Ocean Tsunami of 2004
	In addition to the above six, there were other major disasters which include: Spanish waste water spill, the Baia Mare cyanide spill, the love canal waste dump, Seveso Italian dioxin crisis and major oil spills of twentieth and twenty first century.		

ANTHROPOGENIC ENVIRONMENTAL DISASTERS

1. BHOPAL MIC GAS LEAK TRAGEDY

This is also known to the general public as the 'Bhopal tragedy' of 2nd /3rd December 1984. The event is one of the saddest in the annals of environment disasters – rendered unforgettable for the sudden human tragedy of unprecedented proportions inflicted through human neglect. The present author can still vaguely remember the reports of the newspapers and the heart-rending stories contained therein. I was in my sophomore year of college and was acutely distressed to read about the misery of human beings and cattle alike. The newspaper accounts by themselves were sickening and profoundly disturbing. One question that haunted me time and again, was why at all such hazardous units be allowed to be located near human settlements? I studied the entire Bhopal tragedy during my Environment and Ecological course in the year 1991-1992 again, when as a researcher, I read the updated literature on the subject, googling extensively to retrieve every minute detail. That way, I reconstructed the events leading up to disaster and also its subsequent fallouts. It presents as horrendous a picture today as it did a quarter century ago.

It was around 11:30 P.M. on the fateful night of December 2, 1984. Workers in the Union Carbide unit at Bhopal realized there was a leakage of MIC (Methyl Isocyanate) somewhere in the plant. Their eyes began to water. A few of them walked around the MIC structure and spotted a drip of liquid around 50 meters away accompanied by the oozing out of some yellowish-white gas. They told the shift-in-charge who decided to grapple with the leak after tea break. By the time the tea break ended at 12:40 am (December 3), things started happening very fast.

A worker noticed that the temperature on the gauge of tank 610(containing MIC) had reached 250⁰C, with pressure hovering around 40 psi (pounds per square inch) – the point at which the emergency relief valve opens. He could hear an ominous gurgling sound, resembling a boiling cauldron. Soon there was a white cloud drifting over the plant and prowling across the northern black-blue sky.

The pressure reached 55 psi, the top of the scale; safety valve had opened releasing MIC from the storage tank. It is estimated that the tank contained 90,000 pounds of MIC at the time of the accident. For as long as two hours, the safety value remained open, spewing out over 50,000 pounds of venomous MIC in the atmosphere. Thereafter, the valve closed down as the tank pressure went down below 40 psi.

Thousands woke up between 12:30 am and 1:00 am, by which time the toxic gas was spreading in high concentrations. Whosoever came in contact with the foul gas were seized by bouts of uncontrollable coughing and itching of eyes. In frenzied panic, people ran helter-skelter, many trying to escape the pestilential air on whatever they got – cycles, scooters, bullock-carts, buses, cars, auto rickshaws, mopeds, tempos or trucks. The gas spread over some 40 square kilometre area – affecting people up to 8 km. downwind. People flocked in wave after wave to the over-crowded district hospital for treatment.

The whole city remained in a state of dazed helplessness, suffering the deadly agony for four full days. All around there were hideous sights of bloated carcasses of dead cattle and horrendously distended corpses. Droves of carrion-eating vultures and packs of dogs tore the dead bodies into pieces. Immediate death toll reached around 4000-8000 and over 100,000 were permanently disabled. In the years to come the death from long tern exposure would mount to an unenviable figure of 20,000. Tens of thousands of children would have birth defects and many million would fall gravely ill from drinking contaminated water. Death toll would have been still higher had there not been two lakes that neutralized the poisonous gas to some extent.

After the disaster, investigations were launched into the causes of the incident. It was revealed that water had found ingress in the MIC storage tank, triggering an exothermal reaction that released gas in quantities large enough to open the safety valve. Normally 'Scrubbers' would check escaping gas but they were temporarily out of order for repairs.

The Central Bureau of Investigation (CBI) filed charge sheet on Dec 1, 1987 against Mr Anderson, head of the multinational Union Carbide, and 11 others, including UCE (Union Carbide Eastern, Hong Kong), UCIL (Union Carbide India Ltd), and UCC (Union Carbide Corporation, USA). After four long years of procedure, a settlement was reached in 1989. Union Carbide promised to pay $470 million as compensation, with individual victims receiving 25000 in compensation. Ten years later, the Supreme Court directed the Indian Government to disburse another 330 million.

Dow Chemicals took over the control of Union Carbide in the year2001. Union Carbide sold the Indian unit UCIL to a battery producer. On July 22, 2009 the Chief Judicial Magistrate's court in Bhopal issued a fresh warrant against Anderson and ordered the CBI to produce him before court for trial.

In June 2010, an Indian court convicted seven former managers at the plant, handing down minor fines and brief prison sentences. In December 2010,the attorney general's office filed a case at the

Supreme Court to increase the $470m settlement reached in 1989, seeking to more than double to $1.1bn (£700m) the compensation paid by the US chemical company for the Bhopal gas disaster.

Poisonous wastes are still present in the environment as sordid leftovers of the 1984 disaster. These have the potential to cause failure in nervous system, kidney disease, liver dysfunction, and threat of cancer for many years to come. Local residents still suffer from numerous other health disorders not normally found elsewhere.

Lessons from the Bhopal Tragedy: Many lessons could be learnt from the disaster. It clearly suggested that no squatter settlements ought to be allowed to develop close to units handling hazardous substances and toxic chemicals. Safety aspects should rigorously and continually be reviewed in all major industries handling toxic and hazardous chemicals. Third party review should be made mandatory for industries handling toxic substances. The tragedy highlights the need for accepted standard procedures for dealing with multinational and transnational enterprises. It also brings to sharp focus the need for ecological alternatives such as BPC (biological pest control). There is still a crying need for a directional thrust to research in the area of BPC. By a combination of biotechnology, genetic engineering and biological pest control, we may perhaps obviate the use of chemical pesticides, but it remains an area crying out for proactively intensive research.

2. Chernobyl Nuclear Power Plant Explosion

It has been over 25 years since the Chernobyl accident. It was a disaster that affected not just Ukraine, Belarus and Russia but the whole world, changing attitudes to nuclear safety on a global scale. International radiation standards, strategies for improving nuclear safety, emergency response procedures and mitigation of consequences were all reviewed after the incident. Our understanding of the health effects of ionizing radiation is improving due to continuous research and the knowledge gained from studies carried out on the Chernobyl population.

Judgmental Error: The Chernobyl nuclear power plant located some 128 km away from Kiev undertook some tests on the fateful day of April 26, 1986. Error of judgment coupled with a few other errors led to reactor stress. Temperatures went up beyond 2000 degree Celsius resulting in fuel rods melting and causing the cooling water to boil.

Instant Reaction and Spread of Radioactivity: Fire and explosion instantly killed 31 people. Two days after the explosion, the Swedish national radio reported that 10,000 times the normal amount of Cesium-137 existed in the atmosphere, prompting Moscow to officially respond. The following day over 1.35 lakh people were evacuated from within a 30 kilometre periphery. This area was labelled the 'special zone'. The evacuation of the special zone was made permanent, as the high levels of radioactivity (with long half-life) have been predicted to last for several centuries. The radioactive cloud was blown north and northwest by wind, causing the first mention of the accident to be after radioactivity measurements in Sweden. The cloud covered a large area in Europe. On May 2, the cloud even reached the Netherlands, causing fresh fruit and vegetable consumption to be prohibited.

Varying Death Toll Figures: There are many estimates concerning the number of victims that suffer from symptoms induced by radiation. Reliable data are still lacking. The Ukrainian government figures show that more than 8000 Ukrainians have died as a result of exposure to radiation during the first clean-up operation.

The World Health Organization (WHO) stated that approximately eight lakh people have worked on fire extinguishing, restoring the reactor and cleaning up pollution in the first year after the accident. These people only remained in the area for short periods of time to prevent health problems. It is reported that the eventual death toll resulting from the nuclear explosion might be up to 300,000 and many unofficial sources put the toll over four hundred thousand.

Increase in Radiation-Related Ailments: In Belarus there has been a dramatic increase in cases of thyroid cancer and leukaemia. The extraordinary increase in the incidence of these illnesses can be associated with the exposure of the population to the aggressive radioactive particles released by the Chernobyl explosion. Four dangerous substances were released: Plutonium, Strontium 90, Iodine 131 and Caesium 137, elements that are not compatible even as non-radioactive isotopes with our physiological and nervous systems. Suicide rates have also increased in the area.

Governments in the region estimate that up to seven million people were affected by the accident. Four years after the accident, 6.27 lakhs Soviets were already under permanent observation for symptoms and effects of radiation poisoning. The number of individuals that will ultimately be affected by the Chernobyl disaster has been estimated as high as 11 times that of the cancer deaths expected from the combined 1945 bombings of Hiroshima and Nagasaki. Today it is believed that over 4 million people in the Ukraine, Belarus and western Russia still live on contaminated ground. Chernobyl related health effects and the spread of radiation have resulted in mental defects in many children.

Closure of Reactors: After the Chernobyl disaster, international organizations pressured the Ukrainian government to close the remaining reactors. This was disadvantageous for the country, because it derived 5% of its power supply from the power plant. Eventually, it was decided that the power plant would be closed during the winter of the year 2000. The Ukrainian government tried to obtain a postponement, but the reactor was eventually closed in December 2000.

Environmental & Ecological Effects: Environmental damage was widespread immediately following the accident, stretching from fauna and vegetation to rivers and lakes and all the way down to the groundwater

The Red Forest: The second major plume of radiation released by the Chernobyl nuclear accident was carried directly over what is now called the Red Forest. Radioactive particles settled on trees, ruining approximately 400 hectares of pine forest. The Red Forest is now one of the most contaminated terrestrial habitats on earth.

Fauna & Vegetation: The fallout from the explosion had obvious adverse effects on life in the exclusion zone and the four kilometer red forest, but the current ecological stability seen in those same regions that experienced deadly doses of radioactivity in 1986 is a surprisingly welcome development. In the span of over two decades since the accident, the net effect on the flora and fauna in the highly radioactive, restricted zone has been overwhelmingly positive in favor of biodiversity and abundance of species. For example, researchers have found numerous sightings of moose, roe deer, Russian wild boar, foxes, river otter, and rabbits within the ten km exclusion zone; however, none of these were observed outside the 30 km zone.

Surprising Outcome of Human Exclusion: While exposure to high levels of radiation does have discernible negative impacts on plant and animal life, it is obvious that the benefit of excluding humans from this highly contaminated ecosystem appears to have somewhat offset the otherwise grievous cost associated with Chernobyl radiation. The relocation of hundreds of thousands of Ukrainian citizens, while painful and unfortunate given the circumstances, have allowed ecosystems to flourish in the absence of human activity that is harmful to biodiversity.

New radiation hot spots are still being discovered today in Belarus and Ukraine. There is a critical need for quality scientific information concerning the environmental and health risks associated with nuclear accidents before major decisions regarding remediation are taken.

3. CRIPPLING OF FUKUSHIMA NUCLEAR PLANT, JAPAN

The entire world, for several weeks together, was gripped by the spell of horror caused by this mammoth disaster. The earthquake that hit Japan was several times more powerful than the worst earthquake the nuclear power plant was built to contend with. Within seconds, after the earthquake started, the control rods had been inserted into the core and the nuclear chain reaction stopped. At this point, the cooling system has to carry away the residual heat, about 7% of the full power heat load under normal operating conditions.

The earthquake destroyed the external power supply of the nuclear reactor. It was an ominous situation for a nuclear power plant. The reactor and its backup systems were designed to handle this type of accident by including backup power systems to keep the coolant pumps working. Furthermore, since the power plant had been shut down, it could not produce any electricity by itself. For the first hour, the first set of multiple emergency diesel power generators started and provided the electricity that was needed. However, when the tsunami arrived which was certainly very rare and much stronger than anticipated, it flooded the diesel generators also, causing them to fail.

One of the fundamental tenets of nuclear power plant design is 'Defence in Depth'. This approach leads engineers to design a plant that can withstand severe catastrophes, even when several systems fail. A large tsunami that disables all the diesel generators at once is such a scenario, but the tsunami of March 11 was beyond all reasonable expectations. To mitigate such an event, engineers designed an extra line of defence by bolstering up the containment structure that is designed to contain everything inside the structure.

When the diesel generators failed after the tsunami, the reactor operators switched to emergency battery power. The batteries were designed as one of the backup systems to provide power for cooling the core for 8 hours. And they did. After 8 hours, however, the batteries ran out, and the residual heat could not be drained away any more. At this point the plant operators begin to follow emergency procedures that are in place for a 'loss of cooling event'. These are procedural steps related to the 'Depth in Defence' approach.

However, melting was still a long way from happening and at this time, the primary goal was to manage the core while it was heating up, while ensuring that the fuel cladding remained intact and operational for as long as possible. Because cooling the core was a priority, the reactor was having a number of in-built independent and diverse cooling systems (the reactor water clean-up system, the decay heat removal, the reactor core isolating cooling, the standby liquid cooling system, and others that make up the emergency core cooling system). Which one(s) failed when or how is not clear.

Since the operators lost most of their cooling capabilities due to the loss of power, they had to use whatever cooling system capacity they had to get rid of as much heat as possible. But as long as the heat generation exceeds the heat removal capacity, the pressure starts increasing as more water boils into steam. The priority now is to maintain the integrity of the fuel rods by keeping the temperature below 1200°C, as well as keeping the pressure at a manageable level. In order to maintain the pressure of the system at a manageable level, steam and other gases present in the reactor have to be released from time to time. This process is important during an accident, so that the pressure does not exceed what the components can handle; so the reactor pressure vessel and the containment structure are designed with several pressure relief valves. Hence, to protect the integrity of the vessel and containment, the operators started venting steam from time to time to control the pressure.

As mentioned above, steam and other gases are vented. Some of these gases are radioactive fission products, but they exist in small quantities. Therefore, when the operators started venting the system, some radioactive gases were released into atmosphere in a controlled manner i.e. in small quantities through filters and scrubbers. While some of these gases are radioactive, they did not pose a significant risk to public safety to even the workers on site. This procedure is justified as its consequences are minimal, especially when compared to the potential consequences of not venting and risking the containment structures' integrity.

During this time, mobile generators were transported to the site and some power was restored. However, more water was boiling off and being vented than was being added to the reactor, thus decreasing the cooling ability of the remaining cooling systems. At some stage during this venting process, the water level may have dropped below the top of the fuel rods. Whatever the reason, the temperature of some of the fuel rod cladding exceeded 1200 °C, initiating a reaction between the Zircaloy and water. This oxidizing reaction produces hydrogen gas, which mixes with the gas-steam mixture being vented. This again is a known and anticipated process, but the amount of hydrogen gas produced was unknown because the operators did not know the exact temperature of the fuel rods or the water level. Since hydrogen gas is extremely combustible, when enough hydrogen gas is mixed with air, it reacts with oxygen. If there is enough hydrogen gas, it will react rapidly, producing an explosion. At some point during the venting process, large quantities of hydrogen gas got built up inside the containment, so when it was vented to the air an explosion occurred. The explosion took place outside the containment, but inside and around the reactor building (which had no safety function). A subsequent and similar explosion occurred at the Unit 3 reactor. This explosion destroyed the top and some of the sides of the reactor building, but did not damage the containment structure or the pressure vessel. While this was not an anticipated event, it happened outside the containment and did not pose a risk to the plant's safety structures.

As the temperature of the fuel rod cladding exceeded 1200 °C, some fuel damage occurred. The nuclear material itself was still intact, but the surrounding Zircaloy shell had started failing. At that time, some of the radioactive fission products (caesium, iodine, etc.) started to mix with the water and steam.

Since the reactor's cooling capability was limited, and the water inventory in the reactor was decreasing, engineers decided to inject sea water (mixed with boric acid – a neutron absorber) to ensure the rods remain covered with water. Although the reactor had been shut down, boric acid was added as a conservative measure to ensure the reactor stayed shut down. Boric acid is also capable of trapping some of the remaining iodine in the water so that it cannot escape, however this trapping is not the primary function of the boric acid. The water used in the cooling system is invariably purified, demineralized water. The reason to use pure water is to limit the corrosion potential of the coolant water during normal operation.

The situation at Fukushima is much better and more 'predictable' today than it was in the days and weeks after the quake. However, some 80,000 people remain displaced!

Environmental effect of the Fukushima disaster:
Environmental consequences were unprecedented due to release of various radioactive materials in the ambient atmosphere. The severity of this nuclear accident is provisionally rated 7 on the International Nuclear Event Scale (INES). This scale runs from 0, indicating an abnormal situation with no safety consequences, to 7, indicating an accident causing widespread contamination with serious health and environmental effects. Prior to Fukushima, the Chernobyl disaster was the only level 7 accident on record, while the Three Mile Island accident was a level 5 accident.

Plutonium was detected in small amounts in soil samples collected near the station on 21, 22, 25 and 28 March. Radioactive iodine, caesium, ruthenium, and tellurium were also detected in seawater samples in the vicinity of the station.

Radiation levels higher than 1000 mSv/hour were detected at the surface of water accumulating in the basement of Unit 2 and the piping tunnel outside the Unit 2 building on 27 March. Levels of radioactive Iodine-131, 4,385 times higher than regulatory limits were detected in seawater samples on March 30, 2011.

Radioactive iodine was also found in tap water in some prefectures between 21 and 27 March, prompting government warnings not to drink the water in those regions.

Levels of radioactive caesium above regulatory limits were detected in small fish caught off the coast of Ibaraki on April 4.

Levels of radioactive I-131 between 0.7 and 24 times higher than regulatory limits were detected in seawater samples on May 31.

Lessons from Fukushima: The following are some of the major lessons and follow-up actions.

- ✓ Strengthening of existing 'Response Mechanism' which is quite weak as of now and amply proved to be so in the disaster.

- ✓ Augmenting factor of Safety in future designs.

- ✓ More regular and intense safety checks for all nuclear plants.

- ✓ Constitution of fresh 'Nuclear Safety Agency', bringing in academics and technocrats from expert countries in the field of nuclear energy use.

- ✓ Reactivation and reorganisation of nuclear regulatory body the world over.

The Fukushima disaster prompted the two countries Switzerland and Germany to announce their complete withdrawal from further use of nuclear power by 2034 and 2022, respectively. The bottom line is that the challenges remain high, the risks remain drastically significant, and the inherent risks of nuclear technology, whether for civilian or military purposes still need our constant vigilance.

4. BP Oil Spill in the Gulf of Mexico

An explosion on April 20, 2010, aboard the Deepwater Horizon, a drilling rig working on a well for the oil company BP one mile below the surface of the Gulf of Mexico, led to the largest accidental oil spill recorded in history. It was reported as a classic case of poor maintenance, inadequate training and a lax safety culture that contributed to the lethal explosion and sinking of the BP's rig with the attendant spill. As regards follow up measures, BP clashed with the federal government over its use of dispersants, chemicals sprayed on the spill that were meant to break up the oil in the hope that it would settle to the bottom.

The Underwater Struggle: For several weeks, BP tried without success to reactivate the seal-off valves on the dead blowout preventer. Then it lowered a 40-foot steel containment chamber in an effort to funnel escaping oil to a ship on the surface, but that failed when an icy slush of gas and water clogged up the device.

In a manoeuvre called a 'top kill', BP then planned to pump heavy drilling fluids twice the density of water through two narrow lines into the blowout preventer to plug the runaway well. However, this tactic, though initially promising, failed when it became clear that the pressure of oil and gas escaping from the well was simply too powerful to overcome. With this disappointment, BP and government officials announced they had abandoned efforts to plug the leaking well.

BP engineers used submersible robots to cut off a portion of the pipe through which the oil was gushing out to give a new cap a better target to fit over, and pumped antifreeze down into the space to try to prevent ice build-up. They then eased the cap in place, and slowly began closing vents that had been left open to minimize pressure that might lift it off. By June 5, officials reported that they were siphoning off as much as 10,000 barrels a day, even with only one of four vents closed. In mid-July, after 86 days of oil gushing into the gulf and a series of failed efforts, the leak was finally stopped when BP managed to install a much tighter-fitting cap on the well a mile below the sea floor, and then gradually closed a series of valves.

Nearly five months after it blew out of control, the federal government finally declared the well dead in September, after pressure tests confirmed that cement pumped into the base of the well through a relief well formed an effective, and final, seal. The Macondo well and the two relief wells were to be abandoned, following standard industry practices.

The oil spilled from the BP well first made landfall in Louisiana. But in June, tar balls and oil mousse had reached the shores of Mississippi, Alabama and Florida. Shortly thereafter, it spread on shore, smearing tourist beaches, washing onto the shorelines of sleepy coastal communities and oozing into marshy bays where fishermen have worked for generations.

By August, the slick appeared to be dissolving far more rapidly than anticipated. The long term damage caused by the spill, however, is still uncertain, in part because large amounts of oil spread underwater rather than surfacing. A new study published in the journal Science in late August confirmed the existence of a huge plume of dispersed oil deep in the Gulf of Mexico and suggested that it had not broken down, raising the possibility that it might pose a threat to wildlife for months or even years.

In September 2010, two independent researchers at Columbia University announced that the federal government, after several missteps, had accurately estimated the amount of oil spilled at nearly 172 million gallons; 185 million gallons, a statistical match when the margins of error are figured in, had actually leaked from the broken well, they said.

By November 2010, the emergency program in the Gulf had ended and the settlement phase began.

Aftermath: A year afterward, assessments of the damage to the gulf, its people and their livelihoods have been varied — from reasonably moderated ones to rather undervalued figures to reduce financial compensation. The surface oil has been captured or dispersed, although questions remain about the effect of the vast underwater plumes that spread across the gulf. Hundreds of miles of beaches have been reclaimed, with only a fraction still soiled. Fish are edible. Jobs are returning. The much-maligned federal agency responsible for policing offshore drilling has been restructured, with a tough new director and stricter safety rules.

However, tragedy still haunts in the shape of the damage to the ecology of the Gulf of Mexico, including the enormous dead zone off the mouth of the Mississippi and the alarmingly rapid disappearance of Louisiana's coastal wetlands, roughly 2,000 square miles smaller than they were 80 years ago.

Eclipsed by the spill's uncertain environmental impact is the other fallout: the vast sums in penalties and fines BP will have to pay to the federal government. In addition to criminal fines and restitution, BP is facing civil liabilities that fall roughly into two categories: Clean Water Act penalties and claims from the Natural Resource Damage Assessment process, whereby state and federal agencies tally the damage caused by the spill and put a price tag on it. This could add up to billions, perhaps tens of billions, of dollars.

On April 22, 2011, the Justice Department announced that an agreement had been announced between BP and the trustees who are part of the natural resources damage assessment for BP to provide a $1 billion down payment for early restoration projects, the largest of its kind ever reached.

Many other consequences are likely to ripple out from the spill for a long time to come. Some have already happened: investigations by the Justice Department and Congress into the cause of the spill; new regulations imposing tougher review for deep-water drilling; new leadership for BP as the oil giant struggles to repair a shattered reputation, etc. In December 2010, the Department of Justice filed a civil lawsuit in New Orleans against BP and eight other companies over the Gulf of Mexico oil spill. Although the complaint does not specify the damages that the administration is seeking, the fines and penalties under the laws that are cited in the complaint could reach into the tens of billions of dollars.

On Feb. 2, 2011, a report commissioned by Kenneth Feinberg, the well-known 'pay czar' and government-appointed Administrator of BP Compensation Fund, predicted that the Gulf of Mexico should recover from the environmental damage caused by the enormous BP oil spill faster than many people expected. The prediction, central to Feinberg's plan for paying claimants, is certain to be controversial among those who believe the damage will be longer-lasting and therefore should result in higher pay-outs for the spill's victims. On the same day, BP said it planned to sell half of its refining capacity in the United States while expanding in faster-growing economies, and that it would resume paying a dividend for the first time since the explosion.

Impact on Energy Policy: The deadly explosion and the resulting spill complicated US's plans to expand offshore oil and gas drilling, and doomed a bipartisan energy bill in the Senate in 2010. The US ordered a halt to virtually all current and new offshore oil drilling activity pending a comprehensive safety review, acknowledging that oversight had been seriously deficient and reiterated that offshore drilling would have to remain a dormant part of the nation's sources of energy for at least the near future.

In August, the administration announced that it would revise the process used for granting deep-water drilling permits to require more extensive review. White House officials recommended that the Interior Department suspend use of so-called categorical exclusions, which allow oil companies to sink offshore wells based on environmental impact statements for supposedly similar areas, while the department reviews the environmental impact. Permits for the Macondo well were based on exemptions written in 1981 and 1986. The waiver granted to BP in April 2009, as part of the permitting process for the doomed well, was based on the company's claim that a blowout was unlikely and that if a spill did occur, it would cause minimal damage.

Prospects of Recovery: The effect on sea life of the large amounts of oil that remained below the surface is still a mystery. Two preliminary government reports on that issue have found concentrations of toxic compounds in the deep sea to be low, but the reports left many questions, especially regarding an apparent decline in oxygen levels in the water. Understanding the effects of the spill on the shorelines that were hit, including Louisiana's coastal marshes is expected to occupy scientists for years. Fishermen along the coast are deeply sceptical of any declarations of success, expressing concern about the long-term effects of the chemical dispersants used to combat the spill and of the submerged oil, particularly on shrimp and crab larvae that are the foundation of future fishing seasons.

Evidence is increasing that through a combination of luck (a fortunate shift in ocean currents that kept much of the oil away from shore) and ecological circumstance (the relatively warm waters that increased the breakdown rate of the oil), the gulf region appears to have escaped the direst predictions of spring 2010.

Scientists caution that much remains unknown, and that oil spills can have subtle effects that last for decades. Layers of oil are being found buried beneath the surface, both onshore and deep at sea. In blog posts from a research vessel in the gulf, Samantha Joye, a professor of marine sciences at the University of Georgia, reports that she observed a layer several centimetres thick on the sea floor, 16 miles from the wellhead, that she says was not a result of natural seepage.

In August 2010, top administration officials said that 75 per cent of the oil had evaporated, dissolved or have been collected. But the presidential commission stated in October that the government's own data did not support such sweeping conclusions, which were later scaled back. A number of respected independent researchers have concluded that as much as half of the spilled oil remains suspended in the water or buried on the seafloor and in coastal sludge, and that it will be some time before scientists can paint an accurate picture of the ecological damage.

In an internal report released in early September 2010, BP claimed that it was a series of failures involving a number of companies that ultimately led to the spill. Citing 'a complex and interlinked series of mechanical failures, human judgments, engineering design, operational implementation and team interfaces', the 193-page report deflected attention away from BP and back onto its contractors, especially Transocean and Halliburton.

While it put some responsibility on BP for errors made — such as misreading pressure data that indicated a blowout was imminent — the report tried to gloss over the notion that the company acted with gross negligence. Yet because of its authorship, it was unlikely to carry much weight in influencing the Department of Justice, which was considering criminal and civil charges related to the spill. The report was far from the final word on possible causes of the explosion, as several other divisions of the federal government, including the Coast Guard and Bureau of Ocean Energy Management, Regulation and Enforcement, were also investigating.

A report commissioned by Feinberg predicted that the gulf will recover sometime in 2012. The report, released in February 2011, laid out for the first time the framework for deciding who gets final settlements for spill-related damage and how payments for future losses will be determined. Using the work of environmental scientists, economists and other experts, the study acknowledges that 'prediction is not an exact science', but estimated that the gulf should recover within two years. But the hardest-hit oyster beds could take much longer to come back, it said. Based on those estimates, the damages paid out by the fund would be double the first year's losses for most of those filing claims, less any money previously paid by the fund. Those whose living is tied to oyster beds would receive four times their 2010 losses.

But Gulf Coast residents have become increasingly angry over what they say is the program's shortcomings, including inconsistent payments and an opaque process. The methodology for final settlements is meant to answer those criticisms.

5. London Smog Crisis of 1952

Dr Robert Waller was working at St Bartholomew's Hospital in London in the early 1950s. He says a shortage of coffins and high sales of flowers were the first indications that many people were being killed.

The infamous fog of December 1952 has come to be known as 'The Great Smog'. The term was coined almost half a century earlier, by HA Des Voeux, who first used it in 1905 to describe the conditions of fuliginous (sooty) fog that occurred all too often over British urban areas. It was popularized in 1911 when Des Voeux presented to the Manchester Conference of the Smoke Abatement League of Great Britain a report on the deaths that occurred in Glasgow and Edinburgh in the autumn of 1909 as a consequence of smoke-laden fogs.

The Beginning: During the day on December 5, 1952, the fog was not especially dense and generally possessed a dry, smoky character. When nightfall came, however, the fog thickened. Visibility dropped to a few metres. The following day, the sun was too low in the sky to make much of an impression on the fog. That night and on the Sunday and Monday nights, the fog again thickened. In many parts of London, it was impossible at night for pedestrians to find their way, even in familiar districts. In the Isle of Dogs, the visibility was at times nil. The fog there was so thick that people could not see their own feet! Even in the drier thoroughfares of central London, the fog was exceptionally thick. Not until 9 December did it clear. In central London, the visibility remained below 500 metres continuously for 114 hours and below 50 metres at a stretch for 48 hours. At Heathrow Airport, visibility remained below ten metres for almost 48 hours from the morning of 6 December.

Build-up of Huge Concentration of Air-Pollutants: Huge quantities of impurities were released into the atmosphere during the period in question. On each day during the foggy period, enormous amounts of pollutants were emitted: 1,000 tonnes of smoke particles, 2,000 tonnes of carbon dioxide, 140 tonnes of hydrochloric acid and 14 tonnes of fluorine compounds. In addition, and perhaps most dangerously, 370 tonnes of sulphur dioxide were converted into 800 tonnes of sulphuric acid. At London's County Hall, the concentration of smoke in the air increased from 0.49 milligram per cubic metre on the 4th of December to 4.46 on the 7th and 8th of December.

Follow-up Legislations: Legislation followed the Great Smog of 1952 in the form of the City of London, Various Powers Act of 1954 and the Clean Air Acts of 1956 and 1968. These Acts banned emissions of black smoke and decreed that residents of urban areas and operators of factories must convert to smokeless fuels. As these residents and operators were necessarily given time to convert, however, fogs continued to be smoky for some time after the Act of 1956 was passed. In 1962, for example, 750 Londoners died as a result of a fog, but nothing on the scale of the 1952 Great Smog has ever occurred again.

Consequences: The London Smog is one of the deadliest recorded episodes of urban smog that caused record casualties between 5 December and 9 December 1952. New research indicates that as many as 12,000 people may have died as a result of the smog, and mortality from respiratory illnesses such as bronchitis and pneumonia increased more than seven-fold during the smog. Overall death rates during the first half of that month were three times higher than normal, and morbidity and mortality rates in greater London remained elevated well into March of 1953.

Many of those killed were elderly people or those who were already weak or ill. According to medical staff that treated patients at the time, few people realised the extent of the impact.

6. THE EUROPEAN BSE CRISIS

Mad Cow Disease made strong headlines throughout Europe nearly one and a half decade back. BSE stands for 'Bovine Spongiform Encephalopathy'. It created a sense of terror that lasted for several months. The first diagnosis of BSE was made in November 1986 at Britain's Central Veterinary Laboratory. Although the two cows concerned were from different parts of the country, they displayed the same abnormal neurological symptoms, identified as a spongy-like degeneration of the brain.

The BSE crisis led to the European Union banning exports of British beef with effect from March 1996; the ban would last for 10 years before it was finally lifted on 1 May 2006. Over 18,000 cases related with BSE were reported in different countries.

When the BSE crisis first broke out in the UK, butchers' shops on the continent put up signs saying, 'No British Beef Sold Here'. European governments resorted to jingoistic reaction, extolling the virtues and safety of their own beef, and then banning British imports. However, a general relaxation of safety-critical standards combined with the domination of farming by massive agribusiness is not a purely British affair. This is particularly so in Europe, where the Common Agricultural Policy provides billions in subsidies to protect European farming.

The BSE crisis was both foreseeable and preventable. Its origins lay in the intensified production methods introduced in the mid-1980s, and particularly the practice of adding meat and bone meal to animal feeds. Once cattle that had succumbed to BSE were ground up and used in such high-protein food additives, a cycle was established that ensured the disease multiplied throughout the national herd.

Meat and bone meal additives have been banned in Britain since the 1990s (as were the 'specified risk' materials) but continued to be exported abroad for some time. The EU has only imposed a temporary six-month ban in December last year, with no indication if it will be made permanent.

The EU Commission overhauled food safety mechanisms in the late 1990s, in the wake of the British BSE crisis. But although the new procedures may bring to light more cases of BSE the Commission has no powers of enforcement. Agricultural policy is still a nationally guarded preserve. As an article in Britain's Financial Times newspaper noted, the 'first response (by governments) to outbreaks of BSE elsewhere is not to step up their own safety inspection procedures but to launch campaigns urging consumers at home to boycott foreign beef'.

The BSE crisis is only the most critical in a long line of food safety scandals (which include salmonella and e-coli) and have cost countless lives. As the BSE scandal now spreads across Europe, it confirms tragically that as long as food production and safety are subordinated to the profit system and the market, then public health will continue to suffer.

The disease spread in Britain due to a lack of proper sterilization techniques which gave a chance for the infectious agents to spread. Although by 1996 there was a ban on British meat exports, it was too late to stop the spread of the disease. In 1996 it was also discovered that there was a human equivalent to BSE, which attacked the brain, causing depression, coordination problems, memory loss, mood swings, pain in the limbs, bad headaches and many other problems. Creutsfeldt Jacobs Disease (vCJD) had killed nearly 90 people in the UK by 2003, with deaths also reported in France and Italy. By 2004 a total of 158 people had acquired or died from vCJD, most of whom were Britons. The incidences of the disease are relatively small in number, but the discovery of it had a dramatic effect on European beef consumption. Even after the BSE epidemic is under control, people are still being diagnosed with its human equivalent every year, due to its long incubation period. The full extent of the outbreak may still be unknown.

B. NATURAL ENVIRONMENTAL DISASTERS

Natural disasters are often unpredictable. They are often a result of epidemics, tsunami, volcano, earthquake, hurricane, tornado, storm, flood, wildfire and the like – all 'Acts Of God', to borrow a legalese. Some disasters have atmospheric, geologic and hydrologic origins as well. These catastrophes affected the lives of hundreds of thousands of people the world over. Some of the major natural disasters that have blighted the world since the 14th century are being enumerated here.

1. THE PLAGUE OF THE 14TH CENTURY (BLACK DEATH)

It unleashed a tremendous reign of terror in the minds of people living in the fourteenth century Europe, Asia and Africa. These continents were badly hit with a serious outbreak of the plague, now commonly known as The Black Death. The disease is caused by the bacterium Pasteurella pestis or Yersinia pestis, which is transmitted through rodents to humans by a flea. Symptoms of the disease include fever, delirium, and pneumonia and enlarged pus-filled lymph nodes. These nodes would open to the skin and drain spontaneously.

Background: The deadly disease has been with man and one of the foremost of the world's major pestilences since pre-medieval history. It claimed around 200 million lives the world over. The first ever recorded epidemic of the Bubonic Plague was in Europe during the 6th Century. The disease truly became pandemic in 1328. During this period a third of the world's population died. We tend to associate the history of this terrible disease with Europe; however it originated in the Gobi Desert.

It is believed that the Black Death originated in central China in 1333 as the population succumbed to starvation. The plague spread to the Crimea where Kipchak Mongols or Tartans attacked Genoese traders. The traders escaped by sea, but carried the plague to Messina in Italy. In 1348 the plague spread from Cyprus to Florence which was also suffering from famine. The plague further spread to the English south coast near Southampton in 1348. It affected all walks of life from the rich to the poor. The Black Death ravaged Bristol, killing most of its inhabitants. It reached London around 1 November 1348 and by 2 February 1349, 200 people were being buried every day!

Large Scale Devastation of Human Population: The European population back then counted approximately 100 million people. Between 1347 and 1351, at least 25 and possibly 75 million people died of the plague, practically destroying the European social structure. Death tolls caused the disappearance of law enforcement, religious ceremonies and medical practise in the areas where the plague was at its worst.

Sudden Disappearance: After having killed people by millions it suddenly ceased. Still today, we do not fully understand the reason for this sudden retreat. Possibly, only resistant humans withstood the epidemic – a pre-Darwinian validation of the theory of survival of the fittest. Perhaps, as literally and figuratively suggested in Albert Camus' eponymous novel, reservoirs of the plague are still in waiting, ready to spread when conditions are conducive enough. Fortunately hygiene and medication have been able to prevent a new plague epidemic of equal severity from striking so far.

Social Changes Caused by the Plague: The Black Death caused huge social changes throughout Europe. There were less people to work on the lands and those that survived had more wealth among fewer people. In the Abbey of Ramsay, England, 30 years after the plague, grain production had halved. Such drops in output caused grain prices to rise, and peasants were in higher demand and could attain higher wages, despite laws to thwart them. The Black Death killed may clerics, and children in grammar schools who were taught French were instead taught English due to the lack of French trained clerics.

2. SPANISH FLU (GREAT INFLUENZA EPIDEMIC)
   I had a little bird,
   Its name was Enza.
   I opened the window,
   And in-flu-enza!

This is the rhyme children used to sing in the times of the great Influenza Epidemic. The Spanish Flu, also known as the Great Influenza Epidemic, was an epidemic that killed some 50 to 100 million people worldwide in 1918 and 1919 during the First World

War. Roughly 2.5 per cent of infected people died. The first wave was reported in the late winter, early spring of 1918. A vicious second wave started in late August and early September. It was one of the most deadly global epidemics in human history.

Why 'Spanish' Flu: The disease was called 'Spanish Flu' because it received the greatest media attention in Spain. Spain suffered one of the worst early outbreaks of the disease with some 8 million casualties. Most cases of mortality were among soldiers. Even with treatment it killed one third of those infected. Mortality was mostly caused by pneumonia.

Global Spread: It has been suggested that rapid movement of soldiers and weakened immune systems as a consequence of chemical warfare contributed to the spread of the Spanish Flu during World War I. Mass graves were dug to bury the bodies without even placing them in coffins. After August the disease spread the world over. Global mortality rate from the Spanish Flu was estimated at 2.5-5% of the population, with some 20% of the world population suffering from the disease to some extent. In India 17 million people died, which was 5% of its total population. In the US some 500,000 to 675,000 people died and in Britain some 200.000 were killed. France counted a final death toll of 400,000, while 30,000 to 50,000 Canadians died. The epidemic eventually killed at least as many people as the war itself. In some small towns, the disease wiped out the entire population.

Symptoms: The effect of the infection was so severe that sometimes death was reported within hours of the onset of symptoms. Spanish flu symptoms included extreme coughing fits; sweating; fever; delirium; blood pouring from nose and ears; occasional collapse; meningitis of the brain; and pneumonia of the lungs.

Symptoms of the Spanish Flu also included a blue tint to the face and coughing up blood caused by severe obstruction of the lungs. People tried to stop the epidemic by isolating those that had symptoms, but it did little good. Death rate was highest among young and healthy adults.

Disappearance of the Flu: The Spanish Flu vanished within eighteen months, and the actual cause was not determined at the time. It appears to have been an H1NI virus type. At that time people thought the flu was the result of a bacterial infection, and many years were spent looking for a vaccine in vain.

Possibility of Re-emergence: cannot be predicted with certainty; however, the probability of the 1918 virus re-emerging appears to be remote. Experts believe that a pandemic is most likely to be caused by an influenza subtype to which there is little, or no, pre-existing immunity in the human population. There is evidence that some residual immunity to the 1918 virus, or a similar virus, is present in at least a portion of the human population. Since contemporary H1N1 viruses circulate widely and the current annual influenza vaccines contain an H1N1 component, a 1918-like H1N1 virus would not fit the current criteria for a new pandemic strain.

Efficacy of Currently Available Antivirals & Vaccines to counter the 1918 Virus: Two types of antiviral drugs, rimantadine (Flumadine) and oseltamivir (Tamiflu), have been shown to be effective against influenza viruses similar to the 1918 virus. Vaccines containing the 1918 HA or other subtype H1 HA proteins were effective in protecting mice against the 1918 virus. In fact, the current influenza vaccine provided some level of protection against the 1918 virus in mice.

3. THE DUTCH FLOOD DISASTER 1953

The Netherlands is situated in a low-lying delta where the rivers Rhine, Meuse, Scheldt and Ems debouch into the North Sea. It is accursed by nature to be inundated with flood, about 60% of the country being situated below sea-level. The Dutch have been manfully contending with the flood menace for centuries now, from the heydays of the Holland's United Provinces, when Holland was Europe's most powerful financial centre, to the current post-industrial Netherlands.

After one such big flood in 1916 strong dikes were built that gave people a false sense of safety. But the complacency was badly jolted on February 1 1953. On Saturday, January 31 of that year the Dutch weather service disseminated a warning of an approaching northwester storm on the North Sea. During that night the storm hit the Netherlands with gale force, which started gathering more and more intensity.

Inadequate Communication: Communication means were limited in those times. Most people did not own television, there were no nocturnal radio broadcasts and a large number of people were not connected by basic telephone facilities, causing many to be left unaware of the impending danger. Thus, most people were caught napping when the disaster struck.

Rising Tide Waters: Past midnight, the Netherlands started flooding, causing dikes to break through at more than 60 locations in three provinces. The southern islands were almost completely flooded, causing thousands of houses and farms to be ruined or dragged into sea. People fled to higher places, such as dikes and attics, and were trapped there. On the afternoon of Sunday, the flood increased and water levels were even higher than the previous night.

Widespread Devastation: The floods caused a total of 1,835 deaths. In some villages up to 10% of the population was killed. More than 47,000 cows and pigs and over 140,000 poultry drowned during the flood. A total area of more than 200,000 hectares was flooded and 72,000 people were evacuated from their homes. The 1953 flood became the largest natural disaster to strike the land since the 1570 flood.

Follow- up Measures: A series of measures was taken to rebuild the dikes following the disaster. On February 18, 1953 the Delta Committee was established and in 1955 the Delta law was presented. Starting in 1958, the Delta works were finished in 1986 with the grand opening of the Oosterschelde flood barrier. The Netherlands now has strong dikes and dams that tie together the islands. The flood warning system is improved and the country gained a reputation for its sturdy and effective system of flood protection.

Future Caution: Despite the high level of protection, floods still occur in the Netherlands. In 1993, 1995 and 1998 flooding of the rivers Rhine and Muse caused considerable damage. In 1995 up to 250,000 people were evacuated from their homes. Additionally, global warming may cause sea level rise, resulting in greater inundation of the country in the future, particularly because the height of the western part of the country is slowly decreasing. This warrants and necessitates continuous and relentless monitoring and management of water in flood prone areas of Netherlands.

4. MOUNT PINATUBO VOLCANIC ERUPTION, PHILIPPINES, 1991

Pinatubo Eruption is the second largest eruption of the 20th century in terms of amount of material blown out of the vent which affected global weather. Official figures put the death toll at 722. Mount Pinatubo is an active volcano situated on the isle of Luzon in the

Philippines, on the borders of the Pampagna, Balaan and Zambales provinces. After more than five centuries of dormancy, the volcano erupted in 1991, producing the largest and most violent eruption of the 20th century.

This particular volcanic activity in the Pinatubo was triggered by a series of earthquakes in the area. It caused a 7 km high atmospheric ash column containing 5 billion cubic metres of ash. Ashes reached heights of up to 30 km at the peak of the eruption.

Volcanic deposits, ashes and mudflows destroyed much of the area surrounding the volcano. Thousands of houses were demolished in the eruption. The ash cloud from the volcano covered an area of some 125,000 km², bringing total darkness to much of central Luzon. The Philippine Institute of Volcanology and Seismology issued a warning indicating the possibility of a major eruption within two weeks. As a result of the institute's predictions of the volcanic eruption and the incorporated warning, approximately 200,000 people could be evacuated in time. Had these alerts not been issued, the volcanic eruption would have led to tens of thousands of deaths. The number of deaths was actually restricted to 722 owing to early warning. Some 173 people were injured and 23 went missing. Roofs collapsed under the heavy weight of accumulated ash which caused most of the death cases. Starvation was also a major cause of death, particularly since arable land was covered with ash and there was no harvest. Livestock was killed massively during the eruption. Damage to health facilities in the area caused people to die from disease because of people swarming to the hospitals in large numbers.

The eruption injected thousands of tonnes of aerosols into the atmosphere, causing the impact to be noticeable all over the world. Some 15 million tons of sulphur dioxides were emitted, resulting in acid rain from sulphuric acid formation and in cooling of the earth's temperature by approximately one degree Celsius. It also caused considerable ozone layer destruction.

The eruption of Mount Pinatubo severely hampered the economic development of the affected areas. It cost billions of dollars to repair the damage to surrounding cities. Education and working facilities were disrupted. In all, the eruption ejected about ten cubic kilometres of material, making it the largest eruption since that of Novarupta in 1912 and believed to be ten times larger than the 1980 eruption of Mount St. Helens.

5. TURKISH EARTHQUAKE OF 1999, IZMIT

Turkey has had a long history of earthquakes. Two earthquakes had already occurred on the North Anatolian fault in 1939 and 1967. This earthquake occurred in the wee hours of morning in the northernmost part of North Anatolian fault system on August 17, 1999. A heavy earthquake measuring 7.4 on a Richter scale hit Izmit, a city in Turkey. It occurred on one of the world's best-studied, the east-west trending North Anatolian fault. This fault causes earthquakes at less than 20 km depth, exposing people at the surface to all the hazards of being in close proximity to the subterranean spot where the energy is released.

Casualties: Most of the casualties resulted out of succumbing of residential buildings to powerful tremors. The earthquake killed some 17,000 people and rendered approximately 500,000 homeless. Another tremor of 7.2 on a Richter scale hit the location on November 12, killing 450 more and leaving 3000 people injured.

Eyewitnesses compared the results of the earthquake to the plight of wartime Sarajevo. Power lines were down, roads and rail links smashed and water supplies and telephone communications interrupted. It took a considerable amount of time to repair damages in affected areas.

Environmental Damage: The earthquake caused considerable environmental damage because it set fire to a refinery. By the time the fire had burned out, air, land and water were polluted. According to Greenpeace, the earthquake caused cracks in the Petkim waste dump, exposing chemical waste that was dumped there for years. A PVC factory, waste treatment plant and incinerator were also damaged. Fortunately, despite all these events of pollution, damages to the environment were contained by effective clean-up operation.

Rescue & Relief Work: The relief and rescue work were mainly spearheaded by the 'Turkish Red Crescent' and Turkish Army together with many International Aid Agencies. Survivors of the earthquake were lodged together in temporary camps. Water supplies were arranged to prevent more people dying of dehydration. Fear of epidemics in these camps was very high.

6. INDIAN OCEAN TSUNAMI OF 2004

The December 26, 2004 Indian Ocean Tsunami is considered the fourth largest since 1900. The Indian Ocean tsunami was caused by an earthquake that was believed to possess the energy equivalent to the explosion of 475,000 kilotons of TNT, or 23,000 atomic bombs. The epicentre of the 9.0 magnitude quake was under the Indian Ocean somewhere near the west coast of the Indonesian island of Sumatra.

A severe movement of tectonic plates displaced an enormous amount of water, sending powerful shock waves in several directions. The tectonic plates in this area had been pushing against each other, building pressure for thousands of years – they continue to do so and are likely to cause underwater earthquakes and tsunamis in the future.

The shifting of the earth's plates in the Indian Ocean on December 26, 2004 caused a rupture more than 600 miles long, displacing the seafloor above the rupture by perhaps ten yards horizontally and several yards vertically. That doesn't sound like much, but the trillions of tons of rock that were moved along hundreds of miles caused the planet to shudder and shiver with an earthquake the magnitude of which was the largest in four or five decades.

Within hours of the earthquake, killer waves radiating from the epicentre slammed into the coastline of around one dozen Indian Ocean countries, damaging countries from east Africa to Thailand. Despite a lag of up to several hours between the earthquake and the impact of the tsunami, nearly all of the victims were taken completely by surprise because there were no tsunami warning systems in the Indian Ocean to detect tsunamis or to warn the general populace living around the ocean.

Many people in Indonesia reportedly saw animals fleeing for high ground minutes before the tsunami arrived, very few animal bodies were found afterward! The carcasses rotting in tropical heat further contaminated food and water sources.

Human Crisis: The following statistics speak for themselves.

Death Toll: Latest figures indicate at least 226,000 dead, including 166,000 in Indonesia; 38,000 in Sri Lanka; 16, 000 in India; 5300 in Thailand; and 5000 foreign tourists.

Number of people injured: Over 500,000.

Potential additional deaths from infectious diseases: 150,000.

Number of people affected: Up to 5 million people lost homes or access to food and water.

Number of children affected: Around a third of the dead were children, and 1.5 million wounded, displaced or lost families.

Number of people left without the means to make a living: Around One million.

Affected World Heritage Sites: The list of World Heritage Sites destroyed or damaged include: the Old Town of Galle in Sri Lanka, the Tropical Rainforest of Sumatra in Indonesia, and the famed Sun Temples of Konark in India.

Some Tsunamis in Chronological Order

Year	Casualties	Magnitude	Affected domain
1707	30,000	8.4	Tokaido/Nankaido, Japan
1755	60,000	8.5	Portugal, morocco
1771	13,486	7.4	Ryukyu Trench, Japan
1782	40,000	7.0	South China Sea
1792	15,030	6.4	Kyushu Island, Japan
1868	25,674	8.5	Northern Chile
1883	36000	NA[†]	Krakatau, Indonesia
1896	26,360	7.6	Sanriku, Japan
2004	225,000	9.0-9.3	Indian Ocean

*Data retrieved and rearranged from various sources.

[†] Data Not Available

Richter Scale units and their Significance

It was developed by Charles Richter in 1935 and the scale's name is attributed to him. The following pictorial representation is self-explanatory.

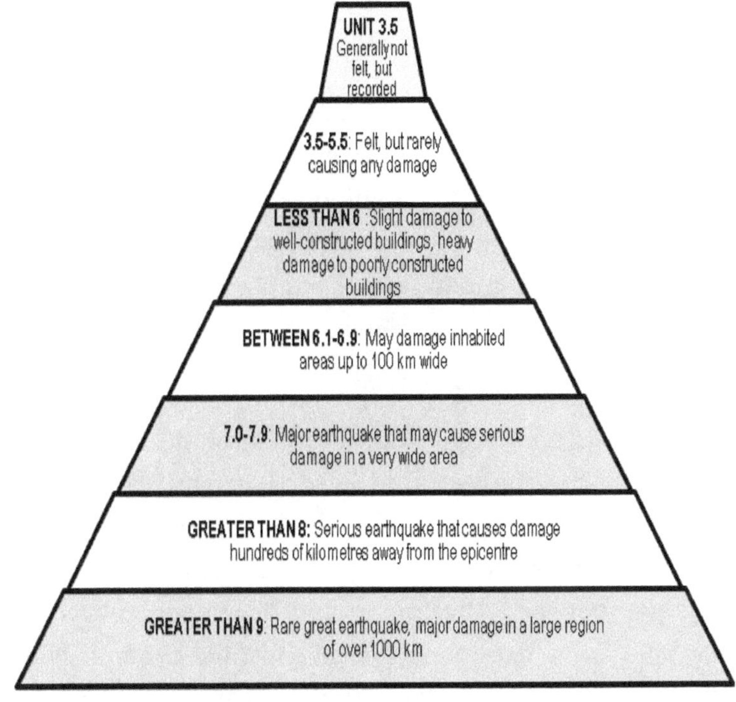

Richter Scale Units & their Connotations

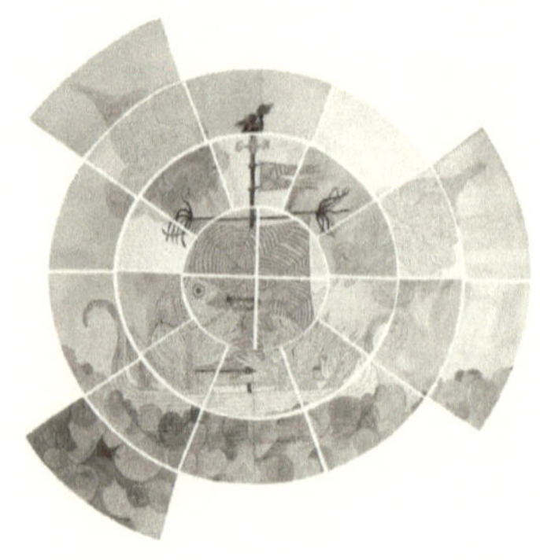

VI
GLOBAL INITIATIVES ON ENVIRONMENT

Umpteen meetings, seminars, and conferences have been held so far to counter environmental degradation. Sincere efforts were also made in some of these meetings to address the menace of pollution and concomitant environmental issues but the success has been modest and a major breakthrough remains elusive.

It was way back in 1972 that the very first time a global concern for environment protection found expression through a convention held at *Stockholm*, the capital of Sweden. In a nutshell it proclaimed man as moulder of environment, and highlighted the urgent need to bring about improvement of human environment, to fill the gap between developing and developed countries and to check population growth. To these ends, the conference exhorted respective governments of the nations to assume direct responsibility for protecting human environment. It also enunciated 26 principles and adopted an 'Action Plan' relating to the key areas of human settlements and health, environment and development, territorial eco-system, energy, ocean and natural disasters.

Ten years later, UNEP convened a session of a special character (SSC) at *Nairobi* in 1982 to commemorate the tenth anniversary of the Stockholm conference. The resultant Nairobi declaration identified the basic orientation of UNEP for the then forthcoming decade, viz. 1982-1992.

Thereafter, the third summit was held at *Rio de Janeiro* (Brazil) in 1992. It adopted the 'Rio Declaration' together with 'Agenda 21' containing a blueprint for sustainable development. The fourth summit took place at *Johannesburg* in 2002, when the participating countries agreed in principle on a sweeping plan to cut poverty while saving the environment. It also touched new issues such as water sanitation, energy, medicine to poor counties, biological diversity, restoring depleted fish stock etc.

Another landmark meeting was the Kyoto meet, the deliberations of which are widely known as the *Kyoto Protocol*. The treaty was negotiated in the city of Kyoto (Japan) in December 1997 and has been in force since Feb16, 2005. This, arguably, was the sincerest and most effective of all climate initiatives so far, wherein a genuine attempt was made towards amelioration of environmental woes that face today's world. Described by many as a real 'trailblazer', the Protocol devised several innovative approaches to stem the environmental rot, such as 'Clean Development Mechanism' (CDM), 'Certified Emission Reduction' (CER) and 'Linking Mechanism'.

As per the extant provisions of the Kyoto Protocol, the developed countries like USA and Canada have the mandate to bring down their emission levels to 93% and 94% respectively, whereas for Britain, Germany and France the target is 92%.(Percentage of Base Year or Period). However, some countries, including Australia, Iceland and Norway, have been allowed percentages higher than that of the base year, viz. 108%, 110% and 101 % respectively for the three specified nations. Overall, as per *Article 3* of the protocol, at least 5% reduction below 1990 levels has been contemplated within the commitment period 2008 to 2012.

Mention may also be made of other meets such as Montreal Protocol (1987), Helsinki Declaration (1989), London Conference

(1990), and Copenhagen Conference (1992), whereby phasing out of CFC, CCl_4 and HCFC was laid down. Brief description of ODS (Ozone Depleting Substance) conferences and their deliberations are enumerated below in chronological order:

Montreal Protocol, 1987

Damage to the Earth's protective ozone layer had sparked unprecedented worldwide concern and action. Since it was agreed internationally in 1987 to phase out ozone depleting substances, 196 countries have ratified the Montreal Protocol so far. In September 2009, East Timor also ratified the Montreal Protocol, making it the first international environmental treaty to achieve complete ratification – a truly remarkable effort that reflects the universal acceptance and success of the agreement.

The Montreal Protocol is widely considered as the most successful environment protection agreement. The Protocol set out a mandatory timetable for the phasing out of ozone depleting substances. This timetable has been reviewed regularly, with phase out dates accelerated in accordance with scientific understanding and technological advances.

The Montreal Protocol sets binding progressive phase out obligations for developed and developing countries for all the major ODSs (ozone depleting substances), including CFCs, halons and less damaging transitional chemicals such as HCFCs.

The Multilateral Fund, the first financial mechanism to be created under such an international treaty, was created under the Protocol in 1990 to provide financial assistance to developing countries to help them achieve their phase out obligations.

The Montreal Protocol targeted 96 chemicals in thousands of applications across more than 240 industrial sectors. The Multilateral Fund has provided more than US $2.5 billion in financial assistance to developing countries to phase out production and consumption of ozone depleting substances since the Protocol's inception in 1987.

The Protocol has been further strengthened through five Amendments – London 1990, Copenhagen 1992, Vienna 1995, Montreal 1997, and Beijing 1999 – which have brought forward phase out schedules and added new ozone depleting substances to the list of substances controlled under the Montreal Protocol.

Helsinki Declaration, 1989

Made on 2 May 1989, this declaration, the operative parts of the text referred to the deliberations at the First Meetings of the Parties (Governments and the European Communities) to the Vienna Convention and the Montreal Protocol, and recorded the following aspects of awareness and agreement.

- ✓ *Aware* of the wide agreement among scientists that depletion of the ozone layer will threaten present and future generations, unless more stringent control measures are adopted.

- ✓ *Mindful* that some ozone depleting substances are powerful greenhouse gases leading to global warming.

- ✓ *Aware* also of the extensive and rapid technological development of environmentally acceptable substitutes for the substances that deplete the ozone layer and the urgent need to facilitate the transfer of technologies of such substitutes especially to developing countries.

✓ *Encourage* all states that have not done so to join the Vienna Convention for the Protection of the Ozone Layer and its Montreal Protocol.

✓ *Agree* to phase out the production and the consumption of CFCs controlled by the Montreal Protocol as soon as possible but not later than the year 2000 and for that purpose to tighten the timetable agreed upon in the Montreal Protocol taking due account of the special situation of developing countries.

✓ *Agree* to both phase out halons and control and reduce other ozone-depleting substances which contribute significantly to ozone depletion as soon as feasible.

✓ *Agree* to commit themselves, in proportion to their means and resources, to accelerate the development of environmentally acceptable substituting chemicals, products and technologies.

✓ *Agree* to facilitate the access of developing countries to relevant scientific information, research results and training and to seek to develop appropriate funding mechanisms to facilitate the transfer of technology and replacement of equipment at minimum cost to developing countries.

The *London Amendment (1990):* changed the ODS emission schedule by requiring the complete phase out of CFCs, halons, and carbon tetrachloride by 2000 in developed countries, and by 2010 in developing countries. Methyl chloroform was also added to the list of controlled ODSs, with phase-out in developed countries targeted in 2005, and in 2015 for developing countries.

The Copenhagen Amendment (1992): significantly accelerated the phase out of ODSs and incorporated an HCFC phase out for developed countries, beginning in 2004. Under this agreement,

CFCs, halons, carbon tetrachloride, and methyl chloroform were targeted for complete phase out in 1996 in developed countries. In addition, methyl bromide consumption of methyl bromide was capped at 1991 levels.

The Montreal Amendment (1997): included the phase out of HCFCs in developing countries, as well as the phase out of methyl bromide in developed and developing countries in 2005 and 2015, respectively.

The Beijing Amendment (1999): included tightened controls on the production and trade of HCFCs. Bromochloro methane was also added to the list of controlled substances with phase out targeted for 2004.

EU (European Union) seems quite proactive as it has incessantly expressed its intents of honouring all its commitments and obligations under the Kyoto protocol but intents and consequent actions should be reflected in the global emission data. It is highly unfortunate that the Annual Emission data ever tend to disappoint year after year!

It is highly unlikely and unrealistic to expect cuts to the tune of 25-40% below 1990 levels by 2020 from key players like the USA. Japan may show some resilience as it has, of late, announced its intentions of imposing 'Carbon Tax' and is extremely considerate on GHGs (Green House Gases) emission issue.

China seems to have principled reservations as its chief climate negotiator Yu Quingtai has stated: 'Each person is entitled to his fair share of global atmospheric space'; he also adds that even today 20% of the world's population living in industrialized countries contributes 70-80% of all the GHG emissions that are leading to climate change. It is apparent that India is also not going to commit to any short term legally binding targets. It is indeed the onus of the developed countries they should take the initiative and declare their immediate short, medium and long term emission reduction targets. Declaration of short term emission reduction targets is absolutely warranted at this stage. Developing countries may express their *long term* targets. Key issues such as 'reform of the international Carbon Market'; finance that developed countries should provide to developing countries 'to adapt and mitigate the climatic change'; 'emission accounting rules for the forestry sector'; future financing of the CDM; implementing REDD (Reducing Emissions from Deforestation and forest Degradation in developing countries), should constitute the agenda for future international forums and concrete solutions ought to be explored at the same time in the forthcoming deliberations. Finally, developed nations should, necessarily and urgently, come forward in unequivocal terms to shoulder the responsibility of fighting the demon of climate change, which has been taking giant strides in pushing the world to its doom. Any more dithering would irrevocably plunge the world into an abyss of ecological hell.

It might be contended that the line of argument relating to 'historical responsibilities of developed nations' suffers from a certain weakness in that the phenomenon of climate change was not explicitly understood in previous times. But then, the 'existing capabilities of developed nations' is something that ought to be reckoned with. The EU, US and other developed countries should step in to financially empower a regime of green technology transfer on softer terms. After all, we have necessarily to fight the great battle against global warming and other related issues collectively as a global citizens and not separately as developing or developed nations.

Various COPs (Conference of Parties) by The UN

In addition to the efforts enumerated above, the United Nations (UN) has organized 17 conferences, better known as COP (Conference of the Parties). Out of all these deliberations, the COP15 held at Copenhagen had generated huge aspirations among masses across the globe; but unfortunately no concrete agreement was arrived at there also, and the mammoth aspirations soon got fizzled out by the concluding day of the meet. The last conference was held in Durban in Nov-Dec 2011. A brief recapitulation is given below of all the conferences held so far from Berlin to Durban:

1995 — COP 1, The Berlin Mandate

The first Berlin Conference of Parties took place in March 1995 in. The Parties agreed that the commitments in the Convention were 'inadequate' for meeting the Convention's objective. In a decision known as the Berlin Mandate they agreed to establish a process to negotiate strengthened commitments for developed countries.

1996 — COP 2, Geneva, Switzerland

The COP 2 took place in Geneva, Switzerland in the month of July 1996. The Geneva Ministerial Declaration was noted, but not adopted. A decision on guidelines for the national communications to be prepared by developing countries was adopted. Among issues also discussed were 'Quantified Emissions Limitation and Reduction Objectives' (QELROs) for different Parties and an acceleration of the Berlin Mandate talks so that commitments could be adopted at COP 3.

It also reflected a U.S. position statement presented by Timothy Wirth, former Under Secretary for Global Affairs for the U.S. State Department at that meeting. The statement

a. accepted the scientific findings on climate change proffered by the Intergovernmental Panel on Climate Change (IPCC) in its second assessment (1995);

b. rejected uniform 'harmonized policies' in favor of flexibility;

c. called for 'legally binding mid-term targets'.

1997 — COP 3, Kyoto Protocol on Climate Change

The COP 3 was an important meet which took place at Kyoto in December 1997. After intensive negotiations, it adopted the Kyoto Protocol, which outlined the greenhouse gas emissions reduction obligation for Annex I countries, along with what came to be known as Kyoto mechanisms such as emissions trading, clean development mechanism and joint implementation. Most industrialized countries and some central European economies in transition agreed to legally binding reductions in greenhouse gas emissions of an average of 6 to 8% below 1990 levels between the years 2008–2012, defined as the first emissions budget period. Issues for future international consideration included developing rules for emissions trading, and methodological work in relation to forest sinks.

The United States was required to reduce its total emissions an average of 7% below 1990 levels; however US Congress did not ratify the treaty after signing by President Clinton. The Bush administration explicitly rejected the protocol in 2001.

1998 — COP 4, Buenos Aires, Argentina

The venue for the COP 4 was Buenos Aires and was held in November 1998. The Buenos Aires Plan of Action, focusing on strengthening the financial mechanism, the development and transfer of technologies and maintaining the momentum in relation to the Kyoto Protocol was adopted. It had been expected that the issues remaining unresolved in Kyoto would be finalized at this meeting. However, the complexity and difficulty of finding agreement on these issues proved insurmountable, and instead the parties adopted a 2-year 'Plan of Action' to advance efforts and to devise mechanisms for implementing the Kyoto Protocol, to be completed by 2000. During COP4, Argentina and Kazakhstan expressed their commitment to take on the greenhouse gas emissions reduction obligation, the first two non-Annex countries to do so.

1999 — COP 5, BONN, GERMANY

COP 5 took place in Bonn during the period October 25 and November 5, 1999. It laid focus on the adoption of the guidelines for the preparation of national communications by Annex I countries, capacity building, transfer of technology and flexible mechanisms. It was primarily a technical meeting, and did not reach any major conclusions.

2000 — COP 6, THE HAGUE, NETHERLANDS

COP 6 was held in Hague from November 13 to November 25, 2000. Consensus was finally reached on the so-called Bonn Agreements. Work was also completed on a number of detailed decisions based on the Bonn Agreements, including capacity-building for developing countries and countries with economies in transition. Decisions on several issues, notably the mechanisms land-use change and forestry (LULUCF) and compliance, remained outstanding.

The discussions evolved rapidly into a high-level negotiation over the major political issues. These included major controversy over the United States' proposal to allow credit for carbon 'sinks' in forests and agricultural lands, satisfying a major proportion of the U.S. emissions reductions in this way; disagreements over consequences for non-compliance by countries that did not meet their emission reduction targets; and difficulties in resolving how developing countries could obtain financial assistance to deal with adverse effects of climate change and meet their obligations to plan for measuring and possibly reducing greenhouse gas emissions. In the final hours of COP 6, despite some compromises agreed between the United States and some EU countries, notably the United Kingdom, the EU countries as a whole, led by Denmark and Germany, rejected the compromise positions, and the talks in The Hague collapsed. Jan Pronk, the President of COP 6, suspended COP-6 without agreement, with the expectation that negotiations would later resume. It was later announced that the COP 6 meetings would be resumed in Bonn, Germany, in the second half of July. The next regularly scheduled meeting of the parties to the UNFCCC – COP 7 – had been set for Marrakech, Morocco, in October–November 2001.

2001 — COP 7, MARRAKECH

Parties agreed on a package deal, with key features including rules for ensuring compliance with commitments, consideration of LULUCF Principles in reporting data and limited banking of units generated by sinks under the Clean Development Mechanism (CDM) (the extent to which carbon dioxide absorbed by carbon sinks can be counted towards the Kyoto targets). The meeting also adopted the Marrakech Ministerial Declaration as an input into the World Summit on Sustainable Development in Johannesburg.

2002 — COP 8, NEW DELHI

The Delhi Ministerial Declaration on Climate Change and Sustainable Development reiterated the need to build on the outcomes of the World Summit. It included 25 decisions and one resolution.

2003 — COP 9, Milan

The COP 9 focused on the institutions and procedures of the Kyoto Protocol and on the implementation of the UNFCCC. The formal decisions adopted by the Conference intend to strengthen the institutional framework of both the Convention and the Kyoto Protocol. New emission reporting guidelines based on the good-practice guidance provided by the Intergovernmental Panel on Climate Change were adopted to provide a sound and reliable foundation for reporting on changes in carbon concentrations resulting from land-use changes and forestry. These reports are due in 2005. Another major advance was the agreement on the modalities and scope for carbon absorbing forest-management projects in the clean development mechanism (CDM). This agreement completes the package adopted in Marrakesh two years ago and expands the CDM to an additional area of activity. Two funds were further developed, the Special Climate Change Fund and the Least Developed Countries Fund, which will support technology transfer, adaptation projects etc.

2004 — COP 10, Buenos Aires

The Parties gathered at COP-10 to complete the unfinished business from the Marrakesh Accords and to reassess the building blocks of the process and to discuss the framing of a new dialogue on the future of climate change policy. They addressed and adopted numerous decisions and conclusions on issues relating to: development and transfer of technologies; land use, land use change and forestry; the UNFCCC's financial mechanism; Annex I national communications; capacity building; adaptation and response measures; and UNFCCC Article 6 (education, training and public awareness) examining the issues of adaptation and mitigation, the needs of least developed countries (LDCs), and future strategies to address climate change. At COP 10 18 decisions were taken and one resolution got passed.

2005 — COP 11, Montreal

COP 11 addressed issues such as capacity building, development and transfer of technologies, the adverse effects of climate change on developing and least developed countries, and several financial and budget-related issues, including guidelines to the Global Environment Facility (GEF), which serves as the Convention's financial mechanism. The COP also agreed on a process for considering future action beyond 2012 under the UNFCC. It proclaimed 14 decisions and took one resolution.

2006 — COP 12, Nairobi, Kenya

COP 12 took place in Nairobi from November 6 to November 17, 2006. At the meeting, one BBC reporter coined the phrase 'climate tourists' to describe some delegates who attended to see Africa, take snaps of the wildlife, the poor, dying African children and women. Despite some criticism, certain strides were made at COP12, including in the areas of support for developing countries and clean development mechanism. The parties adopted a five-year plan of work to support climate change adaptation by developing countries, and agreed on the procedures and modalities for the Adaptation Fund. It was also agreed upon to improve the projects for clean development mechanism.

2007 — COP 13 Bali, Indonesia [Bali Roadmap]

Nusa Dua in Bali was chosen as venue for COP 13 which took place from December 3 to December 15, 2007. It is better known as 'Bali Action Plan'. Agreement on a timeline and structured negotiation on the post-2012 framework (the end of the first commitment period of the Kyoto Protocol) was achieved with the adoption of the Bali Action Plan (Decision 1/CP.13). The Ad hoc Working Group on Long-term Cooperative Action under the Convention (AWG-LCA) was established as a new subsidiary body to conduct the negotiations aimed at urgently enhancing the implementation of the Convention up to and beyond 2012.

2008 — COP 14, POZNAN, POLAND

COP 14 took place in Poznan, Poland during December 1 to 12, 2008. Delegates agreed on principles for the financing of a fund to help the poorest nations cope with the effects of climate change and they approved a mechanism to incorporate forest protection into the efforts of the international community to combat climate change.

2009 — COP 15, COPENHAGEN, DENMARK

COP 15 took place in Copenhagen, Denmark, from December 7 to December 18, 2009. The overall goal for the COP 15 United Nations Climate Change Conference in Denmark was to establish an ambitious global climate agreement for the period from 2012 when the first commitment period under the Kyoto Protocol expires. However, on November 14, 2009, the *New York Times* announced that President Obama and other world leaders have decided to put off the difficult task of reaching a climate change agreement – agreeing instead to make it the mission of the Copenhagen conference to reach a less specific 'politically binding' agreement that would punt the most difficult issues into the future. Ministers and officials from 192 countries took part in the Copenhagen meeting and in addition there were participants from a large number of civil society organizations. As many Annex 1 industrialized countries are now reluctant to fulfill commitments under the Kyoto Protocol, a large part of the diplomatic work that lays the foundation for a post-Kyoto agreement was undertaken in the COP15.

The conference did not achieve a binding agreement for long-term action. A 13-paragraph 'political accord' was negotiated by approximately 25 parties including US and China, but it was only 'noted' by the COP as it is considered an external document, not negotiated within the UNFCCC process. The accord was notable in that it referred to a collective commitment by developed countries for new and additional resources, including forestry and investments through international institutions that will approach USD 30 billion for the period 2010–2012. Longer-term options on climate financing mentioned in the accord are being discussed within the UN Secretary General's High Level Advisory Group on Climate Financing, which is due to report in November 2010. The negotiations on extending the Kyoto Protocol left unresolved issues as did the negotiations on a framework for long-term cooperative action. The working groups on these tracks to the negotiations were due to report to COP 16 and MOP 6 in Mexico.

2010 — COP 16, CANCUN, MEXICO

COP 16 was held in Cancun, Mexico, from November 29 to December 10, 2010. Not contrary to the expectations, consensus on important issues proved elusive. Nothing concrete materialized, and the Cancun meet was a complete failure. It was a fatal disconnect with the call of the time, as the world needed swift and concrete actions but the world's leaders seemed too pre-occupied with other issues.

2011 — COP 17 Durban, South Africa

It was held in Durban, South Africa from Nov 28 to Dec 11, 2012. Prominent among the modest achievements of the conference was, progress toward the creation of a Green Climate Fund, which is to help mobilize a promised $100 billion a year in public and private funds by 2020 to assist developing nations in adapting to climate change and converting to clean energy sources.

Besides this, the agreement in Durban established a new body to negotiate a global agreement (Ad-hoc Working Group on the Durban Platform for Enhanced Action) by 2015. This summit seemed to starkly amplify climate apartheid, whereby 'the richest 1% of the world decided it was acceptable to sacrifice 99%'.

2012 — COP 18 Doha, Qatar

COP 18 is scheduled to take place in Qatar from 26 Nov to 7 Dec, 2012. The Republic of Korea will host a ministerial meeting to prepare for COP 18.

Other Important Conventions

Apart from the above mentioned conferences /meets, two other important conferences are worthy of special mention. These were:
   a. Ramsar Convention on Wetlands 1971.
   b. CBD (Convention on Biological Diversity 1992-93).

1971 — Ramsar Convention

The Convention on Wetlands, called the Ramsar Convention, was held at Ramsar in Iran in 1971. It is an intergovernmental treaty that embodies the commitments of its member countries to maintain the ecological character of their Wetlands of International Importance and to plan for the 'wise use', in a sustainable way, of all of the wetlands in their territories. Unlike the other global environmental conventions, Ramsar is not affiliated with the United Nations system of Multilateral Environmental Agreements, but it works very closely with the other MEAs (Multilateral Environmental Agreements) and is a full partner among the 'biodiversity-related cluster' of treaties and agreements.

Mission of Ramsar Convention: The Convention's mission is 'the conservation and wise use of all wetlands through local and national actions and international cooperation, as a contribution towards achieving sustainable development throughout the world'. The Convention uses a broad definition of the types of wetlands covered in its mission, including lakes and rivers, swamps and marshes, wet grasslands and peat lands, oases, estuaries, deltas and tidal flats, near-shore marine areas, mangroves and coral reefs, and human-made sites such as fish ponds, rice paddies, reservoirs, and salt pans.

Designated Wetlands of International Importance: Ramsar convention has proclaimed 1,951 sites world over as 'Wetlands of International Importance'. The Convention on Wetlands came into force for India on 1 February 1982. India presently has 25 sites designated as Wetlands of International Importance, with a surface area of 677,131 hectares.

1992-3 — CONVENTION ON BIOLOGICAL DIVERSITY

The United Nations Environment Programme (UNEP) convened the Ad hoc Working Group of Experts on Biological Diversity in November 1988 to explore the need for an international convention on biological diversity. Soon after, in May 1989, it established the Ad hoc Working Group of Technical and Legal Experts to prepare an international legal instrument for the conservation and sustainable use of biological diversity. The experts were to take into account 'the need to share costs and benefits between developed and developing countries' as well as 'ways and means to support innovation by local people'.

By February 1991, the Ad hoc Working Group had become known as the Intergovernmental Negotiating Committee. Its work culminated on 22 May 1992 with the Nairobi Conference for the Adoption of the Agreed Text of the Convention on Biological Diversity.

The Convention was opened for signature on 5 June 1992 at the United Nations Conference on Environment and Development, the Rio 'Earth Summit'. It remained open for signature until 4 June 1993, by which time it had received 168 signatures. The Convention entered into force on 29 December 1993, which was 90 days after the 30th ratification. The first session of the Conference of the Parties was scheduled for 28 November – 9 December 1994 in the Bahamas.

The Convention on Biological Diversity was inspired by the world community's growing commitment to sustainable development. It represents a dramatic step forward in the conservation of biological diversity, the sustainable use of its components, and the fair and equitable sharing of benefits arising from the use of genetic resources. The Convention on Biological Diversity (CBD) aims at:

- ✓ The conservation of biological diversity.

- ✓ The sustainable use of the components of biological diversity.

- ✓ The fair and equitable sharing of the benefits arising out of the utilization of genetic resources.

Efforts by Non-Governmental Organizations

Besides the above enumerated efforts, numerous green NGO's, organizations and agencies spread across the globe have been carrying out praiseworthy and commendable work with unflinching zeal. The total number of NGOs in India alone has exceeded 1.5 million; while the world over the number has crossed more than 5 million.

These NGOs have become the watchdogs of the environmental issues. Social development is growing rapidly alongside information Technology. NGOs have been playing a crucial and pivotal role in environmental protection, conservation and development. Greater collaboration of Government, NGO and People is the need of the hour. Multi-sectoral coordination and convergence and holistic and sustainable development can be achieved with greater involvement of NGOs with genuine credentials. Every one of us should join at least one green NGO in order to chip in with our own contribution in the noble mission to heal the blue planet with informed consent.

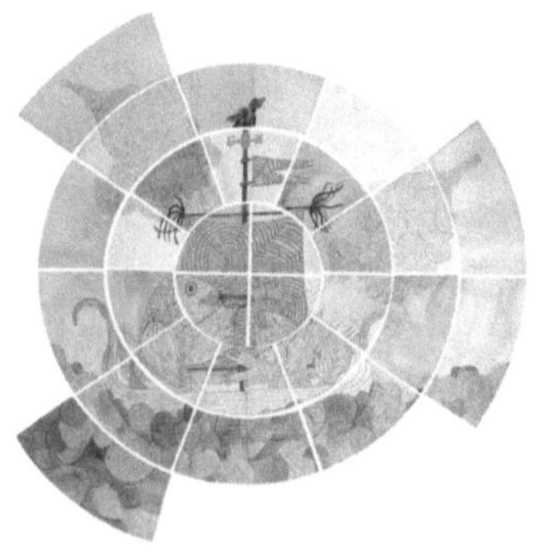

VII
THREATENED & EXTINCT SPECIES

As the human population grows and our demand for natural resources increases, more and more habitats are devastated. Today, we may be losing 30,000 species a year – a rate much faster than at any time since the last great extinction 65 million years ago that wiped out most of the dinosaurs. If we continue on this course, we will destroy even ourselves. American Museum of Natural Histor

We quite often come across the terms 'extinct', 'threatened', 'vulnerable', and 'endangered' through educational channels, TV news and newspapers. Sometimes we are not quite sure of the important differences inherent in the varied use of such terminology. Here is a diagrammatic categorization of some of these key terms understanding of which are crucial in the study of survival of species:

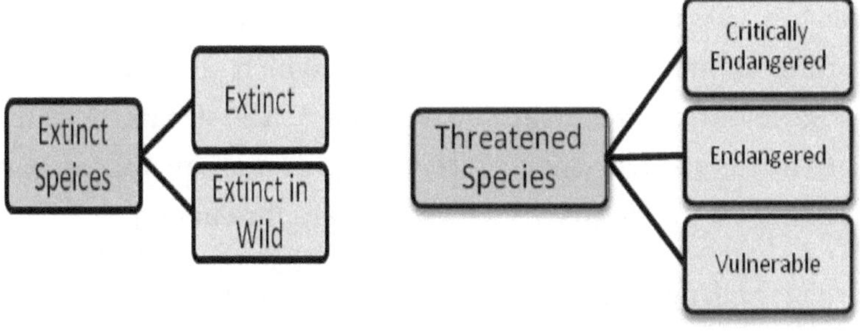

Types of Extinct Species   *Types of Threatened Species*

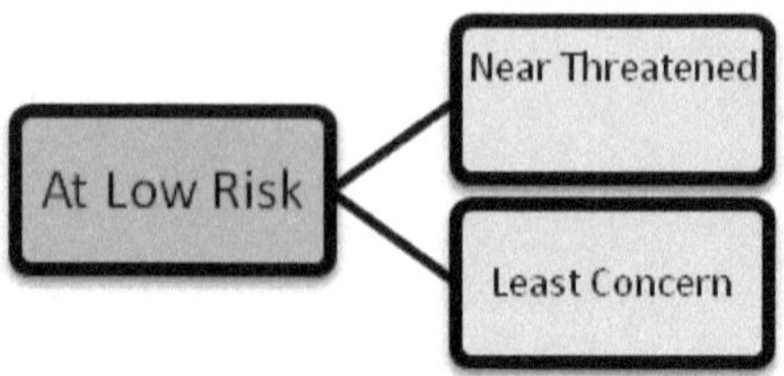

Types of Low-Risk Species

These terms have been further defined by IUCN (International Union for Conservation of Nature). The terms given above are further elucidated here with typical examples:

Extinct: An extinct species is a species of organisms which no longer exists on the planet or has ceased to exist. For Example, Javan Tiger; Thylacine; Dodo; Passenger Pigeon; Caribbean Monk Seal; Dimetrodon; Aurochs; Dusky Seaside Sparrow.

Extinct in Wild: 'Extinct in the wild' connotes that only captive individuals survive, there being no free-living, natural population. Examples: Alagoas Curassow

Threatened Species: Threatened species are any of the species including animals, plants, fungi, etc., which are vulnerable to endangerment in the near future. The IUCN treats threatened species not as a single category, but as a group of several categories, depending on the degree to which they are threatened.

Critically Endangered: 'Critically endangered' is the highest risk category assigned by the IUCN Red List for wild species. Critically Endangered means that a species' numbers have decreased, or will decrease, by 80% within three generations.

Endangered: Under the IUCN Categories and Criteria, endangered species falls in between critically endangered and vulnerable. Critically endangered species may also be counted as endangered species.

Vulnerable: A Vulnerable species is one which has been categorized by the International Union for Conservation of Nature (IUCN) as likely to become endangered unless the circumstances threatening its survival and reproduction improve. Vulnerable species face a high risk of extinction in the medium-term. Examples: Cheetah, Gaur, Lion, Sloth Bear, Manatee, Polar Bear, African Golden Cat, Komodo dragon, Golden hamster

Near Threatened: 'Near Threatened' is a conservation status assigned to species or lower taxa that may be considered threatened with extinction in the near future, although it does not currently qualify for the threatened status. As such the IUCN notes the importance of re-evaluating 'Near Threatened' taxa often or at appropriate intervals.

Examples: Blue-billed Duck, Solitary Eagle, Small-clawed Otter, Manned Wolf, Tiger Shark, Okapi.

Least Concern: 'Least concern' means no immediate threat to the survival of the species. Least Concern is an IUCN category assigned to extant taxon or lower taxa which have been evaluated but do not qualify for any other category. As such they do not qualify as Threatened, Near Threatened, or (prior to 2001) Conservation Dependent. Many common species such as the Rock Pigeon, Honeybee, Asian tiger mosquito, Common Juniper, Snail Kite, Sacred Kingfisher and House Mouse, as well as humans, are assigned the Least Concern category. Others are Nootka cypress, Wood Pigeon, White-tailed Mongoose, House Mouse, and Wolverine.

Animal extinction: a terrible ecological threat! Ecology has its own system of maintaining the balance on earth. But felt necessities of human civilization, greed, and indiscriminate elimination of forests have all combined to upset nature's delicate balance and wreak havoc on the ecosystem upon which we are so heavily dependent. The evolution of a biological species and its end are important attributes of ecology. The moment the last individual of a particular species is dead, it is considered to be an extinct species.

ATTRIBUTING FACTORS FOR ANIMAL EXTINCTION
Several factors are involved in the extinction of animal species ranging from dinosaurs to frogs. Some of them suffered mass-extinction, while others were subjected to extinction because of human destructive activities. Some of the cardinal factors are listed below.

1. Global warming
2. Climate Change
3. Habitat loss
4. Hunting and poaching
5. Deforestation
6. Habitat Fragmentation
7. Other man-made factors

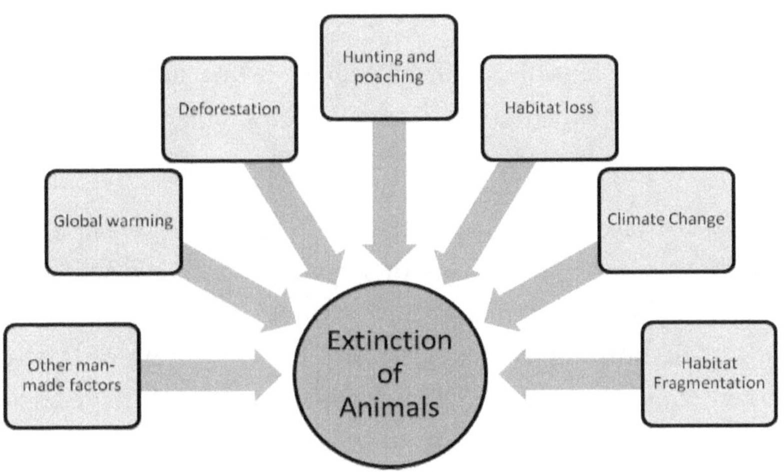

Causative Factors for Extinction of Animals

Habitat loss often emanated from deforestation which brought about shortage of food in the form of declining numbers of their prey. Rapid industrialization and the emission of greenhouse gases have caused global warming. The climate change has affected about 100 to 200 species of animals, and about 70 species of frogs have become extinct. It is largely believed that the threat due to global warming is going to become more intense in future.

Moreover, extensive hunting and poaching of animals for economic gains have led many animal species to become extinct. Apart from this, diseases, threat from predators, competition for food, genetic and demographic phenomena are some of the other factors that have caused extinction of animals.

Some Extinct Animals

Though it is not feasible to describe all the extinct animals at length owing to space constraint, yet some information of select extinct animals is given here in alphabetical order.

Arabian Ostrich: It used to be also known as the Middle Eastern Ostrich. It was a subspecies of Ostrich found in the Arabian Peninsula. The widespread introduction of firearms in the region made their hunting an easy task. By the beginning of the 20th century, this species of bird had become rare, which led to its extinction in the mid-20th century. Its last sighting was in 1966 in Jordan.

Bali Tiger: It was a native of Bali in Indonesia. It is the smallest of the three subspecies of tigers found in the Indonesian archipelago. Loss of habitat due to deforestation and human encroachment is the major factor for their extinction. Moreover, extensive hunting of this animal during the World War II made them extinct.

Barbary Lion: They were also known as the Atlas Lion. They formed a subspecies of lion found in the northern regions of Africa. The heaviest subspecies of lion, these weighed about 440 to 600 pounds. Excessive hunting and loss of habitat due to expansion of agricultural lands have caused their extinction.

Caribbean Monk Seal: It was a subspecies of Seal found in the Caribbean Sea of Mexico. It is also called the West Indian Monk Seal. Pollution of marine waters caused by human activities has led to the extinction of this animal. It was last sighted at the Serramilla bank in the Western Caribbean Sea in 1952.

In the same way, many other animals such as the Caspian Tiger, the Golden Toad, Cape Verde Giant Skink, Carolina Parakeet, Japanese

Sea Lion, Javan Tiger, Laughing Owl, Paradise Parrot, Wake Island Rail, Tasmanian wolf, etc. have become extinct. Therefore, to prevent other animals from joining their list, it is important for us to exercise restraint on our aggressive and selfish activities vis-à-vis other species.

Endangered Species

Man's desire to expand rapidly has destroyed the natural habitat of wild animals, making them homeless. International Union for Conservation of Nature (IUCN) includes the red list names of over 5,000 vertebrate animals, among a total of 15,589 species, as endangered animals. Mammals, Birds, Reptiles, Plants, Fishes, Insects, Amphibians, Snails, Clams, Arachnids, Crustaceans, Worms, Corals, Jellyfish, Sea Anemones, Centipedes and so on, the list susceptible to the threat of extinction continues to grow.

Description of Some Endangered Amphibians

Earth is facing its largest mass extinction since the disappearance of the dinosaurs, with up to half of the world's 6,000 amphibian species in danger of extinction, conservationists warn. Amphibians (frogs and toads, newts, caecilians and salamanders) are being affected by habitat loss, climate change, pollution, pesticides and introduced species, but face an even bigger threat from a deadly parasitic fungus known as amphibian chytrid.

Panamanian Golden Frog: Considered as good luck charm, the Panamanian golden frog is now believed to be extinct in the wild because of chytrid fungus, a deadly disease that scientists say may be exacerbated by climate change. Currently unstoppable and untreatable in the wild, the fungus affects the skin of amphibians through which many drink and breathe.

Wyoming Toad: This toad was a common sight on the Laramie plains of Albany County, Wyoming, until the 1970s, when its population crashed due to a combination of factors such as the spraying of insecticides to control mosquitoes, changes in agricultural practices, an increase in predators and climatic changes. It now exists only in captivity and within Mortenson Lake national wildlife refuge in Wyoming, and is classified as extinct in the wild.

Lehmann's Poison Frog: This brightly colored frog – which comes with red, orange or yellow stripes – is critically endangered. Conservationists say that it lives within a tiny range of less than 10 sq. km in two areas of rainforest in Colombia. The major threats to this species' survival are habitat loss and degradation as a result of agricultural development, illegal crops, logging, human settlement and pollution.

Chinese Giant Salamander: The world's largest amphibian, the Chinese Giant Salamander can reach lengths of up to 1.8 m. Its flesh is considered a delicacy in Asia, and its large size makes it easy and lucrative prey. Critically endangered, illegal hunting is a big threat. But the species also suffers from habitat alteration and loss. The building of dams in China has also changed the natural river flow in some areas where they are found.

Some Endangered Avian Species

Bald Eagle [*Haliaeetus leucocephalus*]: The US prohibited killing the American eagle in 1940. In 1963, 417 nesting Bald Eagle pairs were counted in the lower 48 States of USA. They were listed as endangered south of the 40th parallel in 1967 and in 43 States in 1973. In 1999, it was estimated that almost 6,000 pairs were nesting in the lower 48 States and the U.S. Fish and Wildlife Service proposed to delist the Bald Eagle.

Ivory-Billed Woodpecker: The last confirmed sightings, until February of 2004, were in 1972 in East Texas and Louisiana and in Cuba in 1986. Deforestation caused its decline as each pair required at least ten square miles of low-land hardwood forests. The State of Louisiana ordered a halt to logging while it checked out a reported sighting in 2000.

California Condor [*Gymnogyps californianus*]: California Condors were listed as endangered in 1967. By 1982, there were less than two dozen in the wild. Mating Condor pairs produce only one egg every two years. Rescued from the brink of extinction by an intense captive breeding program, as of October 1, 2003 there was a total wild population of 83 and there were 137 in captivity. With a wingspan of over 9 feet, California Condors can soar more than 100 miles per day on updrafts searching for food. They have a life span of up to 60 years.

Greater Prairie Chicken: The Greater Prairie Chicken was designated endangered in Texas in 1967. It nests in slight, grass lined hollows in the soil sheltered by grass tufts in open coastal grasslands, which have been reduced through cultivation and grazing. Populations have declined to less than 100, making the case strikingly like the story of its extinct cousin, the Heath Hen. It eats grass and flower seeds. Its mating dance has inspired traditional Native American ritual dances. These are preyed upon by hawks and owls, even cats and dogs.

Brown Pelican [*Pelecanus occidentalis*]: Brown Pelicans were designated endangered in 1970 and delisted in 1985 in Florida, Alabama and the Atlantic coast. Inhabiting mostly the coasts (although inland sometimes), from middle and southern North America to South America, they nest in colonies on shores or wetlands, on the ground or in mangrove bushes, usually on islands. Gluttonous, they plunge for fish rather than scooping like the White Pelican.

Red-cockaded Woodpecker [Picoides borealis]: The Red-cockaded woodpecker was designated endangered in 1970. Excavates its own cavities which it returns to for several years in live pine trees in open pine woods, rarely in dense forests, in southeastern US from Oklahoma and Texas to Florida and north to Virginia. They peck hundreds of small holes in the bark from which pine tar seeps, surrounding its cavity entrance hole, deterring insects and some predators. Small groups search tree branches and cones for insects and a few seeds, usually near tree tops. Often mistaken for the Downy Woodpecker, they however, are less likely to roost near humans.

TOP 10 ENDANGERED ANIMAL SPECIES OF ASIA

Snow Leopard [Panthera uncial]: It is mostly found in Afghanistan, Bhutan, China, Kazakhstan, Kyrgyzstan, Mongolia, Nepal, Pakistan, Russian Federation, Tajikistan and Uzbekistan. Unlike their larger cousin, the tiger, Snow Leopards are offered little protection in their native habitats. The Snow Leopard's habitat is closely tied to grazing grounds of its preferred prey, which is also the same land that farmers wish to use for their livestock. This leads to a reduction in prey animals due to competition with livestock, which in turn leads the leopards to hunt the livestock for food. The taking of livestock often leads to retribution killing by farmers. The Snow Leopard is also intentionally hunted for its fur, as well as for other body parts that are used in traditional Chinese medicine as a substitute for much more rare tiger parts, including bones, claws meat and sexual organs. Poaching of live animals for use in circuses and zoos is also depleting the wild populations. Over the past decade, much of the Snow Leopard's native range in the Near East has been an area of major military conflict. Damage to the habitat from military action and the demands of displaced peoples for local resources have had a significant impact on the animals' habitat.

Javan Rhinoceros [*Rhinoceros sondaicus*]: They are mostly found in Indonesia and Viet Nam and have become extinct in Bangladesh, Cambodia, China, India, Laos, Peninsular Malaysia, Myanmar and Thailand. Once the most widespread Asian rhinoceros, the Javan Rhino was hunted to near extinction in the 19th and 20th Centuries, and currently exists in just two isolated areas. There are now less than 100 wild Javan Rhinos – about 40 to 60 on the western tip of the island of Java, and another smaller group in Cat Tien National Park in Viet Nam. The Viet Nam population is believed to contain as few as six animals, and no breeding has been observed in recent years. It's possible that all of the animals who currently survive are too old to breed, and they may all be of the same sex. There are currently no Javan Rhinos in captivity, and historically there have only ever been 22 in zoos, the last one having died in an Australian zoo nearly 100 years ago. Attempts to breed Sumatran Rhinos in captivity failed miserably in the late 20th century, and that expensive experiment is unlikely to make a Javan Rhino breeding program viable. The species will most likely never recover and they will soon be extinct.

Green Turtle [*Chelonia mydas*]: These turtles keep on roaming the oceans of the world and are extensively found in Tropical and subtropical beaches worldwide. The female turtles use soft sandy beaches to lay their eggs in more than 80 countries around the world, and the Green Turtle is believed to inhabit the coastal regions of at least 140 countries.

The single greatest threat to all sea turtles, including the Green Turtle, is intentional human harvesting of their eggs from beach-side nesting areas. They are also often caught by fisherman, both accidentally and intentionally, and then killed for their meat. Human beachfront development often encroaches on nesting sites, and the lights from beach-side communities can fatally disorient newly hatched turtle, drawing them away from the ocean. Turtle egg harvesting has been banned in many countries, but it remains legal in several others despite large reductions in population. The threats to Green Turtles are not reversible and if they are not ended in the near future the Green Turtle faces certain extinction.

Lar Gibbon [*Hylobates lar*]: They could be seen in the countries of Indonesian Sumatra, Laos, Peninsular Malaysia, Myanmar and Thailand. Once plentiful in Southeast Asia, many gibbon species are currently endangered, including the Lar Gibbon. Even though the threat caused by deforestation is on the decline, these animals are still over-hunted for their meat. They are also captured in large numbers for the pet trade, even in protected areas. Gibbons are unlike other apes in that they act as seed carriers for the fruits they eat. They swallow most of the seeds in their diet, and several fruits that gibbons eat are dependent on the digestive process to both remove the outer cover of the seeds and to disperse them through the environment. Without the gibbons, many of these fruit species could also be endangered.

Chinese Pangolin [*Manis pentadactyla*]: Chinese Pangolin can be seen in Bangladesh, Bhutan, China, Hong Kong, India, Laos, Myanmar, Nepal, Taiwan, Thailand and Viet Nam. Populations of all Asian Pangolins have suffered extreme losses in the recent past, and these losses are expected to continue over the coming years. They are hunted throughout Asia for export to China, mostly for medicinal purposes but also for their meat and skins. The pangolins were once hunted for subsistence use, but the exploding demand and high price for the animals has spurred illegal commercial hunting. Pangolins can fetch more than $95 U.S. per kilogram in the open market, so even in protected areas they are being relentlessly hunted. The particular subspecies *Manis pentadactyla* is especially threatened, since it is the easiest to catch. Unlike other tree-dwelling pangolins, *Manis pentadactyla* lives in clearly distinguishable underground burrows that are easily spotted and dug up to capture the animals.

Red Headed Vulture [*Sarcogyps calvus*]: Red Headed Vulture is possibly extinct in Malaysia but can be seen in Bangladesh, Bhutan, Cambodia, China, India, Lao People's Democratic Republic, Myanmar, Nepal, Thailand and Viet Nam. Once widely disbursed and abundant throughout Asia, in recent decades the wild population of Red Headed Vultures, also known as the Indian Black or Pondicherry Vulture, has experienced a rapid decline in range and number. The current wild population is estimated at less than 10,000 individuals throughout Asia, with just a few hundred in Southeast Asia and the rest mostly in India. Like other carrion eaters, vultures are vital to the ecosystem for disposing of dead animals, and their loss has a profound effect on the biosphere. In India, members of the *Parsi* faith also relied on the birds for the disposal of human remains, as burying or burning the bodies was seen as polluting the natural elements.

As recently as in the 1980s there were millions of vultures all over India, but the population suffered precipitous losses and the few remaining birds are mostly found in sanctuaries. The main cause for the rapid decline in Indian vulture populations seems to be the use of a pharmaceutical called *diclofenac*, which was used to prevent colic in cattle. The drug turned out to be lethal to vultures who consumed the flesh of dead cows, which are considered sacred in India and are so are left out in the open when the die. After diclofenac was banned, its replacement drug also turned out to be fatal to vultures, and the remaining populations may not be viable for the species' continued existence. In addition to the deadly drugs used to treat cattle, the overall decline in wild grazing animals in Asia has led to a drop in the available number of dead animal carcasses for the birds to feed on.

Tiger [Panthera tigris]: It can be seen sparsely in countries like Bangladesh, Bhutan, Cambodia, China, India, Indonesian Sumatra, Laos, Peninsular Malaysia, Myanmar, Nepal, Russian Federation, Thailand and Viet Nam. Possibly totally extinct in North Korea, it is extinct in Afghanistan, Indonesia (Bali and Java), Iran, Kazakhstan, Kyrgyzstan, Pakistan, Singapore, Tajikistan, Turkey, Turkmenistan, and Uzbekistan. Multiple tiger subspecies once freely roamed throughout Asia, from Turkey in the west to the Russian coastline in the east. Over the last 100 years tigers have disappeared from 93% of their historic range. The current wild population of all tigers is endangered, with several subspecies considered critically endangered. The entire worldwide wild population is estimated at 3,000 to 5,000 individuals.

Because they are predators that rely mainly on small mammals like pigs and deer for the bulk of their diets, tigers require a large amount of space and a large prey population to survive. Deforestation for farming and commercial development fragments the territory and reduces the number of prey animals, and so directly causes a reduction in the tiger population. Many tigers are killed by farmers to protect their communities as well as their livestock, and the tiger parts from those kills often end up in the black market.

Until very recently it appeared that the tiger would be hunted to extinction for the illegal fur trade and for use in traditional Chinese

Medicine, even though most of the supposed medicinal properties in various tiger parts are either psychosomatic or easily treated with less expensive and destructive alternatives. Even though trade in tiger parts has been banned in every part of the world, a strong illegal trade still exists in Asia, especially in China, Viet Nam and Malaysia. Attempts in China to 'farm' tigers through captive breeding have been made, but the very existence of tiger farms only serves to maintain demand for tiger parts, which in turn fuels illegal trade in other countries.

Bactrian Camel [*Camelus ferus*]: It can be found in China and Mongolia, but has been extinct in Kazakhstan. Once prolific across the Gobi Desert of Mongolia and northwest China, the wild Bactrian Camel population had been reduced to less than 1,000 animals by 2004. Droughts in the Gobi have reduced the amount of water resources for the camels, and predation by wild wolves has increased at the same time. Each year, about 20 Bactrian Camels are intentionally killed by miners and hunters when they migrate out of protected areas across the Mongolian border into China. There are just over a dozen Bactrian Camels in captivity in Mongolia and China – not enough to successfully breed the animals in captivity. If the wild population continues to decline at current rates the species will soon become extinct.

Russian Sturgeon [*Acipenser gueldenstaedtii*]: They can be seen mostly in Russian Federation and its border countries like Azerbaijan and Kazakhstan. It is also found in Bulgaria, Georgia, Iran, Moldova, Romania, Serbia, Turkey, Turkmenistan and Ukraine. It is believed to be extinct in Austria, Croatia and Hungary. The Russian Sturgeon was once prolific throughout the Caspian and Black Seas, as well as many of their tributaries. Due to over-fishing and dam construction in the last 100 years, the wild population has been diminished by

90% of its historic levels. The Russian Sturgeon is now only rarely seen in the Black Sea basin, and spawning grounds have been diminished sharply. Illegal fishing for caviar is expected to continue to reduce the population over time – the only hope for the survival of the species is from captive breeding in fisheries and man-made stocking of formerly rich habitats.

Giant Panda [*Ailuropoda melanoleuca*]: Found exclusively in China. Once ranging throughout China, the current wild population of Giant Pandas is estimated to be around merely one to two thousand. Giant Pandas are completely dependent upon bamboo forests, and in the past they were able to roam from area to area to locate sufficient amounts of food. The combination of deforestation for farming and the breakup of their native range by roads and construction have reduced the Panda population down to smaller numbers.

In the past, poaching was the greatest threat to the Giant Panda, but that threat has been nearly eliminated in recent years. China has imposed stricter protection measures for the Panda's natural habitat, but there is no concrete proof that their population is going to be able to recover in the wild. One such effort is the 'Grain-to-Green' campaign, wherein the government pays farmers to replant trees instead of crops in areas where Pandas might be able to thrive. Whether the Pandas will actual resettle these areas is not yet known.

Man as the Principal Agent of Endangerment
The main reason for endangerment of animals is uncontrolled human activity. To pursue mindless development, man has caused irreparable damage to the fauna. The gases emitted from greenhouses have brought about global climate change affecting everybody. Industrial wastes have polluted the river water and

marine life. Overexploitation of animals to satisfy the needs of humans has led to considerable downfall in their number. Unrestricted hunting of whales during the twentieth-century has made them endangered animals. Poaching of rhinoceros and tigers is another serious cause of their falling numbers. Rhino horns and tiger bones are widely used in making traditional medicines. According to IUCN, one-third of the amphibians, one-half of the fresh water turtles, one-eighth of all the birds, and one-fourth of mammals are in danger. The causes for their endangered lives are directly related to human actions.

PRESSING NEED FOR SAVING ENDANGERED ANIMALS
Although considerable damage has been inflicted, still there is immense scope to reclaim and restore the situation with timely and concrete efforts. It is our moral duty to ensure a safe life to all the creatures, otherwise the coming generations will be deprived of the benefits of the biodiversity that gives natural fullness to the animate world. It is important to save the endangered animals to maintain the ecological balance. Nature has its own way of maintaining the balance. If we do not take steps to prevent the artificial disruption of that balance, we will ultimately have to face the consequences.

By protecting the natural habitats of wild animals, we can do a lot to save them. Greedy advancements of man are endangering animals. Today, most of the animals are in the list of endangered animals. Asian elephant, Blue whale, Brown pelican, Orangutan, Panda, Puma, Rattle snake, Sperm whale, Kangaroo, Bactrian camel, Bengal tiger, Dhole, etc. are some animals endangered by human activity.

Legal private farming for profit has contributed to restoring the situation to some extent. According to IUCN, legal private farming for profit has increased the number of both the Black Rhinoceros and White Rhinoceros in the United States.

WWF (World Wildlife Federation), established in 1961, has played a significant role in conserving the wildlife. It has brought awareness in people by conducting various exercises worldwide.

Special laws for protection of wildlife and checking illegal poaching have been formulated by all the nations. Governments of many nations are discharging their duties for the protection of endangered animals.

TRAGIC COST OF SPECIES' EXTINCTION IN RAINFORESTS

Rainforests are considered the lungs of the Earth and the largest pharmacy of the planet. Tropical rainforests contain at least half of the Earth's species. In Panama, scientists discovered a full 80% of the world's currently known beetle species on only 19 trees. The incredible diversity of the rainforests means that most species have evolved to inhabit very specialized niches in their environment; when humans disrupt that environment, many species cannot survive. Because species depend on each other in a complicated web of inter-relationships, changing just one part of that web harms the entire ecosystem: as people destroy or significantly harm the rainforests, certain species die out, and as they go extinct, other species die out, which in turn leads to further breakdown of the ecosystem. This breakdown of rainforest ecosystems will probably lead to the disappearance of up to 10% of the world's species within the next 25 years unless we act in a concrete and purposeful manner.

Why Extinction is a Danger to Man

Many indigenous people survive directly or indirectly upon the resources available in the rainforests. They eat wild game, use the plants for food and medicine, and may identify certain species as a sacred and essential part of their heritage. When these resources are destroyed, the people lose their homes, their food, and their very culture. And they may be forced to look to protected, endangered areas of forest for shelter and food, leading to further destruction and extinction.

Many medications that we regularly use come from rainforest species. With such a vast number of species still undiscovered, the rainforests are the likely repository of many more important ingredients with which to fight present and future diseases. But with more and more species disappearing from the Earth, more and more sources of possible medicines are forever lost to us.

Prominent Causes of Rapid Extinction

Causes of extinction are numerous and varied. 'Habitat destruction' ranks as the number one among these causes. Habitat destruction is effected especially due to logging, mining, clearing trees for cattle grazing and building dams and highways where rainforests once existed. As the ecosystem shrinks, more and more species lose the resources that they need to survive. Habitat fragmentation was another cause of thinning density of various species. Over-consumption and international trade further endanger certain species. In Africa, commercial hunting is responsible for putting one-third of the currently threatened primary forest at risk. Species populations can also shrink when local people are forced by habitat destruction to rely on a smaller area for their food needs, or when a certain species becomes 'popular' on the international market.

People trap or kill animals and ship them to other countries, where they are taken as pets or used to make other products. Once a species becomes rare or protected the business becomes more lucrative.

IMPORTANCE OF BIOLOGICAL DIVERSITY

Our heritage of biological diversity is an invaluable and irreplaceable resource. Our quality of life and that of future generations depends on our preservation of plant and animal species. Plants and animals hold medicinal, agricultural, ecological, commercial and aesthetic/recreational value. Endangered species must be protected and saved so that future generations can experience their presence and value.

MEDICINAL VALUE

Plants and animals are responsible for a variety of useful medications. In fact, about forty percent of all prescriptions written today are composed of natural compounds of different species. These species not only save lives, but economically they contribute to a prospering pharmaceutical industry worth over $40 billion annually. Unfortunately, only 5% of known plant species have been screened for their medicinal values, although we continue to lose up to 100 species daily.

The Pacific yew, a slow-growing tree found in the ancient forests of the Pacific Northwest, was historically considered a 'trash' tree (to be burned after clear cutting). However, a substance in its bark named 'taxol' has recently been identified as one of the most promising medicinal agents for treatment for ovarian and breast cancer. Even more significantly, more than 3 million American heart disease sufferers would perish within 72 hours of a heart attack without digitalis, a drug derived from the purple foxglove.

AGRICULTURAL ASSETS

There are an estimated 80,000 edible plants in the world. Humans depend upon only 20 species of these plants, such as wheat and corn, to provide 90% of the world's food. Wild relatives of these common crops contain essential disease-resistant material. They also provide humans with the means to develop new crops that can grow in inadequate lands such as in poor soils or drought-stricken areas to help solve the world's hunger problem. In the 1970s, genetic material from a wild corn species in Mexico was used to stop a leaf fungus that had previously wiped out 15% of the U.S. corn crop.

ECOLOGICAL SERVICES

Plant and animal species are the foundation of healthy ecosystems. Humans depend on ecosystems such as coastal estuaries, prairie and other grasslands, and ancient forests to purify their air, clean their water, and supply them with food. When species become endangered, it is an indicator that the health of these vital ecosystems is beginning to unravel. The U.S. Fish and Wildlife Service estimates that losing one plant species can trigger the loss of up to 30 other insect, plant and higher animal species.

The northern spotted owl, listed as threatened in 1990, is an indicator of the declining health of the ancient forests of the Pacific Northwest. These forests are home to over 100 other old-growth dependent species, which are at risk due to decades of unsustainable forest management practices.

Pollution off the coast of Florida is killing the coral reefs along the Florida Keys, which serve as habitat for hundreds of species of fish. Commercial fish species have begun to decline, causing a threat to the multi-million dollar tourism industry, which depends on the quality of the environment.

COMMERCIAL BENEFITS

Various wild species are commercially raised, directly contributing to local and regional economies. Commercial and recreational salmon fishing in the Pacific Northwest provides 60,000 jobs and $1 billion annually in personal income, and is the centre of Pacific Northwest Native American culture. This industry and way of life, however, is in trouble as salmon decline due to habitat degradation from dams, clear cutting, and overgrazing along streams.

Freshwater mussels which are harvested, cut into beads, and used to stimulate pearl formation in oysters form the basis of a thriving industry which supports approximately 10,000 U.S. jobs and contributes over $700 million to the U.S. economy annually. Unfortunately, 43% of the freshwater mussel species in North America are currently endangered or extinct.

WILDLIFE RECREATION

Wildlife recreation is an important activity world over.

> Plant and animal species and their ecosystems form the basis of world's multi-billion dollar, job-intensive tourism industry.

> They also supply recreational, spiritual, and quality of life value.

> Every year millions of people across the globe indulge themselves in wild life recreation.

> Each year over 108 million people from America alone participate in wildlife related recreation including observing, feeding, and photographing wildlife.

People from the US spend over $59 billion annually on travel, lodging, equipment, and food to engage in non-consumptive wildlife recreation

SOBERING PREVIEW OF A POSSIBLE FUTURE SCENARIO

Primate Extinction: The first extinction of a primate species in more than a century is imminent, according to the latest evaluation of the threat posed to the continued existence of monkeys and apes around the world. A detailed assessment of the 394 species of primates from South America to Indonesia has found that 29 per cent are in danger of disappearing due to hunting, habitat loss and climate change. Some are already on the brink of extinction.

Woodland birds join extinction danger list: Both the woodpecker and the willow tit were widespread 40 years ago, but every year since 1970 their populations have declined so they are now in grave danger [*The Independent September 7, 2011*].

Mass Extinction Threat: Earth on Verge of Huge Reset Button? Mass extinctions have served as huge reset buttons, according to a comprehensive study of fossil records. The findings suggest humans will live in a very different future if they drive animals to extinction, because the loss of each species can alter entire ecosystems [*Life Science September 2, 2010*].

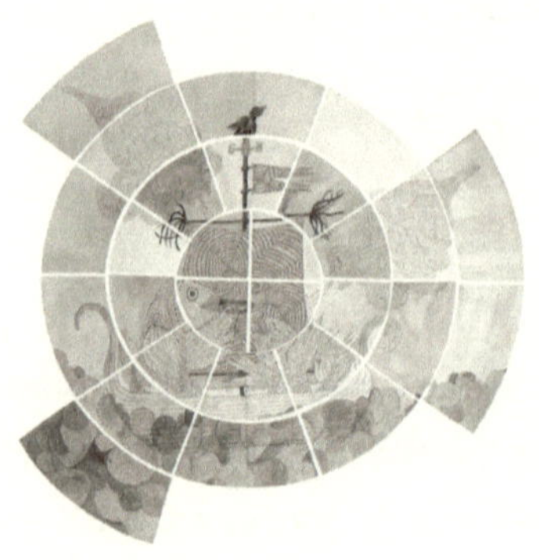

VIII
A Green Protocol for Governments

By now readers would agree that Climate Change and Global Warming are twin monsters that stalk today's world. Fighting such monstrously complex problems confronting the globe ideally requires responses at many levels: individuals, industries and nations.

The first and foremost of many requirements is that Governments the world over ought to step up the pace of negotiations on further reduction of emissions of hazardous greenhouse gases responsible for global warming. States need to agree on the strengthening of international conditions to allow nations to work together to make deeper global emission cuts.

The Kyoto Protocol is an addition to the UNFCCC (United Nations Framework Convention on Climate Change) that contains legally binding measures to reduce greenhouse gas emissions, and whose first commitment period is due to expire in 2012. Negotiations on the second commitment phase of the Protocol are still on in 2011. The world is now facing the possibility of a regulatory gap (in the new phase of the protocol) and the more a consensus is delayed, the more problematic the regulatory gap would be.

Governments need to design new climate institutions that will provide adequate and efficient climate action support to developing countries, including the green climate fund, the technology mechanism, and the setting up of climate change adaptation committees.

It is heartening to note that many large economies have now been giving tremendous impetus to new policies that promote low carbon growth. The private sector is also boosting investments in low carbon business and renewable energy domain.

It is the dire need of the hour to realign our policies in the face of impending disaster which is looming large on the horizon. Governments are the bodies that are in the best position to formulate policies and implement strategies that can reduce the effects of climate change, especially in the following areas:

  i.   Geo-engineering
  ii.   Energy efficiency and conservation
  iii. Alternative energy sources
  iv.   Carbon capture and storage (CCS)
  v.   Governmental and intergovernmental action.

The following is a matrix of possible issues deserving state intervention in the above areas:

Areas requiring State Intervention on Climate Change

Geo-engineering	Energy Efficiency & Conservation	Alternative Energy Sources	Carbon Capture & Storage (CCS)	Governmental & Intergovernmental Action
• Seeding oceans with chalk • Seeding oceans with iron (Iron Seeding/ Iron Fertilization) • Screening out sunlight.	• Better Energy efficiency & conservation • Connecting smart growth and energy efficiency • Better Transport-ation and road network.	• Solar Power • Wind power • Biofuels • Tidal and Wave Energy • Geo-thermal Energy	• Carbon seques-tration	• Incentives for buying 'Carbon Credits' • Encouraging land use changes • Carbon emissions trading • Carbon tax levied on heavy emitting industries • Legal actions and legislations • Encouraging personal choice of t consumers • Technical Support & financial help for mitigation strategies in developing and poor countries. • Kyoto Protocol & its viable and concrete successor.

Some of the listed thrust areas are elaborated in the following sections with other interesting and viable suggestions.

8.01 CARBON CAPTURE & STORAGE (CCS)

- Carbon Capture and Storage (CCS) is in fact the process of capturing carbon dioxide (CO_2) from large industrial sources before it is released to the atmosphere, and then safely transporting the CO_2 and storing it in mature oil and gas reservoirs or in other deep geological formations.

- CCS is a proven, technically viable and environmentally safe means of reducing greenhouse gases (GHG) and should, therefore, be employed extensively.

- There are dozens of projects currently operating or in various stages of development in countries around the world, viz. Canada, the U.S., the Netherlands, Germany, France, Australia, Poland, the U.K., Abu Dhabi, the Czech Republic, Spain, Italy, China, and elsewhere.

- These projects inject CO2 in any of the three storage sinks: sea bed, depleted gas reservoir, mature oil reservoir. At present the operational projects inject in the range of a million tonnes of CO_2 a year. This should be endeavored to be doubled in the next five years.

8.02 SCREENING SUNLIGHT TO MITIGATE CLIMATE CHANGE

This is one of the Geo-engineering approaches that attempt mitigation through changing the Earth's Albedo (reflectivity) to reflect more heat back out into space. A 0.5% Albedo increase would roughly tantamount to halving the effect of CO2 doubling.

Methods in this approach could include: releasing dust, sulfuric acid or reflecting micro-balloons into the stratosphere; enhancing low-level clouds; creating a Saturn-like ring of small particles, or putting a very large mirror or diffraction grating (thin wire mesh) in space, at suitable point between the Earth and the Sun. The cooling effect that volcanic eruptions have on the climate due to ash particles in the upper atmosphere can be cited to illustrate the efficacy of these methods.

A prefatory study by Edward Teller in 1997 had presented the pros and cons of various relatively 'low-tech' proposals to mitigate global warming through scattering/reflecting sunlight away from the Earth by diffusing of various materials in the upper stratosphere.

8.03   IRON SEEDING/IRON FERTILIZATION

Iron fertilization is the intentional and measured introduction of iron to the upper ocean to increase the marine food chain. Thus, in another way it helps sequester carbon dioxide from the atmosphere. Marine phytoplankton annually absorbs and fixes nearly half of all planetary Carbon dioxide emissions, or approximately 50 billion tons.

NASA and NOAA's most conservative estimates of global plankton decline in the last 25 years put the figure around 6%. Simply returning these populations to that of 1980 levels of health and activity could result in incidence of 2-3 billion tons of additional sequestration; in other words, a third to one-half of all current industrial and automotive emissions.

In addition to this, water with more algae population would reflect more sunlight and cause less heating of the ocean.

8.04 CARBON TRADING

Carbon trading or emissions trading is an adjunct of the Kyoto Protocol. The idea is that countries that create more greenhouse gases than allowed can purchase credits from countries whose emissions are much lower.

The most important sources of credits are the Clean Development Mechanism (CDM) and the Joint Implementation (JI) mechanism. The CDM allows the creation of new Carbon Credits by developing emission reduction projects in Non-Annex I countries, while JI allows project-specific credits to be converted from existing credits in Annex I countries.

CDM projects produce Certified Emission Reductions (CERs), and JI projects produce Emission Reduction Units (ERUs).

At present creation of these instruments is subject to a lengthy process of registration and certification by the UN. This has to be simplified and also needs to be rendered less time consuming.

8.05 TRANSPORTATION & ROAD NETWORK

Good roads are essential for the development of a country. The Romans realized this centuries ago. Wherever they established themselves, they tried to improve the road network. Today, the governments of all countries in the world are building more and more roads to gain access to the remotest regions of their countries. Roads typically familiar to us are: NH (National Highways), SH (State Highways), MDR (Major District Roads), ODR (Other District Roads) and VR (Village Roads). We also have different road patterns in place as per location, lay-out of the city, town, and industrial centre as well as roads dictated by the choice of planning.

REDEFINING EXISTING ROADS

Existing roads need redefining and adorning with arboriculture and continuous tree belt alongside city roads and highways. Augmentation in length is also a felt necessity. Apart from this, 'Speed' is paramount and of supreme concern because speed achieved and enhanced is fuel saved which ultimately results in reduction of 'carbon footprints'.

To make a vibrant and dynamic nation, smooth mobility of people is a prerequisite for which there is a greater need for more separate bus corridors and underground metros. We must segregate the freight and passenger corridors. Highways should be rendered unhindered eliminating too much signals. In all developed countries most highways run either above or under intersection, obviating signals and have road signs that are clearly visible from a distance. Rural interiors should be linked by all-weather roads. Our development cannot be called synchronized until we link and interlink all the remote and far-flung areas.

TRAFFIC VOLUME STUDIES

'Traffic volume studies' should be carried out in all prominent cities as well as in cities where such studies have not been carried out so far. This would enable an informed decision where to regulate traffic by means of signals and where to do away with signals. More flyovers need to be constructed in order to approach signal-free crossings and better maneuverings at all intersections. Various cities which have attained 1 million figure or are in the process of doing so badly require mono rails to mitigate their transportation woes.

Odd-Even Protocol

The Odd-Even Protocol ought to be implemented first in select and chosen cities. In a typical Protocol, vehicles ending with odd numbers should be allowed to ply on Tuesday/Thursday and Saturday and those ending with even numbers on Monday/Wednesday and Friday; For vehicles containing Zero at the end – the beginning number should be considered for determining the plying eligibility day; Sunday being the thin traffic day should be open to all vehicles irrespective of odd/even numbers; vehicles complying with Euro III Norms should be allowed on all days and those complying only with Euro-II on alternate days. This should be enforced until all vehicles are Euro-III compliant.

Segregation of Traffic

Multi-level parking should be made at appropriate locations. All vehicles should be segregated and filtered at select locations / reaches where traffic congestion is more pronounced. Very light vehicles (cycles /scooters /motor cycles) in the lower-most layer, heavy to very heavy traffic in middle-layer /course and medium traffic comprising cars/ jeeps etc. should be streamlined in top layer /course.

Speed is the Need

Our best trains have an average speed of 80-90 km per hour. Governments should strive to augment the speed of train. Overhauling /renovation and laying of new tracks is warranted together with electrification of all routes. Advanced signaling should be put in place. Bullet trains may be started to attain electrifying speed. However, cost of laying specialized tracks for such train is somewhat higher, around Rs. 50-65 crore /km. The implementation could be considered via PPP (Public Private Partnership) mode. Upgrading the existing network is not a bad idea either at around Rs 5.0 crore per kilometer.

Heavy Tax Regime

It is high time that we start imposing heavy tax on luxury cars and on possessing more than one car per household.

8.06   SEPARATE CLIMATE CHANGE MINISTRY

Every nation that is concerned about the environment should seriously ponder over having a separate climate change ministry. This would not only help in creating awareness but also in maintaining ecological balance and in imparting momentum to other creative means to get the message across. For any country, having an exclusive climate change ministry would help securing qualitatively sound environmental policies that would put human and environmental interaction at the centre of policy making. For decades and centuries together, policies have been centered on human alone, treating the environment as of little consequence. This kind of approach to policy making has to be abandoned in order to make a substantially positive progress towards environmental enhancement. A sea-change in environmental policy is the need of the hour.

Moreover, environmental issues have now acquired transnational characteristics. Each and every country having a ministry of climate change can help secure a holistic approach towards the environment. Further, for developing countries the ministry of climate change can help analyze the consequences of harnessing certain technologies, with due regard to their pros and cons, so that informed decisions van be taken.

8.07 DE-URBANISATION SATELLITE PROJECTS
[Development of Magnate/Satellite cities]

Growing Urbanization is going to be the next big threat in degrading the environment coupled with Global Warming. Metropolitan cities, across the globe, either have exhausted their accommodating capacity or are in the process of doing so. Governments of all the 236 nations /territories should contemplate extending subsidy for developing satellite cities beside major metros. Such projects, called 'DSPs' [De-urbanization Satellite Projects)] should earn DUC [De-urbanization Credits] just as CER [Certified emission reductions] does. They should be tradable just as Carbon Credits in international markets. The countries that are not able to extend subsidy should receive the same from the international fund which can be created now. REDD projects should receive third priority after CDM & DSP projects. Funds earmarked for CDM and REDD could be dovetailed for meeting the requirements of DSP's. Implementation of such projects can be also considered via PPP [public private partnership] route.

8.08 BIENNIAL & QUINQUENNIAL TARGETS

The cardinal issue of **Emission Cuts and quantum thereof** still remains unresolved at international deliberations. Presently CO_2 concentrations have reached 390 PPM from 300 in 1910, a whopping rise of 30% in one century alone! We had exceeded the tolerable limits of 350 in 1988 itself. All Governments should inevitably and mandatorily draft their Biennial & Quinquennial targets of emission cuts together with **NRMAM** [Nationally Relevant Mitigation & Adaptation Measures]. In no circumstances, the global temperature should be allowed to exceed 1.5^0C from the preindustrial levels, and the measures for the same should be ensured as per feasibility and viability studies in the respective nations.

8.09   BILATERAL & MULTILATERAL FORA

The United Nations is a bigger platform and there is difficulty in arriving at consensus as we have seen from past meetings and conferences. Countries now ought to come together to form, side by side, bilateral or multilateral forums like BASIC (Brazil, South Africa, India & China). Such fora would be more efficient and speedy in resolving the emission cuts /climate change and other concomitant issues. There are dozens of alternatives by which emissions could be reduced /minimized with the help of advanced technology and continuously evolving technological up-gradations. Solutions are within our reach, but we lack strong will, as is apparent from the fate of previous talks which would keep on dithering on a vital issue such as emission, without hard decisions being taken.

8. 10 CRISIS MANAGEMENT PLAN

Globally, around a thousand million people are going to be dislocated in the next couple of decades owing to climate change and related problems. However, no international Crisis Management Plan is available to meet such catastrophic eventualities. The poor and small island nations are going to be hit more severely and it could be an apocalyptic inferno for them. Hence, a global fund to the tune of, say $100 billion should be created and earmarked towards that end. We should be ready for the worst and not wait for crisis to come and knock us out cold.

8. 11 GREEN SCHOOLS

Governments should try to open more and more 'green schools' to produce future 'stewards of the environment'. They would be future torch bearers in the matter of environment conservation, protection and improvement. These schools should impart education right from the nursery to secondary levels. Imparting environmental education right from the childhood would tend to inculcate fine virtues of environmental concerns and attitudes.

8.12 PROMOTION OF E-WASTE PROJECTS

As we have already seen, e-waste or electronic waste is a burgeoning environmental problem the world over. In India it assumes greater significance not only due to generation of significant domestic e-waste but also dumping from the developed countries.

Electronic waste, e-scrap, and WEEE (waste electrical & electronic equipment) is the collective term for a loose category of obsolete, surplus, broken, discarded electrical or electronic devices. The processing of e-waste is turning into a potentially grave health hazard and environmental pollution menace due to lack of containment, unprotected land filling and consequent leaching.

The Basel Convention and regulation by the EU (European Union) and US aim to reduce this problem. Reuse and recycle are promoted as alternative to disposal as trash.

It is estimated that the total obsolete computers originating from government office, business houses, industries and households is around two million in number. Manufactures and assemblers alone in a single year (calendar) are estimated to produce approximately 1200 tons of e-scrap. Due to lack of governmental legislation, and absence of standards for disposal, e-wastes mostly end up in landfills or are partly recycled in unhygienic fashion and partly thrown into river systems or waste streams.

It is now universally agreed that the e-waste, containing substances like Lead (Pb), Cadmium (Cd), Poly Vinyl Chloride (PVC) and Mercury (Hg), poses a clear and present danger of causing enormous harm to human health and the surrounding environment. Exact prescriptions regarding disposal are, at present, inadequate and insufficient. There is an imperative need for early formulation of holistic e-waste legislations and enabling policy. Such policy must appropriately reflect the concerns of all stakeholders together with the views of practitioners both in organized and unorganized sector.

European and some other developed countries have taken a systematic approach towards handling disposal and recycling of e-waste. Several plants have been established for this purpose where large amount of e-waste is recycled, employing the best available technologies.

8. 13   PROMOTION OF VERMICULTURE TECHNOLOGY

Vermiculture technology should receive full boost and subsidy all over the world. In recent times, safe disposal of degradable waste has become a global problem. The rejuvenation of degraded soils by protecting the top soil and ensuring sustainability of productive soil are major concerns at the international level. Vermicomposting is a compatible process encompassing sound environmental principles that value conservation of resources and sustainable practices. Vermicompost is known to be the world's best organic fertilizer.

Vermiculture makes use of worms /earthworms. In this technology, artificial rearing or cultivation is resorted to for betterment of soil fertility and in turn betterment of human life by increasing the productivity.

Vermiculture has been embraced throughout the world, on both sides of the Atlantic, and in developing as also developed countries. It is an essentially and entirely eco-friendly practice and is sustainable as well. Vermicomposting is a panacea for solid waste management. Earthworms serve as 'nature's ploughman' to produce good humus, which has profuse nutritional value for crops. Embracing vermiculture results in multiple benefits to farmers, ecological enhancement and overall boost to the national economy.

8.14 EMPHASIS ON MEDIUM & SMALL IRRIGATION SCHEMES FOR SUSTAINABLE DEVELOPMENT

In India, with the construction of gigantic dams after independence the path to development was paved. Many big dams were constructed and they helped achieve greater hydro-electric potential and irrigation facility. Initially our awareness towards environment was limited and concerns were raised only in the early seventies. By the commencement of the twenty-first century, we have had built around 4000 dams across the length and breadth of the country whereas this number was just 300 in the year of independence. More than 50% of the dams were built during seventies and eighties. Despite all odds, India is today ranked 3rd in the world in dam building after the USA and China. During this great dam building phase, we saw the construction of the highest Bhakra Dam (738 ft. High and 1,699 ft. long) on Sutlej River in Punjab and also the longest Dam, namely the Hirakud Dam on Mahanadi River in Orissa. The longest concrete dam constructed was the Nagarjunasagar dam over Krishana River at Macheria (A.P.) and similarly the longest barrage, Farakka barrage on the Ganga which is 7,364 ft. long.

From the water resources engineering point of view, there are numerous advantages in large dams; but from the point of view of environment and ecology, there are a few shortcomings as well. Still large dams have umpteen economic and other benefits and because of that they cannot just be written off as white elephants. Some of the obvious benefits are generation of hydro-electric power; boosting of irrigation potential; employment generation; enhancement of tourism /eco-tourism; fisheries development; artificial crocodiles sanctuary formation; and augmentation in water table, to name only a few.

On the other hand, voices are often raised against them mainly because of large scale human displacement, loss of employment, depletion of flora &fauna (trees and cattle) and loss of land of farming community, coupled with socio-economic disorientation – and they are valid to some extent in specific cases.

Our pluralistic demography and our democratic polity oblige us to heed the voices of dissent and especially, the concerns for rehabilitation. Construction progress is often hampered by violent agitations as witnessed during 'Narbada Bachao Andolan," and during the construction of Tehri Dam and the Sardar Sarovar Project. Construction of Bisalpur Multipurpose Project (District – Tonk, Rajasthan) also witnessed demonstrations and agitation for proper rehabilitation and higher compensation. Of late, voices have been raised against the Subansiri dam (being constructed on the Arunachal-Assam border), and the Dibang Multipurpose Project (Arunachal Pradesh). The unique feature of these recent demonstrations in North-east India is that this time around, people hailing from the downstream areas are opposing the construction of dams.

Because of sustained demonstrations and agitations against big dams, 'gestation periods' of the projects are prolonged and accrual of benefits is delayed, leading to alteration in cost-benefit ratio largely brought about owing to escalation in costs.

Now what is needed is construction of mid-sized dams and schemes which involve minimum or negligible human displacement. Jawahar Sagar dam (District – Bundi, Rajasthan) could be cited as an ideal example. Mid-sized schemes though are not also always free from troubles, as can be seen from the case of Takali Project (District – Kota, Rajasthan), where construction work was hampered for several months by the people to be affected from future submergence. But, we have to learn and devise ways to cope with such issues, and NGOs should be included for reconciliation and imparting abundant transparency to the projects. In addition to, small water-harvesting structures could be constructed with the caveat that the construction should be according to plan and done only by the department having expertise in such constructions.

Apart from this, there is now greater need to focus upon 'sub-basin' or 'micro-shed level planning' in order to harness water in lean periods. Such planning should be integrated so as to address all issues involving soil and water conservation; land and water management; afforestation and reforestation; regeneration of natural vegetation; drought proofing; productivity enhancement; and market linkage, together with providing for livelihood security. Such a holistic strategy should, in the end, work well.

Recently, most of the proposals under 'Revival of the River Project' are smaller and this reflects a change in focus. From the look of things, it appears in future also only medium or small schemes (barring specific cases in consonance with feasibility and needs) would be planned and executed and that sounds sensible.

8. 15 DEVELOPMENT OF ECO CITIES

The concept of developing sustainable Eco cities is a relatively new one. A few cities are worth mentioning: Waitakere (New Zealand), Curitiba (Brazil), Dongtan (Shanghai, China), and Lavasa India. Immense benefits are associated with development of eco green cities. Governments the world over should look into the prospects of developing such cities through the route of PPP.

The benefits of developing of sustainable, well-conceived and modern eco-cities are numerous. A few are listed here.

1. Improvement in quality of life, living and lifestyle
2. Growth in tax base
3. Growth of Bio-diversity and regulation of certain meteorological parameters
4. Augmentation in GDP
5. Creation of new job Avenues
6. Addition and proliferation of burgeoning middle class
7. A perfectly viable alternative for future 'sustainable development'.

8. 16 ARTIFICIAL RECHARGE OF GROUND WATER

Water is an important abiotic component of environment. Ground water is fast depleting in many countries including India. It is estimated that ground water is depleting at the rate of 1 foot per year in states like Punjab, Haryana and Rajasthan. Ground water has to be judiciously used and water table needs to be augmented. It is all the more important from ecological balance point of view also. Moreover, water itself is scant and precious – an averment which may do with some elucidation, given the fact that nearly 70% of the earth's surface is covered with water. But the reality is that,

97% of the total water on earth (about1400 BCM) is saline, and only 3% is available as fresh water. The bulk (around 77%) of this fresh water is locked up in glaciers and permanent snow; about 11% is known to occur at depths of more than 800 m below ground, and so cannot be extracted economically with the available technology.

About 11% of freshwater resources are available within extractable depth (800 m) and a miniscule fraction of about 1% is available as surface water in rivers and lakes. Around 1,13000 BCM (Billion Cubic Metre) is received from precipitation (rain and snow) out of which, evaporation losses account for about 72000 BCM, leaving a balance of about 41000 BCM, out of which again, 9000-14000 BCM only is considered utilizable.

The Indian scenario is also grim. The annual precipitation is to the tune of 4000 BCM (Billion Cubic Metre) and the natural run-off in the rivers is computed to be about 1869 BCM. The replenishable ground water and utilizable surface water resources are of the order 433 BCM and 690 BCM respectively. The total water resources, thus available for various uses, are of the order 1123 BCM per annum. The per capita availability of water was 5177 (CUM/Yr) in 1951 which went on decreasing. It was 2200 in the year 1991 and subsequently reduced to 1869 in the year 2001. It is estimated that per capita availability of water would further go down to 1341 and 1140 in the year 2025 and 2050 respectively. Gradually, we shall be heading towards water-stressed to water-scarcity conditions. Many basins like Tapi, Pennar and Mahi are experiencing the heat and are presently water stressed.

Ground water could be artificially recharged by various techniques and methods. The following is an abridged enumeration.

1. Direct Methods

i.   Flooding
ii.   Recharge basin
iii. Ditch and furrow
iv.   Bench terracing
v.   Contour bunds and trenches
vi.   Gully plugs, check dams and Nullah bunds
vii. Percolation Ponds
viii. Injection wells
ix.   Gravity head recharge wells
x.   Recharge shafts and pits.

2. Indirect methods

i. Aquifer modification by bore blasting and Hydro fracturing
ii. Induced recharge

3. Combination methods

Many combinations of sub-surface and surface recharge methods could be considered as per hydro-geological conditions of the site. Important techniques under this head are:

i.   Recharge basin with shafts
ii.   Percolation ponds with recharge pits
iii. Induced recharge with wells tapping multiple aquifers.

8.17 TURNING CARBON DI-OXIDE INTO METHANE

Carbon di-oxide buried under the seabed could be transformed into methane which is a major constituent of Natural Gas. Studies and research should be accelerated to identify bacteria which are found in seabed that accelerate the process of formation of methane. In this way, we could dilute the concentration of CO2 in sea and enhance methane production to meet our present and future requirements.

8. 18 MASSIVE IMPLEMETATION OF ROOF-TOP RAINWATER HARVESTING SYSTEM (RRHS)

Rainwater contains small amounts of dissolved minerals that have been blown into the air by winds. Rainwater also contains tiny particles of dust and dissolved gasses, such as carbon dioxide and sulphur dioxide. Still we should not belittle the importance of rainwater on account of such impurities. Normally only about 1/100,000th of the weight of rain comes from these substances.

Rooftop Rainwater Harvesting System ought to be implemented both in urban and rural areas. There is an urgent need to spread awareness, impart technical know-how and specially make it socially acceptable. Need for social acceptance through popular awareness is foremost, because many have prejudices against rainwater. Color, taste and odor are three main considerations for people in choosing drinking water. Clean, odorless water having good taste is normally preferred for drinking purposes. For the purpose of cooking, water having lesser DS (dissolved salts) is preferred because of lesser time taken in cooking. Rainwater contains very little dissolved salt, tastes good and is almost free from pollutants. It is therefore best suited for drinking, bathing and cooking purposes.

In roof top rainwater harvesting system, water is collected in some storage tank during rainy season, and thereafter drawn from the system only when other sources dry up or become inaccessible. As a result, the water collected in RRHS remains stored for a period of 100-180 days before actual utilization. This makes water from RRHS not readily acceptable to many people. Hence, it is imperative to organize mass awareness and education programmes on the potableness of rainwater. People's perceptions and concerns as stakeholders need to be given due importance during such programmes in order to enable them to develop an understanding of the system.

In urban areas, water is mainly required for domestic, industrial, garden and other uses, and is mostly drawn from surface water bodies, river, streams and/or ground water sources. Roof top rainwater harvesting is an ideal alternative in such areas. Appropriate storage facilities can be created to store roof top rainwater depending on availability of space. Rainwater in urban areas would help not only in meeting at least a part of the water requirement but also prevent storm run-off and flooding of roads during heavy rains. It would also reduce pumping cost and consequent reduction on stress upon ground water resources.

In rural areas, streams, ponds and wells have traditionally been used as sources of water for drinking and other uses. In recent years, bore wells with hand pumps and small rural water supply schemes have almost replaced traditional sources of water. However, in many rural habitations, these sources have not been able to supply water to the rural households throughout the year. Domestic RRHS would provide a viable solution to bridge the gap between demand and supply of water in such areas especially during the lean periods of water scarcity. RRHS has numerous advantages over conventional water supply system in rural areas, which are briefly summarized as under:

- Water is made available at the door-step of the householder.

- It requires simple or no maintenance. Maintenance, if any could be carried out by the user itself.

- Water from roof-top is generally free from contamination and pollution hence clean and potable.

- Easy access.

- C & M (construction and maintenance) are simple and do not entail use of sophisticated tools and technology.

- RRHS can provide a dependable, economical and durable source of water for drinking and allied uses.

- Time in fetching from distant water sources is completely eliminated.

8.19 INDEPENDENT STUDIES ON CLIMATE CHANGE

Skepticism does exist on the issue of climate change and global warming. Many scientists question the environmental alarms. A number of Russian scientists have in fact raised their dissenting voice, contending that the world climate changes in recurring cycles are related to solar activity and other natural factors. Hence, there is a felt need for making independent assessments, analysis and conclusion on the basis of exhaustive, objective and authentic information on climate change.

BASIC (Brazil, South Africa, India and China) and BRIC (Brazil, Russia, India and China) countries could take up independent studies. They could take the initiative in launching climate research independent of IPCC (Intergovernmental Panel on Climate Change). India has an Integrated Long Term Programme (ILTP) of scientific collaboration with Russia. Bilaterally they could start studies on climate change drawing scientists from both the countries. Similarly other groups of the world may initiate independent studies on climate change and global warming. In this way, the outcome arrived at from different studies would provide a free, fair and impartial picture of climate change (and concomitant issues), including its genesis and long term impact on human beings, flora and fauna, and so on and so forth.

8.20 ORGANIC FARMING FOR ENVIRONMENTAL ENHANCEMENT

The green revolution laid emphasis only upon hybrid varieties and increased yield with high inputs of toxic fertilizers and pesticides. It totally neglected low input agricultural practices like organic farming.

Let us take the case of Thailand where yield went up by 65%, whereas fertilizer consumption went up by 25%, and pesticides by 50 %.('Lessons from green revolution' by Rosette P Collins J & Lappe F.M.). The continuous use of these harmful toxins has rendered the land barren and affected human health as well. The Green Revolution also brought about the destruction of native seed varieties and gradually relegated to insignificance the local farmers' indigenous knowledge through neglect and disuse.

As of now, organic farming is practiced in less than 1% of farmland area the world over. This has to be increased and awareness incessantly augmented. Capacity building is also an important attribute. Organic farming is the form of agriculture that relies on techniques such as crop rotation, green manure, compost, and biological pest control, to maintain soil productivity and control pests on a farm. Organic farming excludes or strictly limits the use of synthetic fertilizers and synthetic pesticides, plant growth regulators, livestock antibiotics, food additives, and genetically modified organisms.

Readers might have heard of IFOAM (International Federation of Organic Agriculture Movements), which is an international agency headquartered in Bonn, Germany. Its mission is leading, uniting and assisting the organic movement in its full diversity. Its other goals are; worldwide adoption of ecologically, socially and economically sound systems that are based on the Principles of Organic Agriculture.

CROP ROTATION

Values and benefits of Crop Rotation should be inculcated in the minds of farmers. The method of growing different crops in rotation, one after another, in the same field is called crop rotation. Its use are:
- extracting different nutrients thus avoiding deficiency of any particular type;
- reducing pests and insects;
- reducing diseases and wastages
- extracting water from different levels.

The following crop rotation can be adopted depending upon soil suitability.

- Wheat – Juar – Gram
- Rice – Gram

- Cotton – wheat – Gram or sugarcane
- Cotton – Juar – Gram
- Cash crop – fodder crop – soil renovating crop.

BIOLOGICAL PEST CONTROL

[A sound mechanism for Integrated Pest Management]
Biological Pest Control should be promoted extensively. In agriculture it is used to control   insects, mites, weeds and plant diseases that rely on predation, parasitism, herbivory or other natural mechanisms. It can be an important component of integrated pest management (IPM) programs.

Biological Control is also defined as the reduction of pest populations by natural enemies and typically involves an active human role. Natural enemies of insect pests are also known as biological control agents; and include predators, parasitoids and pathogens. Biological control agents of plant diseases are most often referred to as antagonists. Biological control agents of weeds include herbivores and plant pathogens. Predators, such as birds, beetles and lacewings, are mainly free-living species that consume a large number of preys during their lifetime. Parasitoids are species whose immature stage develops on or within a single insect host, ultimately killing the host. Most have a very narrow host range. Many species of wasps and some flies are parasitoids. Pathogens (disease-causing organisms), include bacteria, fungi, and viruses. They kill or debilitate their host and are relatively specific to certain insect groups. There are three basic types of biological control strategies: conservation, classical biological control, and augmentation.

Role of Neem in BPC

Several Neem-based biological pest control (BPC) products have been developed and approved for commercial distribution in some countries. The Neem tree can provide an inexpensive integrated pest management (IPM) resource for farmers. Azadirachtin has been identified as Neem's principal active compound. It acts on insects by repelling them, by inhibiting feeding, and by disrupting their growth, metamorphosis and reproduction. Neem-based formulations do not usually kill insects directly, but they can alter their behavior in significant ways to reduce pest damage to crops, and reduce their reproductive potential. Azadirachtin affects insect physiology by mimicking a natural hormone. It has been shown to affect egg production and hatching rates. In larvae, azadirachtin can inhibit molting, preventing them from developing into pupae.

Some natural, organic, botanical & biological agents for pest control

Agent	Description
Boric Acid	Boron is a naturally occurring mineral and Boric acid is derived from this natural mineral. Boric Acid is a stomach poison for insects. Boric acid is used in many formulations. These products can control common household insects as well as wood-infesting beetles and termites.
Diatomaceous Earth	The fossilized remains of tiny, one-celled organisms are called diatoms. These diatoms kill insects by scratching their waxy outer covering, causing them to dehydrate. Diatomaceous earth is used to control cockroaches, ants, silverfish, fleas & other pests.
Eugenol	Eugenol, extracted from clove oil and cinnamon, is active against ants, fleas, flies, yellow jackets, cockroaches & other crawling insects.

Garlic	Grounded dry garlic cloves are active against ants, aphids, and mosquitoes.
Insect/Rodent Traps	Specially designed traps use mechanical contraptions to monitor & reduce insect and rodent populations.
Limestone	Pulverized limestone is used as a desiccant to control spiders, cockroaches, ants, crickets, silverfish, earwigs, snails, aphids, mites, bed bugs, termites, scorpions, fleas, ticks, flies, bees, yellow jackets, wasps, and other flying insects.
Mint Oil and Peppermint Oil	Extracted from the leaves of the spearmint or peppermint plant. These oils are good repellent for mosquitoes, gnats, ants, flies, cockroaches, mice, yellow jackets and other flying pests.
Nematodes	Nematode is a microscopic worm that lives in soil that acts as a biological control agent. Nematode species can be used to control insect pests. These nematodes carry bacteria that can kill pests like fleas, but do not harm people or pets.
Pheromone Traps	Pheromone traps use 'bug hormones' or scents that stimulate the type of scent produced by the female insect to seduce or lure their male counterparts. Males lured into traps are prevented from mating.
Rodent/Animal Catch and Release Cages	Physical traps and cages are used in a humane manner to catch, transfer and release unwanted animals in or around a home.

Green Manure Crops

GMCs should be widely grown both for its economic and environmental values. Listed here are some popular GMCs that can be extensively grown.

- Alfalfa, which sends roots deep to bring nutrients to the surface.
- Buckwheat in temperate regions.
- Clover
- Fava beans
- Fenugreek
- Ferns of the genus Azolla have been used as a green manure in south-east Asia.
- Lupine
- Mustard
- Sunn hemp, a tropical legume.
- Tyfon, a Brassica known for a strong tap root that breaks up heavy soils.
- Velvet bean (*Mucuna pruriens*), common in the southern US during the early part of the 20th century, before being replaced by soya beans, popular today in most tropical countries, especially in Central America, where it is the main green manure used in slash/mulch farming practices
- Vetch (*Vicia sativa*)
- Winter cover crops such as oats or rye have long been used as green manures.

Good Points of Compost

Compost is composed of organic materials derived from plant and animal matter that has been decomposed largely through aerobic decomposition. The process of composting is simple and practiced by individuals in their homes, farmers on their land, and industrially by cities and factories. Compost can be rich in nutrients. Its application is in gardens, landscaping, horticulture and agriculture. The compost itself is beneficial for the land in many ways, including as a soil conditioner, a fertilizer, as an agent for addition of vital humus or humic acids, and as a natural pesticide for soil. In ecosystems, compost is useful for erosion control, land and stream reclamation, wetland construction, and as landfill cover.

BENEFITS OF ORGANIC FARMING

- ➤ Organic farming enriches 12% to 15% more CO_2 in the soil (this has been confirmed by trials conducted over many years in Switzerland).

- ➤ Organic farming boosts soil fertility and the humus content of soils.

- ➤ Reduces CO_2 emissions by eliminating synthetic fertilizers, and at the same time reduces atmospheric concentration of this gas by storing in the soil.

- ➤ It enriches humus content and at the same time can adapt better to adverse effects of climate change.

- ➤ Soil (rich in humus) stores more water for longer period. It ensures higher yield.

- ➤ Improves water retention, protects against sudden and stress rainfall, as rivers rise less rapidly and erosion is slowed.

- ➤ Organic farming increases soil N, P, K and organic C, and reduces soil pH.

- ➤ It helps restore biodiversity and augments the same.

SOME BENEFICIAL EVIDENCES

A study conducted by FAO records the following findings.

- ➢ Yield of potatoes in Bolivia increased from 4 tons to 15 tons per hectare.

- ➢ Yield of sweet tuber went up from 6 tons to 30 tons.

- ➢ In Pakistan, yield of mangoes shot up from 7 to 20 tons.

- ➢ In Cuba, two time increase in vegetable yield was recorded.

- ➢ Maize yield went up from 2 tons to 9 tons in Kenya.

8.21 IMPETUS TO ALTERNATIVE RENEWABLE ENERGY PROJECTS

The present millennium holds tremendous promise for alternative renewable energy. To mitigate the adverse effects of climate change and global warming, there are increasing calls for alternative energy sources. Alternative energy sources (alternative to fossil fuels) are sources producing little or no GHGs (Green Houses Gases) emissions, while still meeting the current and future energy needs of the World.

Renewable energy sources are sources that are freely available and cannot be easily depleted, while the non-renewable sources can run out and are often not freely available. Among examples of renewable energy are: Solar Energy (solar panels also known as PVCs); Wind Energy; Biomass (Biodiesel, Ethanol, Biogas); Hydroelectric Power; Tidal Energy; Geothermal Energy; Wave Energy etc.

Some technologies such as Clean Coal Technologies (CCTs) have been suggested to make the burning of coal cleaner as well. CCTs are, however, still being researched. In addition to such efforts to clean up the production processes of energy from fossil fuels, several alternative energy sources which are renewable and/or which reduce or eliminate GHGs generation are being researched constantly. Some of these alternative energy sources are:

- ✓ Solar Energy – energy from the Sun
- ✓ Wind Energy – energy due to wind motion
- ✓ Hydrogen Energy
- ✓ Hydroelectric Energy, and
- ✓ Geothermal Energy

Moreover, we have to constantly address issues involved in renewable transport fuel. Nearly one third of global transport fuel would come from renewable sources by 2020. Affordability, development cost, ease of use and consistent availability need to be continuously researched.

8.22 NEED FOR COST EFFECTIVE CONTROL OF INDUSTRIAL POLLUTION

Industrialization has been a continuous process since the later half of the 18th century. Since then, industrial growth has been happening at a breakneck speed and has, in turn, resulted in a significant contribution to the toxicity in the environment. Therefore industrial activities should comply with regulatory norms for prevention and control of pollution. There have been many guidelines for the industries and the pollution caused by them. The implementation and monitoring of these guidelines to curb emissions is the joint responsibility of the central and state governments along with the Central Pollution Control Board. At present, control of pollution from industrial installations ranks among the top-most priorities in the global crusade to save ecology. Cost effective programmes should be formulated and rigorously executed, keeping in view the variegated needs. In effective implementation of such programmes lies the hope of subduing the demon of environmental defilement that has proved to be a 'sordid gift' of the much-vaunted industrial revolution.

8.23 RESEARCH & DEVELOPMENT OF SECOND GENERATION BIOFUELS

Governments across the globe should give a special thrust on development of 'second generation fuel' such as *cellulosic ethanol* and *algal biodiesel*. More research is required in the direction of SVO (straight vegetable oil) and RVO (raw vegetable oil) as fuel source.

All of the vegetable oils are highly viscous and reactive to oxygen. They have high cloud point and pour point temperatures. Diesel engines with vegetable oils offer acceptable engine performance and emissions for short-term operation. Long-term operation results in operational and durability problems. Some investigators have explored modifying the vehicle to preheat the SVO prior to injection into the engine. Others have examined blends of vegetable oil with conventional diesel. These techniques may lessen the problems.

Studies show that carbon build up continues over time, resulting in higher engine maintenance costs and shorter engine life. Another issue that is particularly critical for use of SVO is viscosity. The viscosity of SVO is much higher than that of diesel fuel at normal operating temperatures. This can cause premature wear of the fuel pump, injectors, and also can dramatically alter the structure of the fuel spray coming out of the injectors to increase droplet size, decrease spray angle, and increase spray penetration. All of these changes to the fuel spray would tend to increase wetting of engine internal surfaces with the fuel, leading to increased tendency to form carbon deposits and dilute the lubricant. If these issues are addressed, SVO and RVO could be better alternatives as supplementary/additive fuels.

8.24 NEEDED NEW BIOFUEL POLICY FOR EVERY NATION

Fossil fuels have been depleting fast. There is a great mismatch between global demand and supply. Hence it is an area of critical concern, and the onus is upon governments of the nations to evolve a dynamic and rolling policy on Biofuel. The Government of India has recently (in 2009) come out with one such policy on Biofuel. The highlights of the policy are given below.

- A National Bio-fuel Coordination Committee, headed by the Prime Minister, would be set up to provide policy guidance and coordination, and a Bio-fuel Steering Committee, chaired by Cabinet Secretary, will be set up to oversee implementation of the said policy.

- An indicative target of 20% blending of bio-fuels, both for bio-diesel and bio-ethanol, by 2017 has been proposed.

- Bio-diesel production will be taken up from non-edible oil seeds in waste, degraded and marginal lands.

- Financial incentives, including subsidies and grants, may be considered for second generation bio-fuels. If it becomes necessary, a National Bio-fuel Fund could be considered.

- Major thrust is envisaged on research, development and demonstration with focus on plantations, processing and production of bio-fuels, including second generation bio-fuels.

- Minimum Support Price (MSP) for non-edible oil seeds would be announced with periodic revision to provide fair price to the growers.

- MNRE (Ministry of New and Renewable Energy) will be the co-coordinating ministry for bio-fuel development and utilization.

- MPP (Minimum Purchase Price) for purchase of bio-ethanol and bio-diesel would be announced with periodic revision.

Though biodiesel and ethanol are widely used in Brazil, USA and Europe, but it has not taken off in India and other Asian countries. The blending of bio-ethanol should gradually go up to 62-70%. This would entail constant R & D on our existing engines so that they are well adapted to receive higher blending ratios.

Governments of different nations need to develop their own policies suited to their local conditions, adaptability and preparedness. This would considerably alleviate and mitigate the issue of fossil fuels that has been wreaking havoc. Such policies in the long run will reduce dependence upon fossil fuels as well.

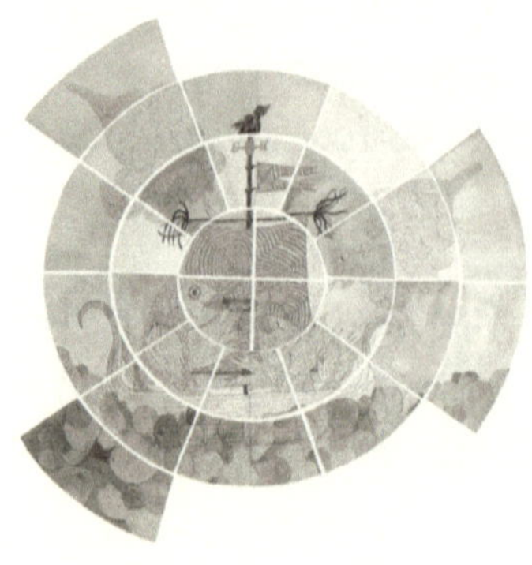

IX
A Green Protocol for Citizens

Climate change and Global Warming are dramatically urgent and serious problems that can lead to calamitous consequences. We do not need to wait for governments alone to find solutions to these terrible problems. Each individual can play an important part by simply adopting a more responsible lifestyle, beginning with some little, everyday Dos and Don'ts. It's the only reasonable way to save our planet, before it is too late

It is important for us all to think in terms of first reducing our emissions of C02 or Carbon Footprints. The carbon footprint is a subset of the ecological footprint. A *carbon footprint* is the total set of greenhouse gas (GHG) emissions caused by an organization, event, product or person. Greenhouse gases can be emitted through transport, land clearance, and the production and consumption of food, fuels, manufactured goods, materials, wood, roads, buildings, and services. For simplicity of reporting, it is often expressed in terms of the amount of carbon dioxide, or its equivalent of other GHGs, emitted.

As one begins this process, it soon becomes evident that there is no way we can currently reduce our emissions of greenhouse gases to zero. Every single aspect of our economy from manufacturing to transportation, and agriculture to health care is dependent on fossil fuel derived energy and resources. As we seek and develop alternative sources of energy, and as we begin to think and live in more efficient ways, we are still left with the undeniable reality that considerable CO_2 emissions from economic activity in the globe will continue and perhaps escalate over the foreseeable future. The only cogent way to take this issue head on is to offset the emissions we cannot yet eliminate.

It is high time that we inculcate strong environmental values among young students. School children should be asked to venture out and take up tasks that make them aware of the major environmental problems of today. They must be encouraged to collage, compile and gather information on areas such as water and energy usage. Young and impressionable minds that would be responsible citizens of tomorrow need to be taught about water audit, energy audit, land audit, waste audit and making the best out of waste. A simple questionnaire carrying theses audits has been generated by some organizations in India which can be filled by a secondary or even an eighth standard student. This concept of GSR (Green School Revolution) needs to be carried further. It would definitely help create awareness, promote values, transmit information, develop skills and provide for environmental solutions in school and in society at large.

Here is a list of simple things that everyone can do in order to fight against the menace of global warming and at the same time reduce carbon footprints. Some of these ideas are at no cost; some others require a little effort or investment but can help save a lot of money in the medium to long term. Some of these hold out a strong appeal to reason and judgement and are worth adopting as a citizens' charter.

1. ETCS ('Earth Tunnel Cooling System') could be deployed for offices / multiplexes / shopping mall / corporate offices. Though one time investment may be higher, but it ensures

consistent power saving. For arid and semiarid zones this may be extremely useful because the system does not make use of water. In addition, ETCS is absolutely free from harmful gases. It would also help protect the ozone layer by obviating the use of CFCs. The first ETCS in India has been successfully installed at CTO Jaipur, Rajasthan.

2. Solar heater should be installed in every household, especially in far flung and remote areas. The newly developed 'Evacuated Solar Technology' should be promoted and given a strong boost.

3. Judicious and Calibrated use of water: Every action pertaining to water consumption should be well calibrated. As we have already seen, water is a scarce and precious commodity. Scarcity is going to be felt more pronouncedly in coming decades. Some of the simple ways could be imbibed and made part and parcel of a simple drill to regulate our life. Like, for example: use a mug while shaving instead of allowing the water tap to gush on; accumulate washable clothes over the week and deploy washing machine only once or twice a week; resort to wet cotton /sponge sweep instead of washing floors quite often; utilise dish-washer instead one to one cleaning of utensils; avoid excessive use of Shampoos and soaps; reutilise water used for bathing, after adding a few drops of anti-septic, for washing clothes. Gradually imbibe the use of toilet papers etc. The whole idea is that fresh water is a priceless resource and in future there is going to be an acute shortage of the same. We should learn to use it judiciously right now so that we might adapt ourselves to even stiffer water scarcities when crunch time comes.

4. Every householder should get *power saver devices* installed in his home. Power savers help reduce 20% to 50% of electricity. It is well known that electricity supply is subject to surges and spikes and the same consume electricity. These devices (power savers) stabilise those surges and optimise the power factor of the electricity drawn by an electric appliance or equipment. It stabilises voltage and current, thereby reducing or eliminating electricity waste. These factors enhance the efficiency of the appliances and extend their life span as well. They are environment friendly also.

5. It is often seen that pamphlets are printed in large numbers and indiscriminately distributed to all and sundry without any regard to their relevance to the recipients. Later on these trash papers lie summarily discarded on streets, leaving an enormous burden of carbon footprint. Such wasteful and polluting habits need to be curbed and printing of pamphlets regulated and disseminated to concerned individuals only, thereby promoting the paper economy so vital to a low carbon regime.

6. People should be encouraged to use battery driven scooters which involve zero-emission. Technological advancements are needed for sure to augment their present single run which is around 70 km at present. Such vehicles should be given government subsidy also because the carbon footprint is negligible.

7. Every householder should develop the habit of using waste-container bags. Cumulative received waste in these bags could be collected on monthly or bimonthly basis. Waste thus collected should be segregated and processed. There is a huge potential of generating power out of such waste.

This would improve cleanliness as well as sanitation in our cities.

8. Present air conditioners carry a lot of carbon footprint. Instead of conventional air conditioners, lower cost air conditioners should be used. It would save electricity up to 50% and do away with CFC. This way we can save energy and emissions, a win-win situation.

9. Print-out should be taken from the printer only when it is absolutely warranted. Complete editing should be done beforehand, and then only print option should be exercised. Reading work could be performed on PC monitor /laptop. This would hugely cut down paper consumption and in turn save numerous trees.

10. Barren stretches of land should be cultivated and cultivation of bio-fuel crops should be encouraged. Ethanol & Jatropha are promising bio-fuels. Farmers at the same time should be assured collection of their crops.

11. Agricultural waste from processing industries / sugar mills / farmyard should be collected and made use of for generation of clean power. This would generate substantial carbon credits as well.

12. Existing gen-sets / engines / tractors can be fitted with new technology kits which are bio-fuel compatible. Such kits can utilize even used cooking oil. This would save wastage and reduce diesel consumption, and in turn help reduce concentration of harmful gases in atmosphere.

13. Extensive use of windmills for agricultural activities like drawing water.

14. Use of waste hair received from saloons/barber shops.

15. Use of bio plastic: Biodegradable plastics certainly have a pronounced ecological edge over conventional plastics. Bio-plastics are derived from renewable bio-mass source such as starch, pea, vegetable oil etc. They have been successfully obtained from crops like maize and soybean. One may find many items made up of bio-plastic, like packaging material, pots, cutlery, bowls, pens, pencil sharpeners, mobile phone casing, car interior and much else. One very recent report indicates that they produce methane gas that could be detrimental to the environment. Extant guidelines require that any product marked as compostable or biodegradable must decompose within 'a reasonably short period of time' after disposal. If we want to maximize the environmental benefit of biodegradable products in landfills 'we need to both expand methane collection at landfills and design these products to degrade more slowly'.

16. Solar Lanterns: Solar Lanterns should be used for households in remote and inaccessible areas. Awareness campaign may be initiated for using solar lanterns. NGO's can play a vital role in this regard. Millions of household are still lacking basic facility of electricity. This will prove a boon for them. Cheap and emission free lanterns could transform the rural lighting scenario. It would definitely ease pressure on coal based thermal plants. A citizen connect initiative to popularize use of solar lamps should be started right now.

17. Our electric appliances should be energy efficient. Profuse use of CFL and LED lamp is highly warranted now and should be made mandatory. Non-compliance should attract heavy penalty. CFLs use 60% less energy than a

regular bulb. This simple switch will save about 300 pounds of carbon dioxide a year. New LED lamps are free from mercury and are highly energy efficient. Their use results in reduced carbon footprint. They are recyclable and of longer duration. A perfectly win-win proposition, indeed!

18. Use of bicycle should be made popular just as in yesteryears. We should observe 'cycle day' once in a month and, on that day cycle riding alone should be allowed barring emergencies. People used to go for their daily chores on cycle in old times. Why can't we do the same today? In recreational trips, we can opt for bicycle instead of car or motorbike. It would greatly save on petrol and diesel bills.

19. Household wet-waste should be composted separately. Pots made for receiving such waste could be purchased from the market and the other material required, viz. sawdust, dry leaves, shredded paper etc. are cheap and eco-friendly. Composting could be done both for individual houses and community dwellings. This way we can produce a lot of useful manure besides achieving cleanliness.

20. Every House should be a modern 'green home', using no outside heavy shades for optimal exploitation of natural light, and using wooden switchboard instead of plastic board. House doors and windows should be made of environment-friendly material like particle boards instead of traditional wood. Some heavy green plant should always find place in the front or at the backyard of the house.

21. E-waste should be systematically collected though the vans specially meant for collecting e-waste. E-Waste should be shredded and segregated to regain useful metal.

22. We should re-orient our electricity consumption habits both at home and office. For instance, we should switch off fan, cooler, or AC whenever not required or not in use. Generally, people are careless at offices. Lights can be seen on even at unwarranted places or hours. Houses and offices should be constructed to receive natural sunlight, obviating use of lamps in the daytime.

23. Imbibe two more R's with respect to water, viz. 'Reclaim' and 'Restore' in addition to the three conventional ones – Recycle, Reduce and Re-use. These five R's should be the buzzwords for the ensuing decades until we restore global environment back on its original track.

24. Events like annual functions, convocations, commemorative anniversary etc. should be held as carbon neutral events. Maximum invitations should be sent via emails, SMS, or through social networking sites in place of physical paper invitation and fax messages. Invited guests should be encouraged to use public transport or share vehicles. This way we could save on paper which in turn reduces our carbon footprints and would also minimise consumption of petrol and diesel further, resulting in cutting down of CO_2 and NO_x etc.

25. We should reduce carbon footprint in our dietary habits. We should avoid, as far as possible, packaged food because extra carbon footprint is attached with them.

26. It has become necessary we develop strong penchant for locally grown /sourced fruits and organic foods. We should endeavour to maximize use of seasonal vegetables and foods. Nowadays vegetables like bitter gourd, bottle gourd

and lady's finger (all summer vegetables) are seen available in winter season also and people buying them with gay abandon. Such unseasonal vegetables should be avoided because they are likely to have been sourced not from a distant place. Heavy transportation is involved in making these fruits and vegetables available leading to extra carbon footprint.

27. Immediately replace corroded water pipes leading to your locality or house.

28. If any public water tap is found leaking, immediately replace the washer or get it fixed by a plumber.

29. For cleaning of car, motorcycle or scooter, use only dry or moist cloth.

30. For gardening, make use of garden sprinkler instead of regular hose pipe.

31. Start following the practice of roof top rain water harvesting.

32. Residual water left after household utilisation should be used for watering plants in kitchen garden or may be utilised in lawn.

33. Hang your clothes outside rather than using the dryer, whereby you can save electricity and time too.

34. Do your grocery in one shopping and if possible couple other things to do. List the things you need, so you would not forget them.

35. Choose energy efficient appliances when making new purchases. Look for the 'Energy Star label' on the new

appliances and white goods and try to choose the most energy efficient products available.

36. Do not leave appliances on standby mode. Use the 'on/off' function on the machine itself. A TV set that is switched on for 3 hours a day (the average time Europeans spend watching TV) and in standby mode during the remaining 21 hours uses about 40% of its energy in standby mode.

37. Placing your fridge and freezer next to the cooker or boiler consumes much more energy than if they were standing on their own. For example, if you put them in a hot cellar room where the room temperature is 30-35ºC, energy use is almost double and causes an extra 160kg of CO_2 emissions for fridges, and 320kg for freezers per year.

38. Use the washing machine or dishwasher only when you accumulate a cost-effective load to use it. If it is half full, then use the half-load or economy setting. There is also no need to set the temperatures high. Nowadays detergents are so efficient that they get your clothes and dishes clean at low temperatures.

39. Cover your pots while cooking; doing so can save a lot of the energy needed for preparing the dish. Even better are pressure cookers and steamers: they can save around 70% in power!

40. Install a low-flow showerhead. A shower takes up to four times less energy than a bath. To maximize energy saving, avoid power showers and use low-flow showerheads, which are cheap and provide the same comfort.

41. Use less hot water. It takes a lot of energy to heat water. You can use less hot water by installing a low flow showerhead

(350 pounds of carbon dioxide saved per year) and washing your clothes in cold or warm water (500 pounds saved per year) instead of hot.

42. Use a clothesline instead of a dryer whenever possible. You can save 700 pounds of carbon dioxide when you air-dry your clothes for 6 months out of the year.

43. Be sure you're recycling at home. You can save 2,400 pounds of carbon dioxide a year by recycling half of the waste your household generates.

44. Recycle your organic waste. Around 3% of the powerful greenhouse gas methane is released by decomposing bio-degradable waste. By recycling organic waste or composting it in a nearby corner, you can help eliminate this problem. Just make sure that you compost is properly constructed, so that it decomposes with sufficient oxygen, otherwise the compost will generate methane and foul emissions.

45. Buy intelligently. One bottle of 1.5 litres requires less energy and produces less waste than three bottles of 0.5 litre; and buy recycled paper products – it takes 70 to 90% less energy to make recycled paper and it prevents the loss of forests worldwide.

46. Choose products that come with little packaging and buy refills when you can. This way you will also cut down on waste production and energy use, and extend another help against global warming.

47. Reuse your shopping bag while shopping; it saves energy and waste to use a reusable bag instead of accepting a disposable one in each shop. Waste not only discharges CO_2

and methane into the atmosphere, it can also pollute the air, groundwater and soil.

48. Reduce waste. Most products we buy cause greenhouse gas emissions in one or another way, e.g. during their production and distribution. By taking your lunch in a reusable lunch box instead of a disposable one, you save the energy needed to produce new lunch boxes.

49. Plant a tree. A single tree will absorb one ton of carbon dioxide over its lifetime. Shade provided by trees can also reduce your air conditioning bill by 10 to 15%. Many websites have information on planting and provide trees you can plant as a service to members.

50. Buy fresh foods instead of frozen. Frozen food takes 10 times more energy to produce.

51. Seek out and support local farmers' markets. They reduce the amount of energy required to grow and transport the food to you by one fifth.

52. Buy organic foods as much as possible. Organic soils capture and store carbon dioxide at much higher levels than soils from conventional farms. If we grew all of our corn and soybeans organically, we could remove 580 billion pounds of carbon dioxide from the atmosphere!

53. Reduce the number of miles you drive by walking, biking, carpooling or taking mass transit facilities wherever possible. Avoiding just 10 miles of driving every week would eliminate about 500 pounds of carbon dioxide emissions a year! So, look for transit options in your area.

54. Start a carpool with your coworkers or classmates: Sharing a ride with someone just 2 days a week will reduce your carbon dioxide emissions by 1,590 pounds a year.

55. Do not leave an empty roof rack on your car. This can increase fuel consumption and CO_2 emissions by up to 10% due to wind resistance and the extra weight – removing it is a better idea.

56. Keep your car in good condition and finely tuned up. Regular maintenance helps improve fuel efficiency and reduces emissions. If only 1% of car owners properly maintain their cars, nearly a billion pounds of carbon dioxide would be kept out of the atmosphere. (At present, the total worldwide emission of CO_2 is hovering around 22 billion tons).

57. Drive carefully and do not waste fuel .You can reduce CO_2 emissions by readjusting your driving style. Choose proper gears, do not abuse the gas pedal, use the engine brake instead of the pedal brake when possible, and turn off your engine when your vehicle is motionless for more than one minute. By readjusting your driving style you can save money on both fuel and car maintenance.

58. Check your tyres weekly to make sure they're properly inflated. Proper tyre inflation can improve gas mileage by more than 3%. Since every gallon of gasoline saved keeps 20 pounds of carbon dioxide out of the atmosphere, every increase in fuel efficiency makes a difference.

59. Try telecommuting from home. Telecommuting can help drastically reduce the number of miles you drive every week.

60. Fly less. Air travel produces large amounts of emissions, so reducing how much you fly by even one or two trips a year can reduce your emissions significantly. You can also offset your air travel carbon emissions by investing in renewable energy projects.

61. Encourage your school or business to reduce emissions. You can extend your positive influence on global warming well beyond your home by actively encouraging others to take action. Just mutually deliberate half an hour a day!

62. Join 'Runs' and 'Virtual Marches'. Such Runs and marches are often sponsored by non-profit media houses or companies. These are often a non-political effort to bring people's concern about global warming together in one place. Add your voice to the hundreds of thousands of other responsible citizens participating is such events.

63. Forests should be protected and conserved by one and all. Forests store huge quantities of carbon, and so play a critical role in Carbon Sequestration. When forests are burned or cut down, their stored carbon is released into the atmosphere. Deforestation now accounts for about 20% of carbon dioxide emissions each year.

64. While investing your money, you should consider the impact that your investments and savings will have on global warming. One should not invest in companies that are heavily polluting and non-compliant of green norms.

Additional Green Tips for Cold Climes

1. Don't let heat escape from your house over a long period: when airing your house, open the windows for only a few minutes. If you leave a small opening all the day long, the energy needed to keep it warm inside during six cold months (10°C or less outside temperature) would result in almost 1 ton of CO_2 emissions.

2. Clean or replace filters on your furnace and air conditioner: cleaning a dirty air filter can save 350 pounds of carbon dioxide a year.

3. Wrap your water heater in an insulation blanket. You would save 1,000 pounds of carbon dioxide a year with this simple action. You can save another 550 pounds per year by setting the thermostat no higher than 50°C.

4. Install a programmable thermostat: such thermostats are popular in many countries. Programmable thermostats will automatically lower the heat or air conditioning at night and raise them again in the morning. They can save you $100 a year on your energy bill.

5. Encourage the shift/switch to renewable energy. Successfully combating global warming requires a national transition to renewable energy sources such as the sun, wind and biomass. These technologies are ready to be deployed more widely, but there are regulatory barriers impeding them. Wherever such barriers do exist citizens should endeavor to eliminate them.

6. Insulate and weatherize your home. Properly insulating your walls and ceilings can save 25% of your home heating

bill and 2,000 pounds of carbon dioxide a year. Caulking and weather-stripping can save another 1,700 pounds per year. Some websites pertaining to energy efficiency have more information on how to better insulate your home. Check them out in case of need.

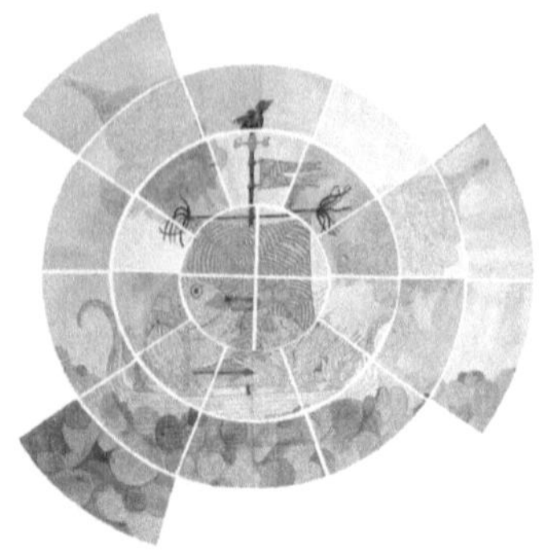

X
FUTURE & DISTANT FUTURE

Time present and time past
Are both perhaps present in time future,
And time future contained in time past.
T.S. Eliot in *Burnt Norton*

Future is not a fixed constant, but rather is a variable of several parameters. Just as future of an individual keeps on changing depending upon his deeds and *'Karma'*, in the same way the collective future of this planet would be shaped and modified by our collective efforts from time to time and by the collective consciousness of the masses dwelling on this earth.

Indeed, there appears to be a striking validity of the 'Karmic' theory when applied in the context of the deterministic results of man's actions on the environmental field. Our future, as I do have my own firm conviction, is largely spawned by our present day actions, choices as well as thought processes. When I conceived and began this mission of writing to foster an informed consent to heal our mother planet, this chapter was at the core of my working hypothesis. It indeed is at the core of the whole green movement, simply because it pertains to the impending tomorrow and the distant day-after of our beloved planet, and to the destiny of this highly advanced civilization of ours. Dozens of questions were to be answered. I marshaled all the questions and jotted all of them down. Here is a glimpse of the questionnaire.

Q1
- What does the planet look like a 100 year from now? (Brief mention of trees, vegetation, rivers, streams, glaciers and Oceans)

Q2
- What does the planet look like after 500 years from now?

Q3
- What does the planet look like after 5000 years from now? (Narration of trees, vegetation, rivers, ocens etc.)

Q4
- What does the planet look like after one millennium from here on?

Q5
- Describe the people of the next century and unfold their specific traits. Do they look 'Super Human'?

Q6
- Do you foresee increased or decreased population on the earth after 1000 years from now?

Q7
- Do you foresee increased or decreased population on the earth after 5000 years?

Q8
- Do you foresee increased or decreased population on the earth after 10,000 years?

Q9
- Can you see any human settlement /colony from earth onto another planet 500/1000 years later?

Q10
- Unfold the future temperature scenario in various parts of the planet.

Q11
- Describe the most common 'transportation system' 100/ 500/1000 years later, and the individual transportation modes most people would use.

Q12
- Can you see 'Immortal Humans' in near/distant future?

Do we have clear- cut answers to the above queries? Let me now retrace the path I followed in searching for an answer.

The climate on this planet has changed significantly over a couple of decades, chiefly due to increased human interference and the mess we have made in the planetary energy balance. Seen from a conscious users' perspective, the specific climate we are having as of now is not the same as the climate that we would have had without human actions. But talking of the future, with changes in human and natural impacts on environment, the probabilities of various outcomes would keep on changing – sometimes towards more extremes and sometimes towards less. We have a great deal of difficulty characterizing these changes because of insufficient observations; insufficient conceptualization of the possible extremes; inaccessibility of model results for extremes; and the basic statistical difficulty in attributing infrequent occurrences. Moreover, results of computer simulation models tend to reveal only an insufficient or sketchy picture.

In a quest to seek answer, I extensively trawled the net and established contacts with several hypnotherapist, psychoanalysts and experts of regression and *FLP (Future Life Progression)*. Although a relatively new and unusual concept, the idea of accepting the possibility of being guided into a possible future life by Hypnotic Progression is gaining interest the world over. Future Life Progression is the opposite of Past Life Regression. FLP is based on the idea that time is circular (spiral), not linear – meaning that past, present and future exist all at the same time like a Parallel Universe – reminiscent of TS Eliot's lines cited at the beginning of this chapter.

Future Life Progression techniques can be used to project an individual or group of individuals forward many years, say

100, 200, 500 years etc. from now. Time is not linear. Studies in Quantum Mechanics have shown this to be true. Yet, we are mostly unaware of this, as we are predominantly focused on the physical senses that follow the laws of three-dimensional reality where time is a linear dimension. However, we are multidimensional beings. Our mind's eye or 'non-physical senses' can access the higher dimensions of reality where time is non-linear. It is therefore possible to experience past, present, and future at the same instant and access the future possibilities and probabilities. We, in a collective sense, are eternal time travellers, and our present depends on both our past as well as our future. In our lives we can easily appreciate the fact that whatever we do at the present is in accordance with our plans for the future. The same is true metaphysically, from the soul's perspective. However, the soul's journey spans many lifetimes. Also, the future exists as a potential field of possibilities, which have not occurred as yet and from which we can choose the future that is desirable! Therefore, looking at future lifetimes helps us to choose desirable future lives and then make changes in our present choices to align ourselves and our world to the chosen future.

FLP could be the right technique to explore the future of a person and for that matter the collective future of our earth. Present day computer simulation models tend to impart erroneous results owing to a number of constraints that make it difficult to predict distant future of 5000, 10000, 50000 years from now. My search produced mixed results. A few of the experts were ready to perform FLP session by which we could get the desired answers and delve into the future of our earth. But most of the professionals hemmed and hawed in regard to the outcome, putting forward a few caveats simultaneously. In fact this technique, as of now, is not so advanced and needs much refinement. Eventually I abandoned the idea of consulting any future life expert until the technique is more refined and advanced.

There are some established FLP experts in the USA. Dr. Brain Weiss is one of them. He experimented with 'group progressions' and tried to explore the collective future of the earth 100, 500 and 1000 years hence. A couple of illustrative excerpts are reproduced here from his renowned book, *Same soul, many bodies*, that are quite startling and thought-provoking:

1. *In 100 years or even 200, the world will be pretty much the same.*

2. *After this period there will be a second dark age. We see a vastly diminished population and a decline in fertility rates because of the poison in the environment.*

Judging by our present callous attitude, the future looks starkly sinister. Can we change that? Yes! We can definitely change and defiantly challenge our future, which is being projected and talked about today! What is required is to firmly recalibrate our actions towards mother earth and discharge our responsibility. We should start making a few sacrifices gradually but consistently. We ought to make drastic cuts on our energy requirements and make genuine efforts to reduce /minimize our 'carbon footprints'. What we need is to be frugal in our energy habits. We can even compensate for our carbon footprints by planting more and more trees and buying 'carbon credits'. 'Environmental Awareness' is a gigantic issue and we should strive hard to be aware ourselves and make many others aware as well. That way we could put up stiff resistance to the twin monsters of 'climate change' and 'global warming', and by so doing change our so called future.

We should rise to the occasion and give a tough fight against all the demons of environment. It is not a fight that can be left to the governments alone. Birds, mammals, reptiles, amphibians, all do share a future in common with the future of mankind! We are common stakeholders in the present and future continuance of good life upon this planet. We have a collective destiny. We all need to be foot soldiers in the battle against the evils ruining the environment and strive hard to reclaim our tomorrow which does not look so rosy at the moment.

As you have cared to read this book, that in itself is ample proof that you are concerned with this planet. I have a strong conviction that readers would be actuated to chip in with their contribution to the cause of the environment after finishing this book, to spread the good word so as to awaken and stir into action thousands of other sleeping minds.

My paramount joy is in the belief that we the citizens of the world would act in unison in healing this blue planet – in the coming decades of storm and *drang* – in the raging battle of humanity against the impending environmental holocaust that was lurking for some time and is now looming large with each passing day!

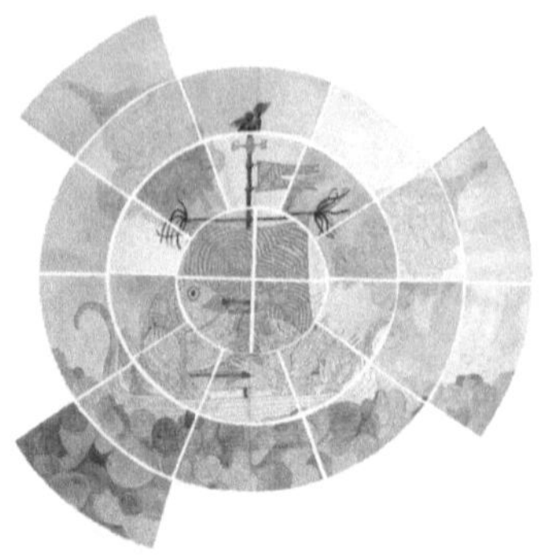

XI
An Environmental Glossary

A lay reader often comes across some technical terms with which he is vaguely familiar, but still its true and exact connotations elude him. Such terms in our present environmental context have been carefully collated and further elucidated here for ready reference. Some new-fangled jargons and acronyms (like EBD, GBD, DALY and YLD) have also been incorporated for better understanding of scientific and environmental studies and reports.

Some words apparently seem identical but differ in meaning e.g. 'sewer' and 'sewerage'; 'tree cover' , 'forest area' and 'open forest'; 'El Niño' and 'La Nina'; 'Biome' and 'Biota'; 'coral reefs' and 'corals'; 'Air Pollution Index' and 'Air Quality Index'. Such words have also been given their due place and explanation in the following Glossary of Terms.

Abiotic: Abiotic means non-biological or not living. The word is generally used in environmental terminology in conjunction with words like components and factors. Abiotic components could mean air, water, soil etc.

Abyssal Zone: The cold and dark water zone of the ocean at a depth below the euphotic zone, where sufficient sunlight is not available. No photosynthesis can take place at this level and marine life is sparsely found in this zone.

Aerosols: collection of airborne solid or liquid particles, with a typical size between 0.01 and 10 micrometer (a millionth of a metre) that resides in the atmosphere for at least several hours. Aerosols may be of either natural or anthropogenic origin. Aerosols may Influence climate in several ways: directly through scattering and absorbing radiation, and indirectly through acting as cloud condensation nuclei or modifying the optical properties and lifetime of clouds.

Afforestation: Planting of new forests on lands that historically have not contained forests for at least half a century.

Air pollutants: Substances that pollute the air, the bulk of which are produced by human activity. Main pollutants are fly-ash, particulate matters, sulphur dioxide, carbon monoxide, hydrocarbons, lead and cadmium.

Air pollution Index (API): Is a generalized way to describe the ambient air quality derived from several sets of air pollution data.

Albedo: A measure of reflectivity of the earth. The fraction of solar radiation reflected by a surface or object, often expressed as a percentage. Snow-covered surfaces have a high Albedo, the surface Albedo of soils ranges from high to low, and vegetation-covered surfaces and oceans have a low Albedo. The Earth's planetary Albedo varies mainly through varying cloudiness, snow, ice, leaf area, and land cover changes.

AQI (air quantity index): Air quality indices (AQI) are numbers used by government agencies to characterize the quality of the air at a given location. As the AQI increases, an increasingly large percentage of the population is likely to experience increasingly severe and adverse health effects. Main pollutants considered could include PM, O_3, SO_2, NOx and CO.

Benthos: The plants and animals that inhabit the bottom of a water body.

Biodegradable: Capable of being broken down by bacteria into basic elements.

Biodiversity: The total diversity of all organisms and ecosystems at various spatial scales (from genes to entire biomes).

Biomass: The total mass of living organisms in a given area or volume; recently dead plant material is often included as dead biomass. The quantity of biomass is expressed as a dry weight or as the energy, carbon, or nitrogen content.

Biome: A major and distinct regional element of the biosphere, typically consisting of several ecosystems (e.g., forests, rivers, ponds, swamps within a region of similar climate). Biomes are characterized by typical communities of plants and animals.

Biota: The animal and plant life found within an environment of geographical region.

Biotic: Pertaining to life.

Biotope: a region of relatively uniform environmental condition occupied by a given plant community and its associated animal community.

Carbon capture & storage (CCS): A process consisting of separation of carbon dioxide from industrial and energy-related sources, transport to a storage location, and long-term isolation from the atmosphere.

Carbon sequestration: The uptake of carbon containing substances, or simply 'the process of removing carbon from the atmosphere and depositing it in a reservoir'.

Catadromous: Diadromous migrating fishes which spend most of their lives in fresh water and migrate to the sea to breed.

Climate change: Climate change refers to a change in the state of the climate that can be identified by changes in the mean and/or the variability of its properties and that persists for an extended period, typically decades or longer. Climate change may be due to natural internal processes or external forcing, or to persistent anthropogenic changes in the composition of the atmosphere or to changed land use.

Coral reefs: Rock-like limestone structures built by corals along ocean coasts (fringing reefs) or on top of shallow, submerged banks or shelves (barrier reefs, atolls), most conspicuous in tropical and subtropical oceans.

Coral: The term coral has several meanings, but is usually the common name for the Order Scleractinia, all members of which have hard limestone skeletons, and which are divided into reef-building and non-reef-building, or cold- and warm-water corals.

DALY: Disability adjusted life years.

Desertification: Land degradation in arid, semi-arid and dry sub-humid areas resulting from various factors, including climatic variations and human activities. Further, the United Nations Convention to Combat Desertification (UNCCD) defines land degradation as a reduction or loss in arid, semi-arid, and dry sub-humid areas of the biological or economic productivity and complexity of rain-fed cropland, irrigated cropland, or range, pasture, forest and woodlands resulting from land uses or from a process or combination of processes, including those arising from human Activities and habitation patterns, such as (i) soil erosion caused by wind and/or water; (ii) deterioration of the physical, chemical, and biological or economic properties of soil; and (iii) long-term loss of natural vegetation.

EBD: Environmental burden of disease.

Ecological Pyramid: A grouping of the successively diminishing trophic levels of an ecosystem.

Ecology: The study of the inter-relations of plants and animals with their environment, including the influences of other plants and animals. This word has its origin in the Greek word *'oikos'* meaning "house". Ecology is literally the study of 'homes' of 'environment', the study and function of nature and the inter-relationships between organisms and their environment.

Ecosystem: The word 'ecosystem' is derived from two words 'ecology' and 'system'. The 'eco' part of the word implies environment while the 'system' part of the word implies an interacting interdependent complex. Ecosystem is a system of living organisms interacting with each other and their physical environment. The boundaries of what could be called an ecosystem are somewhat arbitrary, depending on the focus of interest or study. Thus, the extent of an ecosystem may range from very small spatial scales to, ultimately, the entire Earth.

Ecotone: A transitional zone between two communities containing the characteristic species of each. A zone of transition, in which the conditions of each of the adjacent communities become more adverse and there is often an intermingling of species without loss of fertility.

Edaphic: Of or pertaining to soil, especially with regard to its influence on plants and animals.

El Nino Southern Oscillation (ENSO): The term El Nino was initially used to describe a warm-water current that periodically flows along the coast of Ecuador and Peru, disrupting the local fishery. It has since become identified with a basin-wide warming of the tropical Pacific east of the dateline. This oceanic event is associated with a fluctuation of a global-scale tropical and subtropical surface pressure pattern called the Southern Oscillation. This coupled atmosphere-ocean Phenomenon, with preferred time scales of two to about seven years, is collectively known as El Nino-Southern Oscillation, or ENSO. It is often measured by the surface pressure anomaly difference between Darwin and Tahiti and the sea surface temperatures in the central and eastern equatorial Pacific. During an ENSO event, the prevailing trade winds weaken, reducing upwelling and altering ocean currents such that the sea surface temperatures warm up, further weakening the trade

Endangered species: An endangered species is an organism in danger of disappearing from the face of the earth if its situation is not improved. When its race has not been seen in the wild for over fifty years, we say that it is extinct. Those species that may soon become endangered are called threatened species. Rare animals are species with small populations that may also be at risk.

END: Environmental noise directives.

Endemic Disease: Disease that constantly recurs in a particular locality.

Eutrophication: The process by which a body of water becomes rich in dissolved nutrients, either naturally or by pollution, with a seasonal deficiency in dissolved oxygen.

Exclusive Species: A species confined completely or almost completely to one community.

Facultative: Having the power to live either with or without oxygen.

Fecal Coliform Bacteria: Bacteria that inhabit the intestines of human and animals, including Escherichia coli.

Fauna: The animals of a particular region or period of time.

Flora: The plant life of a geological period or of a region, corresponding term for animal kingdom is fauna.

Fog: Is a collection of tiny water droplets that float in tine air; it is similar to clouds except that clouds do not touch the earth's surface as fog does.

Food security: A situation that exists when people have secure access to sufficient amounts of safe and nutritious food for normal growth, development and an active and healthy life. Food insecurity may be caused by the unavailability of food, insufficient purchasing power, inappropriate distribution, or inadequate use of food at the household level.

Forest Area: The term 'forest area' (or recorded forest area) generally refers to all the geographical areas recorded as forest in government records and are comprised of RF (Reserved Forests) and PF (Protected Forests).

Forest Cover: The term 'forest Cover' connotes presence of trees over any land. It can be further classified as; VDF (Very Dense Forest), MDF (Moderately Dense Forest) and OF (Open Forest).

Fossil: Remains or traces of an organism that have been preserved in the earth's crust by natural processes.

Freon: A trade name for various chlorine and fluorine containing carbon compounds (chlorofluorocarbons) used as a working fluid in refrigerators and in certain air conditioners.

Fungi: Tiny aerobic, heterotrophic, protests containing no chlorophyll. They can tolerate drier and more acid conditions than most bacteria and also are often many celled. They live in the earth, fresh water and seawater. Often they grow so large that they can be seen with the naked eye (mushrooms).

GBD: Global burden of disease.

Glacial Drift: The sediment deposited directly by glaciers or indirectly in melted water streams, lakes or the sea.

Glacial lake: A lake formed by glacier melt water, located either at the front of a glacier (known as a pro glacial lake), on the surface of a glacier (supra glacial lake), within the glacier (en glacial lake) or at the glacier bed (sub glacial lake).

Glacier: A body of ice originating on land by the compaction and recrystallization of snow, and showing evidence of present or past movement. Glaciers occur where winter snowfall exceeds summer melting. A glacier is a mass of land ice, which flows downhill under gravity (through internal deformation and/or sliding at the base) and is constrained by internal stress and friction at the base and sides. A glacier is maintained by accumulation of snow at high altitudes, balanced by melting at low altitudes or discharge into the sea.

Global warming: Global warming refers to the gradual increase, observed or projected, in global average surface temperature, as one of the consequences of discernible increase in anthropogenic emissions.

Grassland: Herbaceous vegetation dominated by grasses. Well over half of the British Isles is grassland.

Greenhouse effect: Greenhouse gases effectively absorb thermal infrared radiation, emitted by the Earth's surface, by the atmosphere itself due to the same gases, and by clouds. Atmospheric radiation is emitted to all sides, including downward to the Earth's surface. Thus greenhouse gases trap heat within the surface-troposphere system. This is called the greenhouse effect. Thermal infrared radiation in the troposphere is strongly coupled to the temperature of the atmosphere at the altitude at which it is emitted. In the troposphere, the temperature generally decreases with height. Effectively, infrared radiation emitted to space originates from an altitude with a temperature of, on an average, –19°C, in balance with the net incoming solar radiation, whereas the Earth's surface is kept at a much higher temperature of, on an average, +14°C. An increase in the concentration of greenhouse gases leads to an increased infrared opacity of the atmosphere, and therefore to an effective radiation into space from a higher altitude at a lower temperature. This causes a radioactive forcing that leads to an enhancement of the greenhouse effect, the so-called enhanced greenhouse effect.

Herbicide: Any chemical substance used to destroy plants.

Herbivore: An organism which obtains energy from the consumption of plants.

Hibernation: Dormancy of animals in winter, during which metabolic rate is much reduced and the body temperature drops to that of the surroundings.

Hydrological cycle: The cycle in which water evaporates from the oceans and the land surface, is carried over the Earth in atmospheric circulation as water vapor, condensates to form clouds, precipitates again as rain or snow, is intercepted by trees and vegetation, provides runoff on the land surface, infiltrates into soils, recharges groundwater, discharges into streams and, ultimately, flows out into the oceans, from which it will eventually evaporate again. The various systems involved in the hydrological cycle are usually referred to as hydrological systems.

Hydroponics: The growing of plants without soil by suspending them with their roots immersed in water enriched with essential nutrients or by rooting them in an inert material and supplying them with a nutrient solution.

Hydrosphere: The total water on earth, including the oceans, the inland lakes, swamps, rivers, and creeks; ground water or water that has soaked into the ground and occupies openings in the lithosphere; water vapor in the atmosphere water enclosed in sediments; and masses of continental ice like those of Antarctica and Greenland.

ICOLD: The International Commission of Large Dams, a body that is particularly interested in dam safety.

Impoundment: A body of water confined by a dam flood gate or other barrier.

Index Species: An organism, species, or community that shows the presence of certain environmental conditions.

Jurassic: Refers to the middle period of Mesozoic Era, 190 to 205 million years ago lasting about 60 million years.

Kelp: brown seaweed. This alga, sometimes used as a biological index of pollution, grows near the low- water mark.

La Nina: La Nina is the cold counterpart of El Nino, meaning sea surface temperatures in the tropical Pacific drop below normal. La Ninas form after some, but not all, El Ninos, and therefore occur less frequently than El Nino. Etymologically it means 'the little girl'.

Lapse rate: The rate of change of an atmospheric variable, usually temperature, with height. The lapse rate is considered positive when the variable decreases with height.

Lentic water: Standing water, generally meaning water in lakes, ponds, marshes, etc.

Littoral: Relating to or taking place on or near the shore.

Lotic: Concerned with flowing water.

Macronutrients: Mineral nutrients utilized by organisms in large quantities, carbon, hydrogen, oxygen, phosphorus, sulphur, potassium and calcium.

Mangroves: Plant communities and trees that inhabit tidal swamps, muddy silt and sand banks at the mouths of rivers and other low lying areas which are protected from strong waves and currents.

Marsh: A term often restricted to water logged ground with a largely mineral basis, in contrast to the peat of bog and fen. It can be destroyed by dredging and filling.

Mass balance [of glaciers, ice caps or ice sheets]: The balance between the mass input to an ice body due to accumulation, and the mass loss caused by ablation, iceberg calving etc.

Macroclimate: A local climate effect, over an area several kilometers wide and one or two hundred metres in height, where climate differs from the regional climate.

Mesosphere: the atmospheric zone or shell located above the stratopause at an altitude of around. 55 to 80 km and characterized by a decrease in temperature with increasing altitude

Metabolism: The sum of the total of the physical and chemical processes by which an organism converts complex compounds into simpler compounds.

Microbe: A tiny plant or animal. Some microbes that cause disease are found in sewage.

Mutation: A sudden change in the chromosomes of a cell. Most mutations are changes in the genetic materials (DNA).

Mutualism: Type of symbiosis in which neither partner is essential for the well-being or life of the other. Any association between organisms of different species including parasitism, Algal Fungi relationship is an example of mutualism.

National Park: A relatively large piece of land set aside for its features of predominantly unspoiled natural landscape, flora, fauna permanently dedicated for public enjoyment and protection from all interference so that natural attributes are preserved e.g. Yellowstone National Park , USA, Kaziranga National Park, Assam India.

North Atlantic Oscillation (NAO): The North Atlantic Oscillation consists of opposing variations of barometric pressure near Iceland and near the Azores. It therefore corresponds to fluctuations in the strength of the main westerly winds across the Atlantic into Europe, and thus to fluctuations in the embedded cyclones with their associated frontal systems.

Noy: A unit of perceived noisiness equal to the perceived noisiness of random noise occupying the frequency band 910-1090 hertz at a sound pressure level of 40 decibels above 0.0002 microbar; a sound that is n times as noisy as this sound has a perceived noisiness of n noys, under the assumption that the perceived noisiness of a sound increases with physical intensity at the same rate as the loudness.

Oil Slick: Oil, discharged naturally or by accident, floating on the surface of water as discrete mass carried by wind currents/tides.

Oil Spills: Accidental or deliberate, dumping of oil or other petroleum products onto the ocean and its coastal waters, bays and harbors or on to land or into rivers or lakes.

Open Cast Mining: The working of a coal seams near their out crops, i.e. near the point where coal appears at the surface.

Pandemic: Widespread throughout an area.

Peatland: Typically a wetland such as a mire slowly accumulating peat.

Pelagic: Relating to communities of marine organisms which belong to open sea, living free from direct dependence on bottom or shore i.e. belonging to that part of the ocean which is deeper than the littoral zone, although shallower than the abyssal zone.

Permafrost: Ground (soil or rock and included ice and organic material) that remains at or below 0°C for at least two consecutive years.

Pest: Any plant or animal that, in its location, is an economic, aesthetic, physical, or biological threat or annoyance to humans or their possessions. Insects and weeds are the two largest groups of pests. Pests can be controlled by physical, chemical, mechanical or genetic methods.

Phenology: The study of the timing of recurring natural phenomena with particular reference to climatological observations.

Photochemical Smog: A smog caused by the effect of sunlight on motor vehicle exhaust gases. The resulting light haze is unpleasant to breathe and cause smarting of the eyes, coughing and soreness of chest. Severe Photochemical Smogs in Los Angles are caused by stable inversions protected by nearby hills.

Photorespiration: Respiration activated by light, characteristic of certain plants (e.g. wheat, sugar beet) but not of others (e.g. maize).

Phytoplankton: The primary basis of animal life in the Sea consisting of passively floating minute plants chiefly diatoms (brownish algae). Many ocean fish feed on phytoplankton which is also the basic food of zooplankton.

PPM: Parts per million, meaning the number of parts of a given pollution in a million parts of air.

PPT: Parts per trillion.

Reclaim: Raw material obtained by reclamation.

Reclamation of Water: The treatment of sewage effluent or other waste so that it can be re-used directly, not necessarily for drinking. Two of the best known examples are at Lake Tahoe, California, and Windhoek, Namibia. In another semi desert country, Israel, sewage effluent is regularly used for irrigation and other purpose. In Europe artificial recharge of ground water with treated effluent is a form of reclamation, since the ground water is later pumped out as raw water. Often the most expensive pollution to be removed from sewage is chloride, because desalination is needed. Reclamation may involve removal, of nitrogen, phosphorus, chlorides and trace organics, followed by conventional treatment for raw water.

Recycling: The return of discarded or waste materials to the production system for utilization in the manufacture of goods, with a view to promoting the conservation as far as practicable of non-renewable and scarce resources. Recycling goes beyond the re-use of a product and involves the return of salvaged materials, such as paper or metals or broken glass, to an early stage of the manufacturing process.

Recycling of Solid Waste: While 're-use' is applied more to the refilling of a bottle or other container, 'recycling' is usually applied to the material of which the container is made. Direct recycling is the reuse of the broken bottle to make similar bottles. Indirect recycling is its reuse for a different purpose usually making something of a lower quality. Pyrolysis and energy recovery are also sometimes regarded as examples of recycling.

Regression: Destruction of vegetation (e.g. by fire, grazing etc.) and subsequent colonization at a lower level (e.g. replacement of forests by grasses following the destruction of trees).

Riparian: Living or situated on the bank of a water course, such as a river of stream; hence the terms 'riparian owner' and 'riparian interests'. It is also defined as 'Relating to or living or located on the bank of a natural watercourse (such as a river) or sometimes of a lake or a tidewater'.

River Basin: The land area drained by a river and its tributaries.

Run-off: That part of precipitation that does not evaporate and is not transpired, but flows over the ground surface and returns to bodies of water.

Salmonella: Enteric bacteria may cause enteric fever, gastroenteritis; the diseases are spread by food or water that has been contaminated by the feces of an infected person.

Saltwater intrusion: Displacement of fresh surface water or groundwater by the advance of saltwater due to its greater density. This usually occurs in coastal and estuarine areas due to reducing land based influence (e.g. either from reduced runoff and associated groundwater recharge, or from excessive water withdrawals from aquifers) or increasing marine influence (e.g. relative sea-level rise).

Saprophyte: Organism (Plant of protista) which obtains food in solution from the dead or decaying bodies of other organisms. Many fungi, bacteria protozoa are saprophyte. Saprophytes break down organic matter into simple substances such as Co2 and nitrates.

Scrub: Scrub is a degraded forest land with canopy density less than 10%. Generally, it is not considered a part of forest.

Sea Lettuce: The sea lettuces comprise the genus ' Ulva', a group of edible green algae that is widely distributed along the coasts of the world's oceans. It gives off hydrogen sulphide when it rots.

Sea surface temperature (SST): The sea surface temperature is the subsurface bulk temperature in the top few metres of the ocean, measured by ships, buoys and drifters. From ships, measurements of water samples in buckets were mostly switched in the 1940s to samples from engine intake water. Satellite measurements of skin temperature (uppermost layer; a fraction of a millimeter thick) in the infrared or the top centimeter or so in the microwave are also used, but must be adjusted to be compatible with the bulk temperature.

Sequestration: Carbon storage in terrestrial or marine reservoirs. Biological Sequestration includes direct removal of CO_2 from the atmosphere through land-use change, afforestation, reforestation, carbon storage in landfills and practices that enhance soil carbon in agriculture.

Sewer: A conduit, culvert or buried pipe that leads away domestic and other waste waters for treatment and disposal.

Sewerage: A physical arrangement of sewer pipes, manholes and plants (oxidation plant, activated sludge plant) for the collection, removal, treatment and disposal of liquid waste. Simply put, a network of sewers.

Silviculture: The management of forest land for timber. Cultivation, development and care of forests.

Sink: Any process, activity or mechanism which removes a greenhouse gas, an aerosol or a precursor of a greenhouse gas or aerosol from the atmosphere.

Smog: Pollutant. It is a combination of smoke and fog. Smog is frequently laden with noxious gases and other irritants produced in the smoke of industrial plants and motor vehicles. Smog causes smarting eyes, fits of coughing and even death in certain instances.

Soil Acidity: As the clay humus particles lose their mineral nutrients, the soil becomes less fertile when these mineral are replaced, however with hydrogen ions the soil becomes more acidic.

Soil conservation: The devising and implementing of systems of land use and management so that there is no loss of stability productivity or usefulness of the soil in relation to the selected purpose.

Soil Erosion: The loss of soil as a result of natural and human activities. Natural erosion is the starting point of pedogensis (Creation of soil) which is indispensable to sustain human life. Erosion results in poor soil deforestation, poor agricultural practices with far reading consequences.

Species: A group whose members have a close mutual resemblance, having a common origin and a continuous breeding system, the smallest unit of classification commonly used.

Specific mass balance: Net mass loss or gain over a hydrological cycle at a point on the surface of a glacier. Total mass balance (of the glacier): the specific mass balance spatially integrated over the entire glacier area; the total mass a glacier gains or losses over a hydrological cycle. Mean specific mass balance: the total mass balance per unit area of the glacier. If surface is specified (specific surface mass balance, etc.) then ice-flow contributions are not considered; otherwise, mass balance includes contributions from ice flow and iceberg calving. The specific surface mass balance is positive in the accumulation area and negative in the ablation area.

Stratification: In ecological terminology, a vertical layering of organisms or environmental conditions within a biotic community, considered as one of the integral properties of nearly every natural community.

Stratosphere: The upper layer of the atmosphere lying above troposphere (above 11 km altitude) in which temperature remains constant up to a height of about 50 Km.

Sullage: Waste water from sinks, baths, wash basins etc. Its volume may form two thirds of domestic sewage.

Swamp: An area which is saturated with water for much of the time but in which the soil surface is not deeply submerged.

Taxonomy: The science of classification usually restricted to mean the classification of plants and animals. The word is derived from the Greek *taxes,* meaning 'arrangement' and *nonos,* meaning 'law'.

Temperature Inversion: A layer in which temperature increases with altitude. The principal characteristic of an inversion is its marked static stability, so that very little turbulent exchange can occur with it.

Thermal Pollution: Discharge of hot water to receiving water. It may be undesirable because warming the water reduces its air saturation value and its capacity to dissolve oxygen. At sufficiently highly temperatures, fish may die.

Thermo cline: The region in the world's ocean, typically at a depth of 1 km, where temperature decreases rapidly with depth and which marks the boundary between the surface and the ocean. The layer of water in a lake which lies between the equlimnion and the hypolimnion; within the Thermo cline the temperature decreases rapidly with increasing depth (usually by more than 10^0 C for each metre).

Thermophile: Any bacterium that thrives at temperatures above 400^0 C.

Threshold of Hearing: The pressure at which a sound source, in the absence of background noise, first becomes audible. In the average young adult with normal hearing, it has been found to be a sound pressure of approximately 0.00002 N/m2. (i.e., a sound of frequency 20 Hz).

Toxic Substance: A substance that acts like a poison. Toxic substances cause adverse environmental effects ranging from mild temporary dysfunction organisms and ecosystem to acute symptoms, disorders, or death. Some cause cancer.

Tree Cover: Tree cover in India is defined as tree patches less than one hectare with canopy density above 10%.

Trophic Level: The transfer of Food energy from the source in plants through a series of organisms with repeated stages of eating and being eaten is known as the food chain. In complex material communities organisms, whose food is obtained from plants by the same numbers of steps are said to belong to the same tropic level.

Tropophyte: A plant which lives under moist condition for part of the year and under dry conditions for the rest of the time (e.g. a deciduous tree, which sheds its leaves for the dry season or for the winter when water may not be available because it is frozen).

Troposphere: The lower layer of the atmosphere extending up to about 11 Kms above the surface of the Earth and in which temperature normally falls with increasing height.

Ultra Violet (UV) Radiation: Invisible rays that are part of the energy that comes from the sun. Ultraviolet radiation can burn the skin and cause skin cancer. Ultraviolet radiation is made up of three types of rays -- ultraviolet A, ultraviolet B, and ultraviolet C. Although ultraviolet C is the most dangerous type of ultraviolet light in terms of its potential to harm life on earth, it cannot penetrate earth's protective ozone layer. Therefore, it poses no threat to human, animal or plant life on earth. UV radiation affects photographic films and plates. They are harmful to the skin of some animals as well as humans. UV is a non-ionizing radiation with less penetrative power in a column of water than visible light, but within cells it can cause chromosome breaks. In man, the radiation is absorbed by melanin in the skin, causing the melanin to darken but excessive exposure in fair skinned people can cause non melanoma skin cancers.

UNEP: United National Environment Programme.

Urbanization: A process leading to a societal change characterized by the movement of people from rural to urban areas. The conversion of land from a natural state or managed natural state (such as agriculture) to cities; a process driven by net rural-to-urban migration through which an increasing percentage of the population in any nation or region come to live in settlements that are defined as urban centres.

Vapor: A substance which through present in the gaseous phase, generally exists as a liquid or solid at room temperature.

Variable: Any quality which can have more than one value; a quantitative characteristic of an individual.

Vector: An organism, often on insect, that carries disease. An organism, such as an insect, that transmits a pathogen from one host to another.

Virus: One of the disease Producing microbes, even smaller than bacteria. They can be from 10 to 250 nanons long (0.01 to 25m) and can be seen only under an electron microscope.

Water Disease: Disease such as cholera, typhoid fever, dysentery, gastroenteritis, hepatitis and biharziasis, which are commonly transmitted through contaminated water supplies.

Water stress: A country is water stressed if the available freshwater supply relative to water withdrawals acts as an important constraint on development. In global-scale assessments, basins with water stress are often defined as having a per capital water availability below 1,000 m^3/yr (based on long-term average runoff). Withdrawals exceeding 20% of renewable water supply have also been used as an indicator of water stress.

Water vapor : The basic atmospheric ingredient from which come such forms of precipitation as rain, snow, hail, and select. These all originate when water vapor is condensed by the cooling process that normally occurs by upward flowing currents of air.

Water-use efficiency: Carbon gain in photosynthesis per unit water lost in evapo-transpiration. It can be expressed on a short-term basis as the ratio of photosynthetic carbon gain per unit transpiration water loss, or on a seasonal basis as the ratio of net primary production/ agricultural yield to the water available.

Wave cloud: A cloud situated in the crest of a mountain or ice wave, and as a consequence almost stationary, with condensation of cloud at the upwind edge and evaporation in the descending air at the downwind edge. Wave clouds usually have a characteristically smooth outline (whale back cloud).

Weather: The condition of the atmosphere at a certain time or over a certain short period as described by various meteorological phenomena such as atmospheric pressure, temperature, humidity rainfall cloudiness and wind speed and direction.

Wetland: An area covered permanently, occasionally, or periodically by fresh or salt water up to a depth of 6 m (e.g. flooded pasture land, marshland, inland lakes, river and their estuaries, intertidal mud flats). A transitional, regularly waterlogged area of poorly drained soils, often between an aquatic and a terrestrial ecosystem, fed from rain, surface water or groundwater. Wetlands are characterized by a prevalence of vegetation adapted for life in saturated soil conditions.

Wild Life : A collective term embracing several thousand different species of mammals, birds and reptiles No two species respond in precisely the same manner and degree to the influences of the environment the differences in responses aspects of competition, selection and evolution.

Wind Erosion: The removal of material from the land or from building by the action of the wind.

Woodland: Vegetation dominated by trees which form a distinct sometimes open, canopy.

World Environment Day: Celebrated on the 5th day of June each year. It was proclaimed by the United Nations Conference on the Human Environments in 1972 to mark the beginning of the First Conference as means of focusing attention on world Environment Problems.

Xenomorphic: Applied to plants that possess the pronounced ability to restrict water loss during adverse conditions. Plants displaying this characteristic are described as xerophytes.

YLD: Years lost due to disability.

Zooplanktons: These are Planktons that are not photosynthetic. Zooplanktons mostly graze upon phytoplankton and can be one of the main constraining factors to the numbers of the latter.

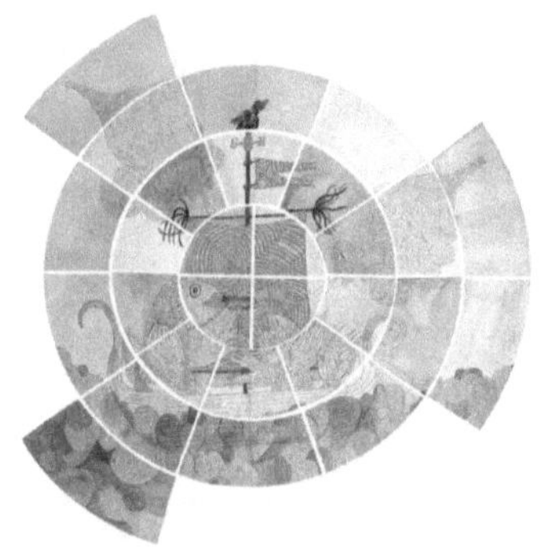

XII
QUOTABLE ENVIRONMENTAL QUOTES

Here is a broad selection of environmental quotes that have a fairly wide currency. They can be seen on green community pages, brochures depicting conservation efforts, international green sites, and non-profit NGO leaflets. They also serve as favourites on the profiles of nature lovers, conservationists, environmentalists et al. Due diligence has been exercised while selecting the quotes and only those have been included which are often heard, read and shared.

❖ *Now I truly believe that we in this generation must come to terms with nature, and I think we're challenged, as mankind has never been challenged before, to prove our maturity and our mastery, not of nature but of ourselves.* Rachel Carson

❖ *We are monumentally distracted by a pervasive technological culture that appears to have a life of its own, one that insists on our full attention, continually seducing us and pulling us away from the opportunity to experience directly the true meaning of our own lives.* Al Gore

❖ *We do not inherit the earth from our ancestors; we borrow it from our children.* Native American Proverb

❖ *What's the use of a fine house if you haven't got a tolerable planet to put it on?* Henry David Thoreau

❖ *Perhaps reluctantly we come to acknowledge that there are also scars which mark the surface of our Earth – erosion, deforestation, the squandering of the world's mineral and ocean resources in order to fuel an insatiable consumption.* Pope Benedict

❖ *A nation that destroys its soils destroys itself. Forests are the lungs of our land, purifying the air and giving fresh strength to our people.* Franklin Delano Roosevelt

❖ *Nature has been for me, as long as I remember, a source of solace, inspiration, adventure, and delight; a home, a teacher, a companion.* Lorraine Anderson

❖ *The ultimate test of man's conscience may be his willingness to sacrifice something today for future generations whose words of thanks will not be heard.* Gaylord Nelson

❖ *Never doubt that a small group of thoughtfully committed citizens can change the world. Indeed, it's the only thing that ever has.* Margaret Mead

❖ *Let every individual and institution now think and act as a responsible trustee of Earth, seeking choices in ecology, economics and ethics that will provide a sustainable future, eliminate pollution, poverty and violence, awaken the wonder of life and foster peaceful progress in the human adventure.* John McConnell

❖ *Only when the last tree has been cut down,*
only when the last river has been poisoned,
only when the last fish has been caught,
only then will you find that money cannot be eaten.
Cree Indian Prophecy

❖ *The more clearly we can focus our attention on the wonders and realities of the universe about us, the less taste we shall have for destruction.* Rachel Carson

❖ *I have come to terms with the future. From this day onward I will walk easy on the earth. Plant trees. Kill no living things. Live in harmony with all creatures. I will restore the earth where I am. Use no more of its resources than I need. And listen; listen to what it is telling me.* MJ Slim Hooey

❖ *To waste, to destroy, our natural resources, to skin and exhaust the land instead of using it so as to increase its usefulness, will result in undermining in the days of our children the very prosperity which we ought by right to hand down to them.* Theodore Roosevelt

❖ *Let us permit 'Nature' a bit to take her own way....she better understands her own affairs than we do!* [Translation] Michel de Montaigne

❖ *Earth provides enough to satisfy every man's need, but not every man's greed.* Mahatma Gandhi

❖ *When you defile the pleasant streams and the wild bird's abiding place, you massacre a million dreams and cast your spittle in God's face.* John Drinkwater

❖ *Would I a house for happiness erect, Nature alone should be my architect, she'd build it more convenient than great, And doubtless in the country choose her seat.* Horace, 20 BC

❖ *Most of the luxuries and many of the so called comforts of life are not only not indispensable, but positive hindrances to the elevation of mankind. Henry* David Thoreau

❖ *We won't have a society if we destroy the environment.* Margaret Mead

❖ *The amount of sunshine energy that hits the surface of the Earth every minute is greater than the total amount of energy that the world's human population consumes in a year!* Home Power Magazine

❖ *After one look at this planet any visitor from outer space would say 'I want to see the manager'.* William S. Burroughs

❖ *In our every deliberation, we must consider the impact of our decisions on the next seven generations.* Great Law of the Iroquois Confederacy

❖ *In the end, our society will be defined not only by what we create, but by what we refuse to destroy.* John C. Sawhill

❖ *Unless someone like you cares a whole awful lot, Nothing is going to get better, it's not.* The Lorax, *by* Dr. Suess

❖ *I feel most emphatically that we should not turn into shingles a tree which was old when the first Egyptian conqueror penetrated to the valley of the Euphrates. Theodore Roosevelt*

❖ *I'd put my money on the sun and solar energy. What a source of power! I hope we don't have to wait till oil and coal run out before we tackle that.* Thomas Edison

❖ *Today's mighty oak is just yesterday's nut that held its ground.* Anon.

❖ *Great spirits have always been met with violent opposition from mediocre minds.* Albert Einstein

❖ *Not to have known, as most men have not, either the mountains or the desert, is not to have known oneself.* Joseph Wood Krutch

❖ *Now I see the secret of the making of the best persons; it is to grow in the open air and eat and sleep with the Earth.* Walt Whitman

❖ *I do not believe in the collective wisdom of individual ignorance.* Thomas Carlyle

❖ *He who is in harmony with Nature hits the mark without effort and apprehends the truth without thinking.* Confucius

❖ *The causes that lie behind much sickness and human suffering are short - sightedness and greed. Health for all can be achieved only through the organized demand by people for greater equality in terms of land, water, services, and basic rights. More power to the people!* Dr. David Werner

❖ *No one person has to do it all but if each one of us follows our heart and our own inclinations we will find the small things that we can do, and together we will come up with enough to create a sustainable future and a healthy environment.* John Denver

❖ *A person is either the effect of his environment or is able to have an effect upon his* environment. L Ron Hubbard

❖ *It isn't pollution that's harming the environment. It's the impurities in our air and water that are doing it.* George W Bush

❖ *It's incredible to see labor unions and environmentalists getting together to stop the corporate mentality that destroys both jobs and the environment.* Bonnie Raitt

❖ *Lack of awareness of the basic unity of organism and environment is a serious and dangerous hallucination.* Alan Wilson Watts

❖ *The differences between a competent person and an incompetent person are demonstrated in his environment (surroundings).* L Ron Hubbard

❖ *Man must cease attributing his problems to his environment, and learn again to exercise his will – his personal responsibility.* Albert Schweitzer

❖ *Man's characteristic privilege is that the bond he accepts is not physical but moral; that is, social. He is governed not by a material environment brutally imposed on him, but by a conscience superior to his own.* Emile Durkheim

❖ *Perhaps catastrophe is the natural human environment, and even though we spend a good deal of energy trying to get away from it, we are programmed for survival amid catastrophe.* Germaine Greer

❖ *The most important issue of the 21st century will be the condition of the global environment.* Ian Mcharg

❖ *Touring does so much damage to the Earth, and that's one of my favorite things to do. I'm really into the whole environment thing, so we're always thinking of ways to conserve energy and just do things in a different way and figure out how you can go about it.* Kelly Clarkson

❖ *We all live every day in virtual environments, defined by our ideas.* Michael Crichton

❖ *I think it's crazy for us to play games with our children's future. We know what's happening to the climate, we have a highly predictable set of consequences if we continue to pour greenhouse gases into the atmosphere.* Bill Clinton at the UN Climate Conference 2005

❖ *We have modified our environment so radically that we must now modify ourselves to exist in this new environment.* Norbert Wiener

❖ *Thank God men cannot fly, and lay waste the sky as well as the earth.* Henry David Thoreau

❖ *When we heal the earth, we heal ourselves.* David Orr

❖ *I'm not an environmentalist. I'm an Earth warrior.* Darryl Cherney

❖ *Our environmental problems originate in the hubris of imagining ourselves as the central nervous system or the brain of nature. We're not the brain; we are a cancer on nature.* Dave Foreman

❖ *Sooner or later, wittingly or unwittingly, we must pay for every intrusion on the natural environment.* Barry Commoner

❖ *I think the environment should be put in the category of our national security. Defense of our resources is just as important as defense abroad. Otherwise what is there to defend?* Robert Redford

❖ *Strict economy in the use of natural resources has not been practiced, but it must be henceforth unless we are immoral enough to impair conditions in which our children are to live.* Daniel Burnham

❖ *Research has shown that a barren environment is much more damaging to baby animals than it is to adult animals. It does not hurt the adult animals the same way it damages babies.* Temple Grandin, Doctor of Animal Science

❖ *As you may know, some of the stereotyped behaviors exhibited by autistic children are also found in zoo animals who are raised in a barren environment.* Temple Grandin, Doctor of Animal Science

❖ *Each one (of the Earth's 5 million invertebrate species) plays a role in its ecosystem. It's like we're tearing the cogs out of a great machine. The machine might work after you tear out ten cogs, but what happens when you tear out a hundred?* Scott Black

❖ *People are becoming more environmentally aware and caring more for animals and really wanting to improve their health.* Heather Mills

❖ *Give a man a fish, and he can eat for a day. But teach a man how to fish, and he'll be dead of mercury poisoning inside of three years.* Charles Haas

❖ *Those who wish to pet baby wild animals "love" them. But those who respect their natures and wish to let them live normal lives, love them more.* Edwin Way Teale

❖ *The animals of the planet are in desperate peril... Without free animal life I believe we will lose the spiritual equivalent of oxygen.* Alice Walker

❖ *The difference between animals and humans is that animals change themselves for the environment, but humans change the environment for themselves.* Ayn Rand

❖ *If all mankind were to disappear, the world would regenerate back to the rich state of equilibrium that existed ten thousand years ago. If insects were to vanish, the environment would collapse into chaos.* Edward O. Wilson

❖ *The earth we abuse and the living things we kill will, in the end, take their revenge; for in exploiting their presence we are diminishing our future.* Marya Mannes

❖ *Will urban sprawl spread so far that most people lose all touch with nature? Will the day come when the only bird a typical American child ever sees is a canary in a pet shop window? When the only wild animal he knows is a rat — glimpsed on a night drive through some city slum? When the only tree he touches is the cleverly fabricated plastic evergreen that shades his gifts on Christmas morning?* Frank N. Ikard

❖ *For me, going vegan was an ethical and environmental decision. I'm doing the right thing by the animals.* Alexandra Paul

❖ *The only way to save a rhinoceros is to save the environment in which it lives, because there's a mutual dependency between it and millions of other species of both animals and plants.* David Attenborough

❖ *The real cure for our environmental problems is to understand that our job is to salvage Mother Nature. We are facing a formidable enemy in this field. It is the hunters... and to convince them to leave their guns on the wall is going to be very difficult.* Jacques Yves Cousteau

❖ *I don't consider you green if you eat meat.* Christian Serratos

❖ *I think if everyone chilled out on eating animals and the way they treat them it would help global warming, people would be incredibly healthy.* Constance Marie

❖ *How many people have hybrids in this town, how many people recycle? Being vegetarian is so much more eco-conscious. And it's lovely to know that when you are eating it's ethical and nothing had to die.* Owain Yeoman

❖ *We can debate this or that aspect of climate change, but the reality is that most people now accept our climate is indeed subject to change as a result of greenhouse gas emissions.* Tony Blair

❖ *All across the world, in every kind of environment and region known to man, increasingly dangerous weather patterns and devastating storms are abruptly putting an end to the long-running debate over whether or not climate change is real. Not only is it real, it's here, and its effects are giving rise to a frighteningly new global phenomenon: the man-made natural disaster.* Barack Obama

❖ *What's now urgently needed (to stop environmental disaster) is the international political commitment to take action to avoid dangerous climate change.* David Miliband

❖ *Today we're seeing that climate change is about more than a few unseasonably mild winters or hot summers. It's about the chain of natural catastrophes and devastating weather patterns that global warming is beginning to set off around the world, the frequency and intensity of which are breaking records thousands of years old.* Barack Obama

❖ *Global warming is one of those things, not like an earthquake where there's a big bang and you say, 'Oh, my God, this really has hit us.' It creeps up on you. Half a degree temperature difference from one year to the next, a little bit of rise of the ocean, a little bit of melting of the glaciers, and then all of a sudden it is too late to do something about it.* Arnold Schwarzenegger

❖ *We've got to ride the global warming issue. Even if the theory of global warming is wrong, we will be doing the right thing — in terms of economic policy and environmental policy.* Timothy Wirth

❖ *The issue of climate change is one that we ignore at our own peril. There may still be disputes about exactly how much we're contributing to the warming of the earth's atmosphere and how much is naturally occurring, but what we can be scientifically certain of is that our continued use of fossil fuels is pushing us to a point of no return. And unless we free ourselves from a dependence on these fossil fuels and chart a new course on energy in this country, we are condemning future generations to global catastrophe.* Barack Obama

❖ *Climate change is and will be a significant threat to our national security, and in a larger sense to life on earth as we know it to be.* Gen. Gordon R. Sullivan

❖ *Climate change is for real. We have just a small window of opportunity and it is closing rather rapidly. There is not a moment to lose.* Dr. Rajendra Pachauri

❖ *The good news is we know what to do. The good news is, we have everything we need now to respond to the challenge of global warming. We have all the technologies we need; more are being developed. And as they become available and become more affordable when produced in scale, they will make it easier to respond. But we should not wait, we cannot wait, we must not wait.* Al Gore

❖ *Yet, despite our many advances, our environment is still threatened by a range of problems, including global climate change, energy dependence on unsustainable fossil fuels, and loss of biodiversity.* Dan Lipinski

❖ *I have long been something of a climate change skeptic, but my views in recent years have shifted. For me, the most convincing evidence that something worrying is going on lies right here in the arctic.* Michael Hanlon

❖ *But reducing harmful emissions, abating our dependence on foreign oil and developing alternative renewable energy sources have benefits that go beyond environmental health, they improve personal health, enhance national security and encourage our nation's economic viability.* Jim Clyburn

❖ *Earth Day 1970 was irrefutable evidence that the American people understood the environmental threat and wanted action to resolve it.* Barry Commoner

❖ *In every case, the environmental hazards were made known only by independent scientists, who were often bitterly opposed by the corporations responsible for the hazards.* Barry Commoner

❖ *The environmental crisis arises from a fundamental fault: our systems of production – in industry, agriculture, energy and transportation – essential as they are, make people sick and die.* Barry Commoner

❖ *The environmental crisis is a global problem, and only global action will resolve it.* Barry Commoner

❖ *I am on the board of corporations who contribute both to environmental problems and their solutions. And I am on the NGO side: the Earth Council and other organizations.* Maurice Strong

❖ *Moral codes adjust themselves to environmental conditions.* Will Durant

❖ *More than ever before, there is a global understanding that long term social, economic, and environmental development would be impossible without healthy families, communities, and countries.* Gro Harlem Brundtland

❖ *In a few decades, the relationship between the environment, resources and conflict may seem almost as obvious as the connection we see today between human rights, democracy and peace.* Wangari Maathai

❖ *What we've proven is that you can protect the environment, use it wisely and grow the economy and that there is no conflict between the two.* Bruce Babbitt

❖ *I think the greatest and the most rewarding challenge in environmentalism is trying to figure out how humans can meet their needs while protecting the environment.* Gale Norton

❖ *The earth we abuse and the living things we kill will, in the end, take their revenge; for in exploiting their presence we are diminishing our future.* Marya Mannes

❖ *The insufferable arrogance of human beings to think that Nature was made solely for their benefit, as if it was conceivable that the sun had been set afire merely to ripen men's apples and head their cabbages.* Savinien de Cyrano de Bergerac

❖ *Drive Nature forth by force, she'll turn and rout the false refinements that would keep her out.* Horace

❖ *Nature always strikes back. It takes all the running we can do to remain in the same place.* Rene Dubos

❖ *Nature favors those organisms which leave the environment in better shape for their progeny to survive.* James Lovelock

❖ *The more we exploit nature, the more our options are reduced, until we have only one: to fight for survival.* Morris K. Udall & Stewart L. Udall Foundation

❖ *A margin of life is developed by Nature for all living things — including man. All life forms obey Nature's demands — except man, who has found ways of ignoring them.* Eugene M. Poirot

❖ *The magnificence of mountains, the serenity of nature — nothing is safe from the idiot marks of man's passing.* Loudon Wainwright

❖ *Understanding the laws of nature does not mean that we are immune to their operations.* David Gerrold

❖ *Nature's laws affirm instead of prohibit. If you violate her laws you are your own prosecuting attorney, judge, jury, and hangman.* Luther Burbank

❖ *It appears to be a law that you cannot have a deep sympathy with both man and nature.* Henry David Thoreau

❖ *The system of nature, of which man is a part, tends to be self-balancing, self-adjusting, self-cleansing. Not so with technology.* E. Schumacher

❖ *This is a beautiful planet and not at all fragile. Earth can withstand significant volcanic eruptions, tectonic cataclysms, and ice ages. But this canny, intelligent, prolific, and extremely self-centered human creature had proven himself capable of more destruction of life than Mother Nature herself. We've got to be stopped.* Michael L. Fischer

❖ *The frog does not drink up the pond in which he lives.* Native American Proverb

❖ *We all moan and groan about the loss of the quality of life through the destruction of our ecology, and yet every one of us, in our own little comfortable ways, contributes daily to that destruction. It's time now to awaken in each one of us the respect and attention our beloved Mother deserves.* Ed Asner

❖ *As the human population grows and our demand for natural resources increases, more and more habitats are devastated. Today, we may be losing 30,000 species a year – a rate much faster than at any time since the last great extinction 65 million years ago that wiped out most of the dinosaurs. If we continue on this course, we will destroy even ourselves.* American Museum of Natural History

❖ *The environment is where we all meet; where we all have a mutual interest; it is the one thing that all of us share. It is not only a mirror of ourselves, but a focusing lens on what we can become.* Lady Bird Johnson

❖ *These sprays, dusts, and aerosols are now applied almost universally to farms, gardens, forests, and home – nonselective chemicals that have the power to kill every insect, the 'good' and the 'bad,' to still the song of birds and the leaping of fish in the streams, to coat the leaves with a deadly film, and to linger on in soil – all this though the intended target may be only a few weeds or insects. Can anyone believeit is possible to lay down such a barrage of poisons on the surface of the earth without making it unfit for all life? They should not be called 'insecticides,' but 'biocides'.* Rachel Carson

❖ *Take a course in good water and air; and in the eternal youth of Nature you may renew your own. Go quietly, alone; no harm will befall you.* John Muir

❖ *I go to nature every day for inspiration in the day's work. I follow in building the principles which nature has used in its domain.* Frank Lloyd Wright

❖ *One touch of nature makes the whole world kin.* William Shakespeare

❖ *The supreme reality of our time is.....the vulnerability of our planet.* John F. Kennedy

❖ *On Spaceship Earth there are no passengers; everybody is a member of the crew. We have moved into an age in which everybody's activities affect everybody else.* Marshall McLuhan

❖ *When you plant a tree, never plant only one. Plant three – one for shade, one for fruit, one for beauty.* African proverb

❖ *When one tugs at a single thing in nature, he finds it attached to the rest of the world.* John Muir

❖ *Approximately 72 percent of the waste currently being land filled or incinerated consists of materials that could be put to higher and better use through recycling or composting. Most of this material is office paper, cardboard, non-recyclable paper, and food waste.* Minnesota Office of Environmental Assistance

❖ *What is a weed? A plant whose virtues have not yet been discovered.* Ralph Waldo Emerson

❖ *All things share the same breath — the beast, the tree, the man . . . the air shares its spirit with all the life it supports.* Chief Seattle

❖ *Water and air, the two essential fluids on which all life depends, have become global garbage cans.* Jacques Cousteau

❖ *In the end we will conserve only what we love. We love only what we understand. We will understand only what we are taught.* Baba Dioum

❖ *The nation behaves well if it treats the natural resources as assets which it must turn over to the next generation increased, and not impaired, in value.* Theodore Roosevelt

❖ *If there is magic on this planet, it is contained in water.* Loren Eiseley

❖ *Water is the most critical resource issue of our lifetime and our children's lifetime. The health of our waters is the principal measure of how we live on the land.* Luna Leopold

❖ *What we are doing to the forests of the world is but a mirror reflection of what we are doing to ourselves and to one another.* Gandhi

❖ *It's the flock, the grove that matters. Our responsibility is to species, not to specimens; to communities, not to individuals.* Sara Stein

❖ *Don't it always seem to go that you don't know what you've got till it's gone. They paved paradise and put up a parking lot.* Joni Mitchell

❖ *The most alarming of all man's assaults upon the environment is the contamination of air, earth, rivers, and sea with dangerous and even lethal materials. This pollution is for the most part irrecoverable; the chain of evil it initiates not only in the world that must support life but in living tissues is for the most part irreversible. In this now universal contamination of the environment, chemicals are the sinister and little-recognized partners of radiation in changing the very nature of the world – the very nature of its life.* Rachel Carson

❖ *Nature provides a free lunch, but only if we control our appetites.* William Ruckelshaus.

❖ *Rapid environmental change is all around us. The most obvious example is climate change. .. But that is not the only threat. Many other clouds are on the horizon. .. This assault on the global environment risks undermining the many advances human society has made in recent decades. .. It could even come to jeopardize international peace and security!* Ban Ki-Moon

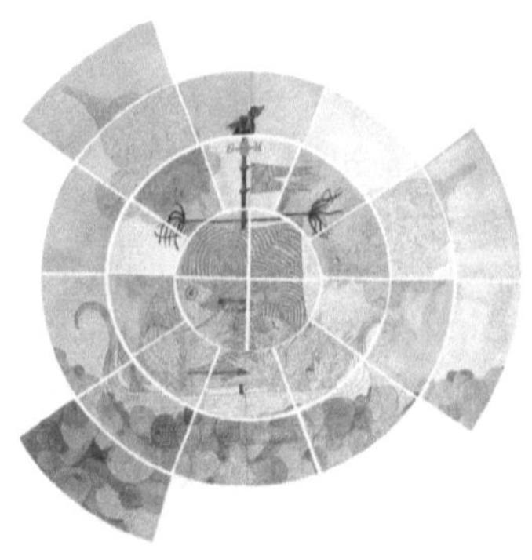

XIII
LAGNIAPPE

It is considered smart these days for authors or publishers to add a *Lagniappe*, as icing on the cake, at the end of a book. Merriam Webster dictionary defines 'Lagniappe' as 'something given or obtained gratuitously or by way of good measure'. In simpler terms, it means an added gift for a valued customer. In the same manner, this whole chapter is presented as an added gift of significant information offered to the worthy reader to honour his concern for the environment.

Although serious effort has been made to impart much of the available environmental information in the preceding twelve chapters, yet some interesting bits and pieces could not be adequately covered in those chapters in the absence of specific context for elaborating on these aspects. Epistemological considerations demand that such missing links in the chain of environmental knowledge should be provided at one place for ease of reference. This being as good a place as any, the following collage of supplementary points is presented here by way of abundant information for the interested reader.

➢ According to the Kyoto Protocol, **the dirty half-dozen**, defiling our environment are the six greenhouse gases:

- Carbon dioxide (CO2)
- Methane (CH4)
- Nitrous oxide (N2O)
- Hydrofluorocarbons (HCFs)
- Perfluorocarbons (PFCs)
- Sulphur hexafluoride (SF6)

➢ There is a thermal tie between the years 2005 and 2010, the two having differed by less than 0.018 degrees Fahrenheit. The difference is smaller than the range of uncertainty in comparing the temperatures of recent years, putting the two years in question in a bracket of statistical tie.

➢ The warmest years since 1990 are – 1995, 1997, 1998, 1999, 2000, 2001, 2002, 2003, 2004, 2005, 2006, 2007, 2009 and 2010 – revealing the apparently inexorable march of global warming.

➢ The CO_2 level in year 1910 was 300ppm. In 1930, the level recorded was 310ppm; then in 1980, it was 340ppm. In year 2010, it reached as high as 390ppm. The tolerable limit is 350 PPM which was exceeded way back in the year 1988.

➢ Oceans are becoming more acidic than ever in the last 50 million years or so.

➢ Oceanic acidity has increased 30% since the pre-industrial years; some effects of acidification are permanent and some are expected to aggravate.

➢ As per one report of United Nations Convention on biological diversity, oceans would be more acidic by 150% just by 2050.

➢ Here is a plausible case for artificial volcano to offset global warming. A volcano erupted on Mt. Pinatubo (Philippines) in

1990. Its debris shielded earth from solar energy, which resulted in global temperature falling for two years before rising again.

➤ Charles Keeling (U.S.A.) made the first measurement of atmospheric CO_2 at Mauna Loa, Hawaii in 1958. He indeed was the whistle blower of carbon emission.

➤ Mauna Loa constitutes the longest record of direct measurements of CO_2 in the atmosphere. After the measurements were started by Keeling of the Scripps Institution of Oceanography in March 1958 at a facility of the National Oceanic and Atmospheric Administration, the NOAA started its own CO_2 measurements in May 1974; since then they have run in parallel with those made by Scripps.

➤ Is CFC (chlorofluorocarbon) the chief villain? So it seems, since one molecule of CFC has the same greenhouse effect as have 10,000 (ten thousand) molecules of CO_2.

➤ Sulphate and Nitrate particles in the atmospheric brown cloud act as mirror and absorb the sunlight, thus heating up the blanket of greenhouse gases. They also create acid when mixed with rain.

➤ IPCC stands for the Intergovernmental Panel on Climate Change, which was founded by UN in 1988 for collating and analysing evidence on global warming.

➤ Bio-plastic products like spoon, plates, crockery etc. which are now available, should preferably be used instead of conventional plastic.

➤ As plastic grows older it releases various harmful ingredients, such as polyvinyl chloride, phthalates, BPA and DEHA.

Note BPA stands for bisphenol-A and DEHA stands for diethylhexyladipate; Bioplastic stands for biodegradable plastic.

➢ Tomato, lemon and other citrus items increase BPA leaching from plastics.

➢ Mineral water, juice, and soft drink bottles use PET which stands for Polyethylene terephthalate. Antimony (Sb) is also used in making PET and over the time it is released in the liquid contained in the bottle.

➢ TR [thermally rearranged] plastic can be used for curbing CO_2 pollution. It is nearly 4 times more affective and about 100 times faster in detecting CO_2 than traditional membranes.

➢ Plastic wares and containers often bear a triangle at the bottom and some number is engraved inside the triangle. Exercise caution when the number so displayed is 7 [BPA], 6 [polystyrene] or 3 [polyvinyl chloride, PVC].

➢ Freon is the trade name (DuPont) commonly used for various chlorine and fluorine containing carbon compounds, used as a working fluid in traditional refrigerators and in certain air conditioners. It wreaks havoc on environment by eating up the stratospheric ozone.

➢ Difference between fog and cloud: fog is a collection of tiny water droplets that float in the air; it is similar to cloud except that clouds do not touch the earth's surface as fog does.

➢ Lentic and lotic water: The prefix 'Lentic' means standing water (lakes/ponds) whereas 'Lotic' refers to flowing water.

➢ Mangroves are plant communities and trees that inhabit in

swamps, muddy silt and sand banks at the mouth of a river and other low-lying areas which are protected from strong waves.

➤ PAN stands for peroxyacyl nitrates, one of a family of compounds present in photo-chemical smog. Complex chemical reaction between partially oxidised hydrocarbons (from auto exhausts), oxygen, ozone and nitrogen oxide produce PAN. It is an eye irritant as well.

➤ The term 'Pelagic' relates to communities of marine organism belonging to open sea. They live free from direct dependence on bottom or shore. They belong to that part of ocean which is deeper than the littoral zone but shallower than the abyssal zone. Abyssal zone extends to depths greater than 2000 metres.

➤ It takes around 100 years or more to build one inch (2.54 cm) of top soil.

➤ It takes a few millennia or so to decompose plastic bags. However, artificial ways have been discovered to decompose plastic in around 3 months.

➤ 'Sodding' means grassing a target area to prevent erosion

➤ The acronym 'dBA' means 'decibel a-weighted', which signifies 'noise level'. It is called 'a-weighted' because sound meters have a-weighted network, thus yielding a-weighted DB reading.

➤ 'TTS' is a type of hearing change caused by noise exposure. It stands for Temporary Threshold Shift.

➤ 'NIPTS' is short for Noise-induced Permanent Threshold Shift, and represents irreparable hearing loss.

➤ According to researches many monkey species of Africa would face the risk of extinction if the global warming continues at the current pace.

➤ In India, the year 2009 received deficient rainfall by 22%. It can be called as one of the biggest deficient years. Historically (from 1901 to 2009), the year 1918 was the biggest deficient year (25% deficiency) followed by 1972 which recorded 24% less rainfall than average.

➤ The USA, which has just about 4% of the world's population, contributed 30% of greenhouse gases in the atmosphere.

➤ AOSIS- It stands for Alliance of Small Island States and includes Barbados, Cuba, Fiji, Jamaica, Tonga, Solomon Island, and Antigua, Cape Verde etc.

➤ Waste plastic could be recycled for making *'Nanotubes'* which could further be utilised as an anode in cell phone battery.

➤ Plants could be the next generation plastic factories. Scientists have discovered a gene that allows plants to make plastic. The generated plastic could be stored in their stalks and leaves. Maize and Soy-bean are promising plants for future plastic generation.

➤ Experimental studies have been carried out for making use of waste polythene bags in construction of water proof roads.

➤ Researchers at Wolfgang Kiessling of the Humboldt University of Berlin have found that the coral reefs not only harbour amazing bio-diversity but are also active at generating biodiversity in the oceans; further, they export biodiversity to other ecosystems. This overturns the old belief that coral life originated elsewhere.

➢ Arctic sea ice cover in December 2010 was the smallest since records began in 1979, with an average monthly extent (of the area of ocean where there is at least some ice) of 12 million square kilometres – some 270,000 square kilometres less than the previous low of 2006. The ice cover is considered a marker of climate change as global warming tends to be seen first at the poles.

➢ Based on a range of models, it is likely that future tropical cyclones (typhoons and hurricanes) will become more intense, with larger peak wind speeds and more heavy precipitation associated with on-going increases of tropical SSTs. There is less confidence in projections of a global decrease in numbers of tropical cyclones. The apparent increase in the proportion of very intense storms since 1970 in some regions is much larger than simulated by current models for that period.

➢ *79% of Himalayan Glaciers are in retreating mode:* ISRO (Indian Space Research Organisation) and GSI (Geological Survey of India) jointly conducted a research on retreating Himalayan Glaciers and found that as many as 2184 glaciers were retreating out of 2767 studied. This means around 79% of Himalayan glaciers are retreating – a cause for immense concern indeed.

➢ *A wake-up call from the Arctic Sea:* The extent of the Arctic sea ice has reached a historic minimum (4.24 million km ^{2}) on Sep. 8, 2011. The ice melt in the Arctic could further go on and even exceed the previous historic minimum of 2007. It seems clear that this is an extended outcome of the man-made global warming with global repercussions. As a consequence, the sustenance of many small animals, algae, fishes and mammals like polar bears and seals would continue to be heavily affected.

➤ *3600 International Water Sharing Treaties:* As per FAO (Food & Agriculture Organization) there are over 3600 international water sharing treaties dating as far back as 805 AD. These treaties mainly pertain to water sharing, hydro-power, navigational issues, flood management, fishing rights etc.

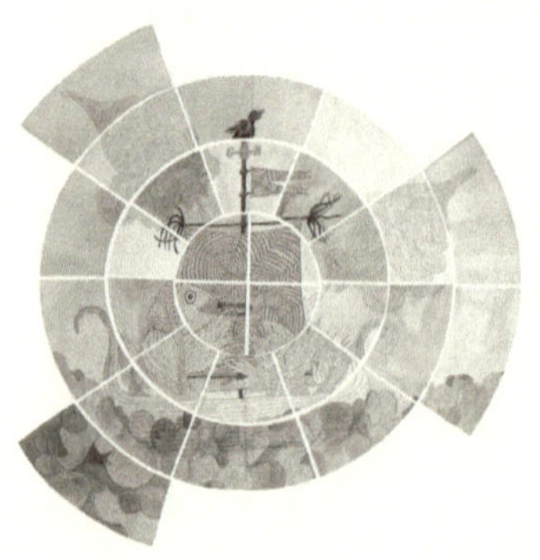

APPENDIX-1[A]
THE NOISE POLLUTION (REGULATION & CONTROL) RULES, 2000

MINISTRY OF ENVIRONMENT & FORESTS

[NOTIFICATION] New Delhi, the 14 February, 2000

S.O. 123(E) Whereas the increasing ambient noise levels in public places from various sources, inter-alia, industrial activity, construction activity, generator sets, loud speakers, public address systems, music systems, vehicular horns and other mechanical devices have deleterious effects on human health and the psychological well being of the people; it is considered necessary to regulate and control noise producing and generating sources with the objective of maintaining the ambient air quality standards in respect of noise;

Whereas a draft of Noise Pollution (Control and Regulation) Rules, 1999 was published under the notification of the Government of India in the Ministry of Environment and Forests vide number S.O. 528 (E), dated the 28 th June, 1999 inviting objections and suggestions from all the persons likely to be affected thereby, before the expiry of the period of sixty days from the date on which the copies of the Gazette containing the said notification are made available to the pubic;

And whereas copies of the said Gazette were made available to the public on the 1 st day of July, 1999;

And whereas the objections and suggestions received from the public in respect of the said draft rules have been duly considered by the Central Government;

Now, therefore, in exercise of the powers conferred by clause (ii) of sub-section (2) of section 3, sub-section (1) and clause (b) of sub-section (2) of section 6 and section 25 of the Environment (Protection) Act, 1986 (29 of 1986) read with rule 5 of the Environment (Protection) Rules, 1986, the Central Government hereby makes the following rules for the regulation and control of noise producing and generating sources, namely:

The Noise Pollution (Regulation & Control) Rules, 2000

1. **Short-title and commencement**
   1. These rules may be called the 'Noise Pollution (Regulation and Control) Rules, 2000.
   2. They shall come into force on the date of their publication in the Official Gazette.

2. **Definitions** In these rules, unless the context otherwise requires,-
   a. "Act" means the Environment (Protection) Act, 1986 (29 of 1986);
   b. "area / zone" means all areas which fall in either of the four categories given in the Schedule annexed to these rules;
   c. "authority" means and includes any authority or officer authorized by the Central Government, or as the case may be, the State Government in accordance with the laws in force and includes a District Magistrate, Police Commissioner, or any other officer not below the rank of

the Deputy Superintendent of Police designated for the maintenance of the ambient air quality standards in respect of noise under any law for the time being in force;

d.   "court" means a governmental body consisting of one or more judges who sit to adjudicate disputes and administer justice and includes any court of law presided over by a judge, judges or a magistrate and acting as a tribunal in civil, taxation and criminal cases;

e.   "educational institution" means a school, seminary, college, university, professional academies, training institutes or other educational establishment, not necessarily a chartered institution and includes not only buildings, but also all grounds necessary for the accomplishment of the full scope of educational instruction, including those things essential to mental, moral and physical development;

f.   "hospital" means an institution for the reception and care of sick, wounded, infirm or aged persons, and includes government or private hospitals, nursing homes and clinics;

g.   "person" shall include any company or association or body of individuals, whether incorporated or not;

h.   "State Government" in relation to a Union territory means the Administrator thereof appointed under article 239 of the Constitution.

3.   Ambient air quality standards in respect of noise for different areas/zones

1.   The ambient air quality standards in respect of noise for different areas / zones shall be such as specified in the Schedule annexed to these rules.

2.   The State Government shall categorize the areas into industrial, commercial, residential or silence areas / zones

for the purpose of implementation of noise standards for different areas.

3. The State Government shall take measures for abatement of noise including noise emanating from vehicular movements and ensure that the existing noise levels do not exceed the ambient air quality standards specified under these rules.

4. All development authorities, local bodies and other concerned authorities while planning developmental activity or carrying out functions relating to town and country planning shall take into consideration all aspects of noise pollution as a parameter of quality of life to avoid noise menace and to achieve the objective of maintaining the ambient air quality standards in respect of noise.

5. An area comprising not less than 100 metres around hospitals, educational institutions and courts may be declared as silence area / zone for the purpose of these rules.

4. Responsibility as to enforcement of noise pollution control measures

1. The noise levels in any area / zone shall not exceed the ambient air quality standards in respect of noise as specified in the Schedule.

2. The authority shall be responsible for the enforcement of noise pollution control measures and the due compliance of the ambient air quality standards in respect of noise.

5. Restrictions on the use of loud speakers / public address system

1. A loud speaker or a public address system shall not be used except after obtaining written permission from the authority.

2. A loud speaker or a public address system shall not be used at night (between 10:00 p.m. to 6:00 a.m.) except in closed premises for communication within, e.g. auditoria, conference rooms, community halls and banquet halls.

3. Notwithstanding any thing contained in sub-rule (2), the State Government may subject to such terms and conditions as are necessary to reduce noise pollution, permit use of loud speakers or public address systems during night hours (between 10.00 p.m. to 12.00 midnight) on or during any cultural or religious festive occasion of a limited duration not exceeding fifteen days in all during a calendar year.

6. **Consequences of any violation in silence zone/area**
Whoever, in any place covered under the silence zone / area commits any of the following offence, he shall be liable for penalty under the provisions of the Act:-
   i. whoever, plays any music or uses any sound amplifiers,
   ii. whoever, beats a drum or tom-tom or blows a horn either musical or pressure, or trumpet or beats or sounds any instrument, or
   iii. whoever, exhibits any mimetic, musical or other performances of a nature to attract crowds.

7. **Complaints to be made to the authority.**
   1. A person may, if the noise level exceeds the ambient noise standards by 10 dB (A) or more given in the corresponding columns against any area/zone, make a complaint...
   2. The authority shall act on the complaint and take action against the violator in accordance with the provisions of these rules and any other law in force.

8. Power to prohibit etc. continuance of music sound or noise

1. If the authority is satisfied from the report of an officer in-charge of a police station or other information received by him that it is necessary to do so in order to prevent annoyance, disturbance, discomfort or injury or risk of annoyance, disturbance, discomfort or injury to the public or to any person who dwell or occupy property on the vicinity, he may, by a written order issue such directions as he may consider necessary to any person for preventing, prohibiting, controlling or regulating:-

   a. the incidence or continuance in or upon any premises of-

      i. any vocal or instrumental music; ii. sounds caused by playing, beating, clashing, blowing or use in any manner whatsoever of any instrument including loudspeakers, public address systems, appliance or apparatus or contrivance which is capable of producing or re-producing sound, or

   b. the carrying on in or upon, any premises of any trade, avocation or operation or process resulting in or attended with noise.

The authority empowered under sub-rule (1) may, either on its own motion, or on the application of any person aggrieved by an order made under sub-rule (1), either rescind, modify or alter any such order: Provided that before any such application is disposed of, the said authority shall afford to the applicant an opportunity of appearing before it either in person or by a person representing him and showing cause against the order and shall, if it rejects any such application either wholly or in part, record its reasons for such rejection.

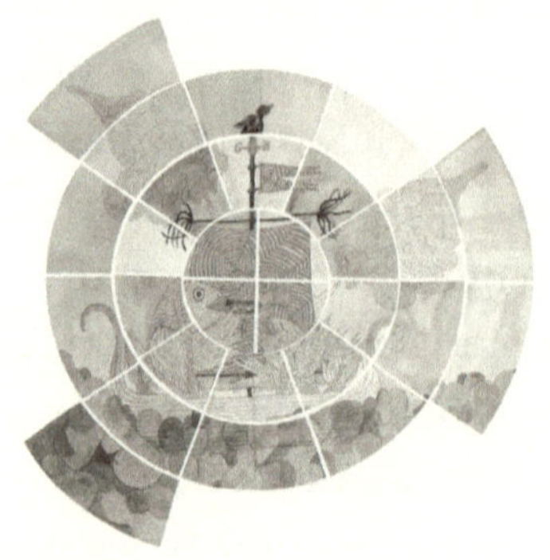

APPENDIX-1[B]
NOISE POLLUTION (REGULATION & CONTROL) (AMENDMENT) RULES, 2010

Notification No :SO50(E)

Ministry of Environment and Forests

Notification No: SO50 (E)

Date of Notification: 11.01.2010

Date of Publication: 11.01.2010

Notification/ Circulars Referred: number S.O. 123 (E), dated the 14th February, 2000, S.O.1088 (E), dated the 11th October, 2002; S.O.1569 (E), dated the 19th September, 2006; G.S.R. 158(E), dated the 9th March, 2009

Noise Pollution (Regulation and Control) (Amendment) Rules, 2010

Whereas, the Central Government has notified the Noise Pollution (Regulation and Control) Rules, 2000 vide notification number S.O. 123 (E), dated the 14th February, 2000, which has been amended vide S.O. 1046(E), dated the 22nd November, 2000, S.O.1088 (E), dated the 11th October, 2002 and S.O.1569 (E), dated the 19th September, 2006;

And, whereas, the Central Government had received representations from Non-Government Organisations and individuals requesting for certain amendments in view of various difficulties being faced in the society due to noise pollution;

And , whereas, the Central Government in exercise of the powers conferred by sub-section (2) of section 3 and section 25 of the Environment (Protection) Act, 1986 (29 of 1986), read with rule 5 of the Environment (Protection) Rules, 1986, further to amend the Noise Pollution (Regulation and Control) Rules, 2000 published the draft rules in the Gazette of India, Extraordinary, vide G.S.R. 158(E), dated the 9th March, 2009 for the information of all persons likely to be affected thereby; and notice was given that the said draft rules would be taken into consideration by the Central Government on or after the expiry of a period of sixty days from the date on which copies of the Gazette containing this notification are made available to the public ;

And, whereas, the copies of the said Gazette notification were made available to the public on the 27th March, 2009;

And, whereas, objections and suggestions received in response to the above mentioned draft rules have been duly considered by the Central Government;

Now, therefore, in exercise of the powers conferred by clause (ii) of sub-section (2) of section 3, sub-section (1) and clause (b) of sub-section (2) of section 6 and section 25 of the Environment (Protection) Act, 1986 (29 of 1986) read with rule 5 of the Environment (Protection) Rules, 1986, the Central Government hereby makes the following rules further to amend the Noise Pollution (Regulation and Control) Rules, 2000, namely:

The Noise Pollution (Regulation and Control) (Amendment) Rules, 2010

1. (1)These rules may be called the Noise Pollution (Regulation and Control) (Amendment) Rules, 2010.
(2) They shall come into force on the date of their publication in the Official Gazette.

2. In the Noise Pollution (Regulation and Control) Rules, 2000, (hereinafter referred to as the said rules), in the opening portion, after the words "construction activity", the words "fire crackers, sound producing instruments" shall be inserted;

3. In the said rules, in rule 2, after clause (h), the following clauses shall be inserted, namely:
"(i) "public place" means any place to which the public have access, whether as of right or not, and includes auditorium, hotels, public waiting rooms, convention centers, public offices, shopping malls, cinema halls, educational institutions, libraries, open grounds and the like which are visited by general public; and
(j) "night time" means the period between 10.00 p.m. and 6.00 a.m.".
4. In the said rules, in rule 3, in sub- rule (3), after the words "noise emanating from vehicular movements", the words "blowing of horns, bursting of sound emitting fire crackers, use of loud speakers or public address system and sound producing instruments" shall be inserted.

5. In the said rules, in rule 5,-
(i) in the heading, after the words "PUBLIC ADDRESS SYSTEM", the words "AND SOUND PRODUCING INSTRUMENTS" shall be inserted;
(ii) for sub-rule (2), the following sub- rule shall be substituted, namely:-
"(2) A loud speaker or a public address system or any sound

producing instrument or a musical instrument or a sound amplifier shall not be used at night time except in closed premises for communication within, like auditoria, conference rooms, community halls, banquet halls or during a public emergency.";

(iii) In sub-rule (3),-

(a) for the words "public address systems during night hours", the words "public address system and the like during nights hours" shall be substituted;

(b) after the words "a limited duration not exceeding fifteen days in all during a calendar year.", the words "The concerned State Government shall generally specify in advance, the number and particulars of the days on which such exemption would be operative." shall be inserted;

(iv) after sub-rule 3, as so amended, the following sub-rules shall be inserted, namely:-

"(4) The noise level at the boundary of the public place, where loudspeakerorpublicaddresssystemoranyothernoisesourceisbeing used shall not exceed 10 dB (A) above the ambient noise standards for the area or 75 dB (A) whichever is lower;

(5) The peripheral noise level of a privately owned sound system or a sound producing instrument shall not, at the boundary of the private place, exceed by more than 5 dB (A) the ambient noise standards specified for the area in which it is used.".

6. In the said rules, after rule 5, the following shall be inserted, namely:-

"5A. RESTRICTIONS ON THE USE OF HORNS, SOUND EMITTING CONSTRUCTION EQUIPMENTS AND BURSTING OF FIRE CRACKERS.-

(1) No horn shall be used in silence zones or during night time in residential areas except during a public emergency.

(2) Sound emitting fire crackers shall not be burst in silence zone or during night time.

(3) Sound emitting construction equipments shall not be used or operated during night time in residential areas and silence zones.".

7. In the said rules, in rule 6, after the clause (iii), the following clauses shall be inserted, namely -

"(iv) whoever, bursts sound emitting fire crackers; or

(v) whoever, uses a loud speaker or a public address system.".

8. In the said rules, in rule 7, in sub-rule (1), after the words "in the corresponding columns against any area/ zone" the words "or, if there is a violation of any provision of these rules regarding restrictions imposed during night time" shall be inserted.

9. In the said rules, in rule 8, in sub-rule (1), in clause (a),-

(i) in sub-clause (ii), for the words, "public address systems, appliance or apparatus" the words "public address systems, horn, construction equipment, appliance or apparatus" shall be substituted;

(ii) after sub-clause (ii), the following sub-clause shall be inserted, namely:-

"(iii) sound caused by bursting of sound emitting fire crackers, or,".

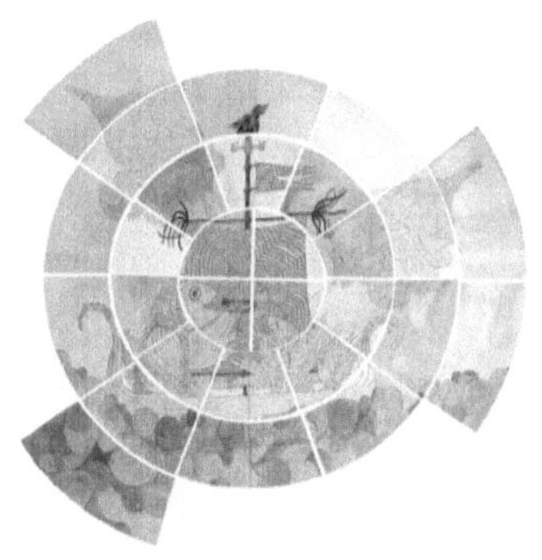

APPENDIX-1[C]

WATER QUALITY STANDARD

	Characteristic	Impurity	Max Permissible Limit
1	Physical	Turbidity	5-10 mg/l (Silicascale)
		Color	10-20(Cobalt scale)
		Taste & odour	1.0-3.0
2	Chemical	Total s olids	500-1000 mg/l
		pH Value	6.6-8.0
		Hardness	75-115 mg/l
		Chloride	250 mg/l
		Nitrate(NO_3)	45 mg/l
		Iron	0.3 mg/l
		Manganese	0.05 mg/l
		Lead	0.05-0.1 mg/l
		Arsenic	0.05 mg/l
		Selenium	0.05 mg/l
		Barium	1.0 mg/l
		Cadmium	0.01 mg/l
		Chromium	0.05 mg/l
		Silver	0.05 mg/l
		copper	1.0-3.0 mg/l
		Zinc	15 mg/l
		Magnesium	125 mg/l
		Sulphate	250 mg/l
		Phenolic Substances	0.001 mg/l
		Fluoride	1.5 mg/l
		Cyanide	0.02 mg/l
		B O D	NIL

3	Biological & Micro Organic	Coliform Bacteria	MPN of B-coli shold not exceed 1 per 100 ml
4	Radiological	α emitters	1μμc/litre
		β emitters	10 μμc/litre

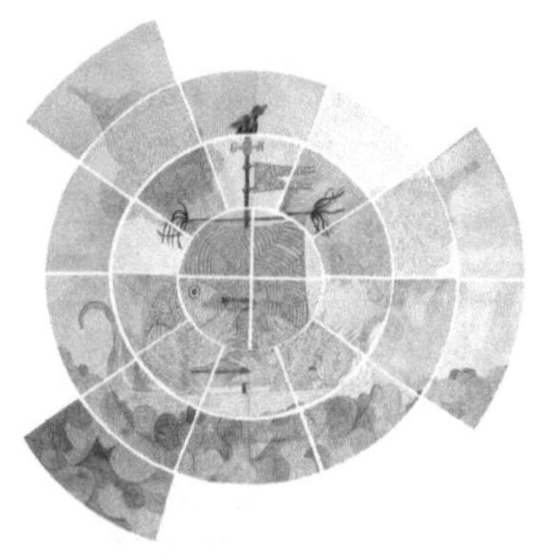

APPENDIX-1[D]

TOLERANCE LIMIT FOR RIVER WATER

Parameter	Value	Unit
Arsenic (As)	0.2	(Max) mg/L
BOD	3.0	(Max) mg/L
Boron (B)	2.0	(Max) mg/L
Cadmium (Cd)	0.01	(Max) mg/L
Calcium (Ca)	80	(Max) mg/L
Chloride (Cl)	600	(Max) mg/L
Chromium (Cr)	0.5	(Max) mg/L
Conductivity	2250	(Max) Micromhos/cm.
Copper (Cu)	1.5	(Max) mg/L
Cyanide (Cn)	0.5	(Max) mg/L
DO	6.0	(Max) mg/L
Fluoride (F)	1.5	(Max) mg/L
Free Ammonia (NH_3)	1.20	(Max)
Iron (Fe)	50	(Max) mg/L
Lead (Pb)	0.10	(Max) mg/L
Magnesium (Mg)	24	(Max) mg/L
Manganese (Mn)	0.50	(Max) mg/L
Mercury (Hg)	0.001	(Max) mg/L

Nitrate (NO$_3$)	50	(Max) mg/L
pH	6.5-8.5	-
SAR	26	(Max) mg/L
Sodium (Na)	60	Percentage (%)
SOU	1000	(Max) mg/L
TDS	500-2100	(Max) mg/L
Total Coli form	5000	(Max) mg/L
Total Hardness	3000	(Max) mg/L
Zinc (Zn)	15	(Max) mg/L

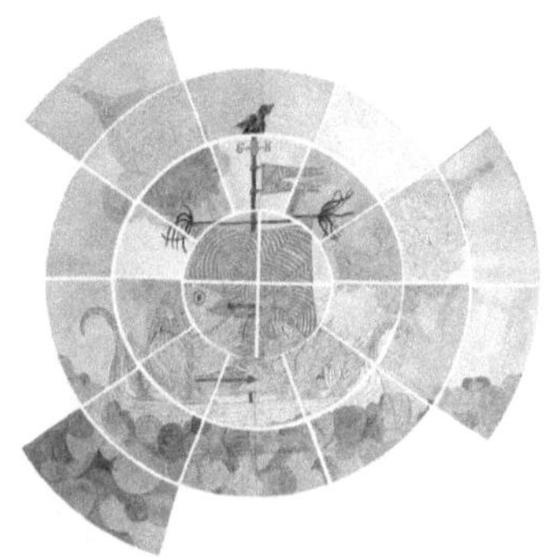

APPENDIX-1[E]

PRIMARY WATER QUALITY CRITERIA IN INDIA

	Designated Best Use	Water Class	Criteria
1	Drinking water source without conventional treatment but after disinfection	A	1. Total Coliforms Organism MPN/100ml shall be 50 or less 2. pH between 6.5 & 8.5 3. Dissolved Oxygen 6mg/l or more 4. Biochemical Oxygen demand 5 days 20°C 2mg/l or less.
2	Outdoor bathing (organized)	B	1. Total Coliforms Organism MPN/1 100ml shall be 500 or less. 2. pH between 6.5 & 8.5 3. Dissolved Oxygen 5mg/l or more 4. Biochemical Oxygen demand 5 days 20° C 3mg/l or less.
3	Drinking Water Source	C	1. Total Coliforms Organism MPN/1 100ml shall be 500 or less. 2. pH between 6 & 9 3. Dissolved Oxygen 5mg/l or more 4. Biochemical Oxygen demand 5 days 20° C 3mg/l or less.
4	Propagation of Wild Life	D	1. pH between 6.5 & 8.5 Fisheries 2. Dissolved Oxygen 4mg/l or more 3. Free Ammonia (as N) 1.2 mg/l or less
5	Irrigation, Industrial Cooling, Controlled Waste	E	1. pH between 6.0 or 8.5 2. Electrical Conductivity at 25°C Micro mhos/cm Max 2250. 3. Boron, Max 2mg/l

*Source Central Pollution Control Board India

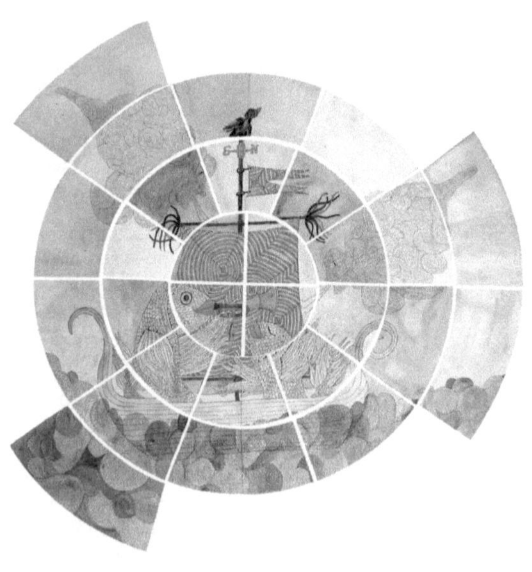

www.ingramcontent.com/pod-product-compliance
Lightning Source LLC
Chambersburg PA
CBHW051244250726

48656CB00004B/1117